ACKNOWLEDGMENTS

The National Park Service and its personnel should receive prime credit for the instigation and accomplishment of the Chapin Mesa Survey. Mesa Verde National Park Superintendent Oscar W. Carlson allowed his interpretive staff to conduct most of the fieldwork as part of their regular duties and later granted permission for me to conduct test excavations and to use park facilities while analyzing the materials recovered. Park Archaeologist Don Watson exercised general supervision over the project, and his successors Carroll A. Burroughs and Jean M. Pinkley were most cooperative during my phase of the work.

James A. Lancaster directed the fieldwork itself, devising the specific techniques employed and using his uncanny skill for deciphering the clues encountered on the ground's surface. His ingenuity kept the overall expense of the operation to a minimum, thus making its successful completion possible. Assisting Lancaster in the field were Fred Peck, Robert Bradley, and Leland J. Abel who kept the bulk of the records.

My work began in 1958 with a program of test excavations, general collation of the mass of data that had accumulated since the beginning of survey activities in 1951, and study of the ceramics and other artifacts collected during fieldwork. Financial support for this program has been provided by the Milton Fund of Harvard University, the Wenner-Gren Foundation for Anthropological Research, and the Mesa Verde Museum Association. J. O. Brew and Watson Smith gave general guidance and stimulation.

Throughout the preparation of this report, as well as in the final stages of artifact analysis, Douglas Osborne permitted my use of facilities of the Wetherill Mesa Project laboratory. The fine quality of the photographs is the work of Fred Mang, Jr., who took approximately half of the pictures.

In addition to those individuals already mentioned above, Richard P. Wheeler and Lewis D. Anderson require separate mention for their contributions of willing assistance and encouragement. Dorcas S. Rohn has assisted in typing, editing, and criticizing the manuscript. William D. Lipe provided an invaluable assessment of content. Cherie A. Rohn drafted the better maps and diagrams, standardized them all, and proofread the final copy. Patty Hess Killman achieved the remarkable typing of the finished version. Many other persons have also offered suggestions and help that is gratefully acknowledged even though they cannot all be mentioned by name.

CULTURAL CHANGE AND CONTINUITY
ON CHAPIN MESA

Cultural Change and Continuity on Chapin Mesa

by

ARTHUR H. ROHN

THE REGENTS PRESS OF KANSAS
Lawrence

CONTENTS

LIST OF FIGURES

LIST OF TABLES

I

INTRODUCTION

Chapin Mesa is one of several long narrow tongues of relatively high and flat land that constitute the Mesa Verde in southwestern Colorado (fig. 1). Subdivision of this large erosional remnant into its finger-like constituents has resulted from the cutting of deep steep-sided north-south canyons draining intermittently southward into the Mancos River and ultimately through the San Juan and Colorado Rivers to the Gulf of California.

Detailed descriptions of Mesa Verde's geology and physiography and of its natural environment are readily available in published form (e.g., Wanek 1959; Osborne 1964; O'Bryan 1950; Erdman, Douglas and Marr 1969; among others), so I shall not repeat them here. It is sufficient to characterize the setting as a semi-arid pinyon-juniper woodland where precipitation is adequate for dry farming, yet erratic enough to pose a serious threat. Permanent water is available only from springs for the streams in the canyons flow only after rainstorms. There are abundant wild sources of food and raw materials, and natural conditions would permit farming with a primitive technology.

The environmental factor of primary importance to this study is physiography. Travel and communication along the flat mesa tops are easy, but the steep canyon walls hinder foot traffic from one finger mesa to the next. The canyons do not prevent travel across them; rather, several times as much time and energy is required to cross a canyon than to cover an equal distance on the mesa top. Thus, the physiography must have influenced to a degree the extent of interpersonal contacts in prehistoric times. The effects of environment receive fuller attention in the chapters where they are pertinent.

Mesa Verde National Park occupies a large portion of the Mesa Verde extending from the high north rim down to and including its middle elevations. Chapin Mesa, the largest of the finger mesas in area, extends well south of the south park

1

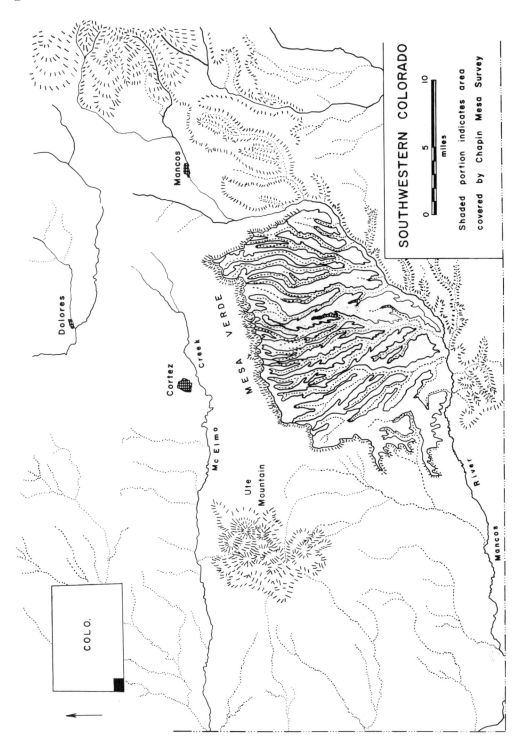

Figure 1. Southwestern Colorado

boundary. Soda and Little Soda Canyons demarcate the eastern
side of Chapin Mesa with Navaho Canyon on the west. Rainwater
runs off into one or the other of these through numerous tributaries including Cliff and Fewkes Canyons to the east and
Spruce and Pool Canyons on the west.

History of Chapin Mesa Archaeology

        Following the discoveries and initial explorations by
Richard Wetherill and his brothers (e.g., see McNitt 1957),
Gustav Nordenskiöld dug in several of Mesa Verde's cliff houses
during the summer of 1891. On Chapin Mesa, John Wetherill
helped him clear most of Painted Kiva House (Site 557) and
guided him to other large ruins which he described in the first
scientific publication on Mesa Verde prehistory (Nordenskiöld
1893).
        Although each successive year witnessed much unre-
corded digging, it was not until the establishment of Mesa
Verde National Park in 1906 that systematic studies resumed.
Jesse Walter Fewkes assumed the task of preparing the major
ruins on Chapin Mesa for the edification of visitors to the new
park. Between 1907 and the early 1920's, Fewkes excavated 18
sites in addition to re-excavating Painted Kiva House (Fewkes
1909, 1911, 1915, 1916a, 1916b, 1916c, 1917, 1920, 1921, 1922,
1923; Linton n.d.).
        In 1910, Jesse L. Nusbaum excavated and stabilized
Balcony House (Site 615) under the sponsorship of the Colorado
Cliff Dwellers' Association (Nusbaum 1911). Subsequently, during his tenure as superintendent of Mesa Verde National Park in
the 1920's, he searched for traces of Basket Maker occupation
in several cave sites. On Chapin Mesa, Nusbaum worked in Sites
510 and 519 as well as the refuse behind Spruce Tree House
(Site 640). None of this work has so far been described in
print.
        In 1934 with the help of Robert F. Burgh and James A.
Lancaster, Earl Morris carried out extensive stabilization work
at Cliff Palace (Site 625) and at Far View House (Site 808).
Although never published, records from this work provide the
most exact information available on the latter site.
        Development of a dating method by A. E. Douglass
through the study of tree-rings brought about the sampling of
well-preserved timbers from Mesa Verde's dry cave sites by
several of Douglass's co-workers during the early 1930's. Tree-
ring dates for logs from various Chapin Mesa sites appeared in
several issues of the Tree-Ring Bulletin (Douglass 1938;

Schulman 1946; Smiley 1950), but only one site, Spruce Tree House, contained a number of datable timbers in situ large enough to provide dependable dating of the ruin (Getty 1935a and 1935b).

As part of Gila Pueblo's comprehensive coverage of the Southwest, Harold S. Gladwin began in 1941-42 a gross reconnaissance of non-cliff sites on the Mesa Verde, especially on Chapin Mesa. Excavations in five sites on and near Chapin Mesa by Deric O'Bryan followed in 1947-48. In his published report (O'Bryan 1950), O'Bryan described the results of both his work and Gladwin's survey and attempted to synthesize Mesa Verde prehistory in terms of the Gila Pueblo classificatory system (Gladwin and Gladwin 1934).

Beginning in this same period and continuing to the present time, the staff at Mesa Verde National Park has conducted a series of small excavations, either to salvage sites threatened with destruction or to enhance the Park interpretive program. Most of these have been reported in print (Lancaster and Watson 1942; Smiley 1949; Lancaster, Pinkley, Van Cleave and Watson 1954; Cassidy 1960; Luebben, Herold and Rohn 1960; Luebben, Rohn and Givens 1962; and Hayes and Lancaster 1962). Descriptions of several others, located on Chapin Mesa, appear in this volume.

After the beginning of the Chapin Mesa Survey in 1951, the University of Colorado excavated four sites near Far View House from 1953 through 1955 (Lister 1964; 1965; and 1966). More recently, the expansion of facilities at Mesa Verde National Park led to the Wetherill Mesa Archaeological Project and necessitated the salvage of additional small sites. Since 1965, the University of Colorado has conducted excavations at numerous Mesa Verde sites including several on Chapin Mesa.

The Archaeological Site Survey

In October 1951 Mesa Verde National Park initiated a survey of its archaeological resources to improve its plan for future development. Efforts were first concentrated on Chapin Mesa where the then existing exhibits and accommodations were located and where the bulk of previous archaeological attention had been focused. As new facilities were developed--such as the campground in Morfield Canyon--additional portions of the park were also surveyed. Wetherill Mesa was incorporated into the Archaeological Site Survey as the second major physiographic segment of the Mesa Verde to be intensively surveyed.

The present study encompasses only those sites

recorded on Chapin Mesa, as previously delineated, in order to provide a physiographic unity for the problem and to delimit its scope. Standard field survey techniques were employed, and only clearly recognizable sites were recorded.

Each location of unquestioned human activity was assigned a consecutive site number, starting with "1", in the order they were recorded. This number was stamped on a steel stake that was implanted near the center of the site for later identification. All written records, maps, photographs, and collected specimens bear the appropriate site number. A single number generally includes only contiguous remains; spatial discontinuity unless it appeared unimportant usually occasioned the use of additional numbers. As we shall see from the results of the Chapin Mesa Survey, this practice proved quite useful in an area where prehistoric remains of human activity are found so heavily concentrated and intermingled.

Cautions in the Use of Survey Data

The part of Chapin Mesa within the national park boundaries has been intensively searched for signs of prehistoric occupation or use. In spite of this, many remains have certainly escaped notice. Dense vegetation prevented thorough examination of the ground surface in some places-- especially the chaparral-covered zones toward the north, both on the mesa top and on the lower canyon slopes. Erosion probably damaged some sites beyond recognition to judge by various suspicious-looking situations where no positive evidence was visible. In this vein, the presence of several scattered sherds or stone chips could not be regarded as a site because of the many potential upslope sources from which they could have drifted.

Still other sites left no traces whatsoever on the ground surface, having been obliterated by later deposition. The accidental discoveries through construction of pipelines, roads, and houses of Sites 117, 354, 405, 1032, and 1060, among others, in previously surveyed areas, demonstrate this point. Furthermore, re-examination of once surveyed ground frequently resulted in the recording of additional sites. It may even be quite presumptuous to estimate that 80 per cent of the sites on Chapin Mesa have been recorded.

The inability of a site survey to discover all sites of past human activity is only one weakness of this field technique. An archaeologist can only guess as to the precise nature of any given site when limited to its surface appearance

after centuries of decay.   Nearly every excavation or test conducted on a surveyed site showed discrepancies between what
actually was found and the surveyor's estimate of what he would
expect to find.

The Problem of Culture Change

        In spite of these various limitations, data acquired
from intensive archaeological survey can be applied against
many kinds of problems. The most general problem and perhaps
the most difficult to treat concerns the nature of cultural
evolution and change.   By its very complexity, this problem
defies full understanding from the results of a single research
project. Instead we must first isolate for examination various
aspects of the ways in which cultures change almost as a laboratory scientist would isolate variables that might affect the
outcome of an experiment. The analogy is greatly oversimpli-
fied, as the reader will realize by attempting merely to
comprehend the nature of culture itself, much less the process
by which it may alter its content.
        For any student of culture change, archaeology serves
as an excellent approach by providing data in chronological
context.   Since the archaeological record lacks many cultural
segments that can be observed by ethnologists, who in turn
suffer from a lack of time depth for their data, it would seem
axiomatic that useful studies might avail themselves of the
knowledge and theoretical concepts of both these sub-disci-
plines of anthropology.
        Ethnologists have tended to concentrate on aspects of
social organization and religion, while archaeologists, by
necessity, have concentrated on durable elements of material
culture.   Each group has tended to overlook the chief subject
matter of the other.   (There are some notable exceptions, of
course.) In this study I intend to focus prime attention
on two aspects of culture change that could be examined by both
ethnologists and archaeologists, possibly even jointly. The
first of these aspects concerns recognition of continuities in
a cultural pattern through times when marked changes are taking
place; the second attempts to decipher changes in nonmaterial
culture as interpreted through analyses of archaeological
remains.
        The magnitude of culture change can only be assessed
realistically in contrast to cultural continuity through the
same period of time. This is not a simple matter. For example,
the shapes and decorative styles of pottery vessels may change,

while the tradition of pottery making and its technology show no change. It would be equally justifiable to consider this same situation as a continuity in pottery manufacture and use with the recognition of stylistic evolution. Because virtually every published discussion of Mesa Verde prehistory has pointed out the changes through time in ceramics, stoneworking, architecture, settlement pattern, and economy, I shall emphasize both specific and general continuities in these same aspects of culture. All continuities will be set against the framework of a suggested phase sequence for Chapin Mesa in which the main changes will be summarized.

Intensive archaeological survey produces data especially applicable to the interpretation of some nonmaterial aspects of culture. An intensive survey records all traces of human activity, not just loci of habitation. On Chapin Mesa, non-habitation sites included devices for the management of water resources, temporary shelters in field areas, shrines, and other structures that appear to have had ceremonial connotations. From the distributions of habitation sites, it is possible to recognize different locations chosen for house placement. Clusters of contemporary houses presumably represent communities of people whose locations and relative sizes may be seen to fluctuate. Finally, estimates of population and population density can be made, at least on a relative scale.

The chapters that follow present the descriptions of what the Chapin Mesa Survey found. Habitation sites are separated from non-habitation sites and each of these categories is further subdivided into groups of similar sites. The bases for interpreting each group as I do are presented along with the descriptions. Previously unreported excavations are summarized in their respective site groupings. Ceramics and other material findings are considered as they contribute toward the general knowledge of Mesa Verde prehistory and to the major theme of this study. The final chapters contain interpretations of this mass of data as they seem to reflect continuity and change in the prehistoric Indian culture of Chapin Mesa.

II

HABITATION SITES

In the ensuing two chapters, the archaeological sites recorded on Chapin Mesa are described primarily according to their surficial appearance, and specific location, or situation. Thus, "burned stone mounds" are distinguished from "rubble mounds" and from "talus sites." The size and content of surface collections also helped characterize site categories, but ceramic styles were employed mainly for subsequent chronological assignments.

The reader will eventually discover many of the habitation site categories fit into a single chronological unit. On the Mesa Verde, architectural practices seem to have changed as markedly as ceramics through time, and the variously-built distinctive structures tended to collapse into distinctive patterns. The plan of a mound, or the presence of distinctive building stones, possesses both descriptive and chronological significance. The first category of Basket Maker III pithouse sites deviates most from these principles because the sites are virtually invisible on the ground surface.

Basket Maker III Pithouse Sites

An accurate count of the number of Basket Maker III pithouses on Chapin Mesa is practically impossible. The surface indications of such a structure may be nonexistent or so indistinct as to be unrecognizable from the natural ground surface. Almost all pithouses that have so far been excavated or located by testing lacked any outward evidence of their presence until the ground surface was disturbed. However, several untested sites with a few surface signs probably represent Basket Maker III pithouses too.

These last are characterized by a small cluster of fire-reddened stones, not over seven yards in diameter, lying on the level ground (no mound), with some sherds, stone chips, and occasionally tiny lumps of burned adobe intermingled. The potsherds, with few exceptions, are classifiable as Chapin

Gray or Chapin Black-on-white. Occasionally upright slabs are
visible, forming arcs, which suggest a slab-lined pithouse like
Site 283 (Lancaster and Watson 1942: Pithouse C). Most sites
in this category appear to represent a single structure, but a
few, such as Sites 715 and 13, consist of several clusters of
burned stones and sherds and may represent as many as six pithouses. It is, of course, possible that any site may include
several pithouses not discernible on the surface.

Most other Basket Maker III houses have been found by
accidental means, such as ditching for water lines or building
and road construction, or by programs of organized testing.
Apparently only Sites 118 and 283 showed surface indications
before they were dug. Sites 405, 1060, and 1061 were cut by
pipeline ditches; Site 354 was salvaged from road construction;
Site 364 showed up under a concessioner's cabin location.
O'Bryan trenched a large area to locate two pithouses at Site
145 (O'Bryan 1950), and a determined National Park Service
program to locate a late pithouse for exhibit turned up 12
structures before Site 101 was chosen for excavation. Two pithouses were found beneath later houses at Site 16 (Lancaster
and Pinkley 1954) and another beneath a masonry pueblo at Site
59.

While the survey has recorded 52 Basket Maker III
sites consisting of possibly 65 individual pithouses (table 1),
only a fraction of the real total is probably represented. Who
knows how many do not show at all on the surface, as at the 22
sites found by methods other than survey? Secondly, there are
many small concentrations of burned stones and potsherds that
have not been grouped with the pithouses for various reasons.
Any site yielding Pueblo I or later pottery, which did not
appear to be obvious drift from other sites, was excluded.

No cluster of burned stones occurring in a mound has
been included in this grouping; these frequently contained
later pottery. Many sites of this sort are described as Basket
Maker III-Pueblo I burned stone mounds and are lumped in the
general category of miscellaneous burned stone mounds and other
sites. In spite of these limitations, the 52 recorded sites
represent a sizable number in the Mesa Verde district.

Since no more can be said about unexcavated sites,
the following descriptions are limited to those sites that have
been excavated but never reported fully in print.

Site 118 (Earth Lodge A). During the field season of
1919, Ralph Linton served as assistant to J. W. Fewkes at Mesa
Verde and excavated two sites on the mesa top near Square Tower
House, which he described in an unpublished manuscript entitled
"The Small Open Ruins of the Mesa Verde." One of these was a

Table 1
PITHOUSE SITES

Site No.	No. Houses 3-4	Excavated By	Tested By	Size of Burned Rock Area	Burned Adobe	Upright Slabs	Remarks	POTTERY Chapin Gray	Chapin B/W	Abajo R/O	Others	Total Sherds
13				15' dia.	yes			34	2		5	41
16	2	Lancaster 1950(1)		covered by later site								
35	1		O'Bryan	20 yds.dia.	yes	yes	T-R dates— A.D. 653+	33	2			35
59	1		Lancaster 1941				T-R dates— A.D. 626	32	1	1	70	104
60	1		Lancaster 1941(2)	35' dia.				6			6	12
68	1		Lancaster 1950	None								
101	2	Lancaster 1950(3)		None			T-R dates— ca.A.D. 675 & 700					
104	1		Lancaster 1950	None	yes			23	1		1	25
105	1		Lancaster 1950	10' X 15'				10	1			11
106	1		Lancaster 1950	None			burial trough metate	2 jars 67	4		4	75
108	1		Lancaster 1950	None				4				4
109	1		Lancaster 1950	None				4	1			5
110	1		Lancaster 1950	None				7	1		1	9
112	1		Lancaster 1950	None								
113	1		Lancaster 1950	None								
114	1		Lancaster 1950	None								
115	1		Nusbaum & Morris 1933 Lancaster 1950	None			trough metate	½ bowl 1 effigy				
116	1		Lancaster 1950	None								
117	1	Lancaster 1941(4)		None	yes		T-R dates— A.D. 595					
118	1	Linton 1919 Nusbaum & Morris 1933 Lancaster & Watson 1941						10				10
145	2	O'Bryan 1947(5)										
283	1	Lancaster & Watson 1941(6)		None		yes	T-R dates— A.D. 612 or 650					
285	1			5 X 5 yds.				15				15

Table 1 (cont.)
PITHOUSE SITES

Site No.	No. Houses	Excavated By	Tested By	Size of Burned Rock Area	Burned Adobe	Upright Slabs	Remarks	POTTERY: Chapin Gray	Chapin B/W	Abajo R/O	Others	Total Sherds
320	1	Lancaster 1948(7)		7 yds.dia.	yes			25	2	2		29
354	1		Lancaster & Abel 1953	None		yes	T-R dates- A.D.629+ or 688		1 bowl		2	
364	1?	Smiley 1939(8)			yes		burial	72				74
405	1			None				18	3			21
412	1			5 yds.dia.	yes			13				13
414	1			20 yds.dia.				4				4
416	1			5 X 5 yds.				10				10
433	1			5 X 5 yds.				15	1			16
435	1			10 X 10yds.				9				9
442	1			5 X 5 yds.				12				12
443	1			5 yds.dia.				10	1			11
467	1			10 yds.dia.	yes			3				3
701				ca.5yds.dia.				7			2	9
702	2 clusters			10 X 30yds.				12				12
712	1?			Indef.		yes		13	1			14
715	6 clusters			ea. cluster 3 to 5yds.dia.		yes		16				16
731	1			12 yds.dia.				5				5
734	1			10 yds.dia.				12	1		3	16
735	2 or more clusters			7 yds.dia.	yes	yes		21	1		1	23
771	1			5 yds.dia.		yes		16	1			17
784	1			5 yds.dia.	yes			22			3	25
787	1			5 yds. dia.				25			2	27
792	1			5 yds.dia.	yes		1 point	17				17
847	1?			5 yds.dia.				16			1	17
848	1			5 yds.dia.	yes							
996	1			5 yds.dia.	yes			61	8		1	70
1048	1			5 yds.dia.				11	1			12
1060	1	Lancaster & Hayes 1959(9)		None								
1061		Lancaster & Rudy 1959		None								

Table 1 (cont.)
PITHOUSE SITES

NOTES:

(1) Lancaster and Pinkley 1954

(2) Jennings 1968

(3) Lancaster and Watson 1954

(4) Lancaster and Watson 1942

(5) O'Bryan 1950

(6) Lancaster and Watson 1942

(7) Lancaster 1968

(8) Smiley 1949

(9) Hayes and Lancaster 1962

Basket Maker pithouse. When in the course of excavating it
Linton encountered a crude circle of sloping charred beams, he
apparently assumed these to be the side walls and stopped his
investigation there. But once other pithouses had been excavated in Step House and in the La Plata District, Jesse L.
Nusbaum and Earl Morris returned to "complete" the excavation,
probably in 1934. Several additional details were exposed by J.
A. Lancaster and Don Watson in 1941.

A combination of the discoveries by all these workers
furnishes the following picture. The house was nearly circular,
approximately 19 feet in diameter, with a narrow banquette set
only slightly below the ground surface. Most of the wall was
clay-lined, but several upright stone slabs helped form the
southern portion. The roof once rested on four upright posts,
set in the floor, with secondary poles sloping between the
basic framework and the banquette. An antechamber on the south
side had almost completely eroded away. Other features
included an upright slab deflector, mud wing walls, circular
clay-lined hearth, sipapu, and a large bell-shaped cist.
Although no accurate floor plan of this house has ever been
made, figure 2 depicts the probable appearance of such a plan
based on fragmentary data.

Site 364. This badly eroded site was tested twice;
once, revealing groups of upright sandstone slabs but no
definable floor, and the other time, producing a burial
surrounded by refuse 25 yards to the south (fig. 3). The
skeleton was that of a man about 40 years old resting on his
back with legs drawn up into a semi-flexed position and arms
laid across his abdomen. Two Chapin Black-on-white bowls
flanked the undeformed skull which pointed to the west. From
the sherds recovered in the burial excavation, part of a Chapin
Gray--Chapin Variety seed jar was restored.

Site 106. One of the structures encountered by the
National Park Service Testing program in 1950 contained a
burial in its fill about four inches above the floor (fig. 4).
An adult male whose skull was long and undeformed lay on his
back, head to the north, his legs in a flexed position with the
knees pointing at right angles to the trunk. The right arm
rested along his side and the left across the abdomen. There
were no grave offerings. On the pithouse floor beneath the
grave, a trough metate propped up for use and a small Chapin
Gray--Chapin Variety seed jar were found by excavator Jean
Pinkley.

Site 1061. In October 1959 a ditching machine, working on a new water line to Cliff Palace, cut through the ventilator of a deep unburned pithouse. Subsequent excavation

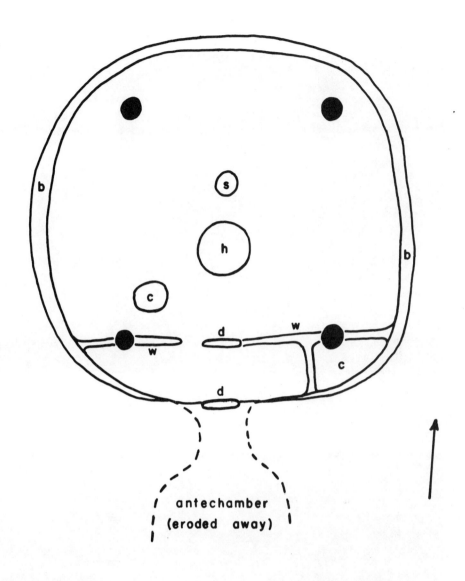

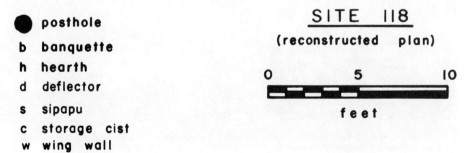

Figure 2. Site 118 (reconstructed plan).

Figure 3. Burial from Site 364.

Figure 4. Burial from Site 106.

revealed a squarish plan, 10 feet across, with well rounded
corners (fig. 5). Its ancient builders had dug through 2½ to
3 feet of red loess and hard caliche before making their floor.
Features included an extremely large ventilator, two upright
slabs both of which apparently functioned as deflectors, a slab
wing wall, a circular mud-lined hearth, sipapu, five floor pits
or cists, two wall cists, and four large postholes for roof
supports. There was no banquette. The floor pits ranged from
2½ to 8 inches deep; the four shallow ones contained sand
perhaps to accomodate round-bottomed pots, while the deep pit
may have been for storage. None of the roofing material
remained.

The fill did not appear to be refuse although sherds
appeared throughout it. No other artifacts were found. Only
two pottery types were present--Chapin Black-on-white (13
sherds) and Chapin Gray (205)--with one unclassified sherd. All
of the Chapin Black-on-white sherds represented bowls decorated
with organic paint, and five had a fugitive red wash on their
exteriors. Two of four rims were painted solid. Crushed rock
temper predominates, but two sherds contain sand. Twenty-two
sherds of Chapin Gray including three bowl rims, show fugitive
red coloring. The twenty rim sherds include ten from necked
jars, four from seed jars, and six from bowls. Although it is
unlikely, these six bowl rim sherds could simply be undecorated
portions of black-on-white vessels. Prominent crushed rock
temper and rough surfaces characterize most sherds, but a
significant number of surfaces were well smoothed and even
polished. It would be impossible to draw a line through the
broad transition zone between rough and polished surfaces.

Slab-based Houses - Pueblo I

Three chief characteristics served to identify Pueblo
I house sites: 1) a long narrow mound of burned stones; 2) the
presence of upright slabs; and 3) pottery. The mounds measure
up to 70 yards long, average 3 to 6 yards wide, and stand
normally 6 to 18 inches higher than the surrounding ground
level. They consist of small irregular fragments of fire-
reddened sandstone, frequently chunks of burned adobe, with
some potsherds and stone chips, carried in a relatively loose
dark gray soil. Masonry-size building stones are always absent
unless the remains of a masonry pueblo stand nearby. Upright
slabs were visible on 90 of 123 sites and burned adobe was
recorded for about one-fourth of them (table 2).

These features all imply wattle-and-daub wall con-

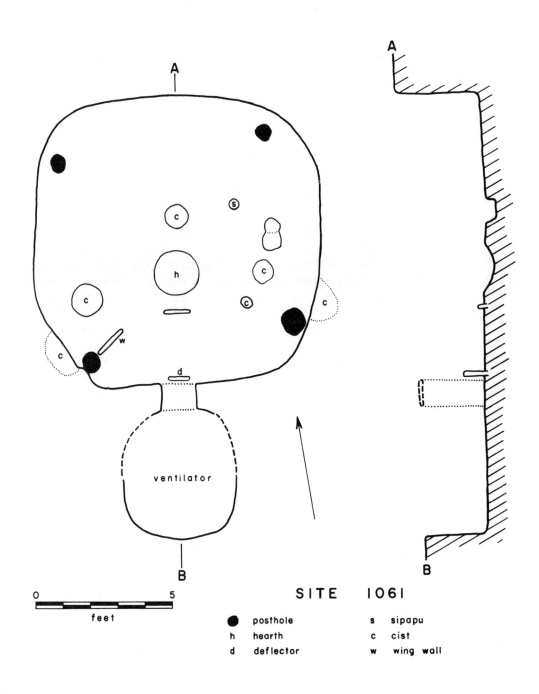

Figure 5.

Table 2
SLAB–BASED HOUSE SITES

Site No. (PH = Pithouse)	Room Estimate (R = Rooms)	Excavated (E) Or Tested (T) By	Size Of Mound (Yards)	Burned Adobe	Upright Slabs	Remarks	Chapin Gray	Chapin Gray-Moccasin Var.	Chapin B/W	Piedra B/W	Reds	Cortez B/W	Mancos Gray	Corrugated	Other B/W's	Unclassified	TOTAL SHERDS
1	5+ R	E – O'Bryan 1947[1]					22		1		2			2			27
16	1+ PH	E – Lancaster 1950[2]			yes		16			1				1		3	21
20	ca. 4-8 R		13 X 7 yds.		yes		9										9
22	ca. 2-3 R		8 X 4 yds.		yes												
33	ca. 3-4 R		5 yds. dia.	yes													
45	ca. 3-5 R		5 X 5 yds.		hearth		8			1							9
46	ca. 2-3 R		3 yds. dia.	yes	yes		17			1	3					2	23
58	ca. 4-6 R / 2 PH	T – Pinkley 1947	12 yds. long		yes	T-R date A.D. 847 / Ref. mound	27	8	4	9	16			1		4	69
64	ca. 4-5 R		15 yds. long		yes	Ref. mound	19		2						1		23
78	ca. 3-4 R		14 X 5 yds.		yes		8							1			9
84	ca. 5 R?				yes		13		2								15
90	ca. 3 R?						13		2				1				16
95		ca. 5 R?			yes	Twin Trees Village	14									4	19
103	4+ ca. 6-10 R / 4+ ? PH	E – O'Bryan 1947[3]				(See table 4)											
107		T – Lancaster 1950			yes		3			1							4
111	2+ ca. 6-10 R	T – Rohn & Lancaster 1959	20 X 7 yds.			under PII house											
125						Ref. mound	9			2	2	20	16	3	8	11	71
131	ca. 5-7 R	T – Gila Pueblo	15 X 3 yds.		yes	trough metate / Ref. mound	50		4		1	1			7	6	69
137	ca. 4-6 R			yes	yes	point / Ref. mound	82		4		1				1	4	92
154			5 X 3 yds.	yes	yes		5			2		1		1		1	3
159	ca. 3-5 R		5 X 3 yds.		yes		28							2		2	32
175	ca. 2 R		8 X 3 yds.		yes		4										6
180	ca. 2-3+ R		5 X 3 yds.		yes		10								2	1	11
185	ca. 2-3 R				yes	Ref. mound	30				2					2	32
187							7										8
209	ca. 10-20 R		33 X 5 yds.			Ref. mound	12		4	1				1	2	2	22
224	ca. 8-15 R		25 X 5 yds.		yes	Ref. mound	23		2						1	1	27

Table 2 (cont.)
SLAB-BASED HOUSE SITES

Site No.	Room Estimate (R = Rooms) (PH = Pithouse)	Excavated (E) Or Tested (T) By	Size Of Mound (Yards)	Burned Adobe	Upright Slabs	Remarks	Chapin Gray	Chapin Gray-Moccasin Var.	Chapin B/W	Piedra B/W	Reds	Cortez B/W	Mancos Gray	Corrugated	Other B/W's	Unclassified	Total Sherds
225	ca. 3–5 R		10 X 5 yds.		yes	Ref. mound	14		2					1		1	15
242	ca. 4–6 R		15 X 5 yds.		yes	Ref. mound	25							1	2	1	29
249	ca. 2 R		5 X 2 yds.			trough metate	10									2	12
250	ca. 1 R		2 X 2 yds.		yes							1			1	1	4
251	ca. 2–3 R		7 X 5 yds.			Ref. mound	9										9
254	ca. 7–10 R		22 X 8 yds.	yes			17					1			1		23
259	ca. 2 R		7 X 5 yds.	yes			13					1				1	15
260	ca. 5–8 R		14 X 5 yds.		yes	Ref. mound	31		3						1	2	39
264	ca. 2 R		5 X 2 yds.		yes		10			2					1		11
271	ca. 4–6 R		12 X 7 yds.	yes	yes	Ref. mound	23		5						1		24
277	ca. 3–4 R		8 X 5 yds.	yes	yes?		4		2		1				1	2	7
280	ca. 4–8 R		12 X 9 yds.	yes	yes	Ref. mound	30		4		1				1	1	34
288	ca. 3–6 R		11 X 8 yds.		yes	under later houses	42			2						1	48
Subtotal								1	2	2	3	30	32	71	141	7	**314**
299	ca. 2 R		6 X 2 yds.	yes	yes		21		2	2							28
300	ca. 3 R		10 X 2 yds.		yes		13		1	1				3	2	1	13
302	ca. 2–3 R		5 yds. dia.		yes		10										11
310	ca. 7–10 R		23 X 4 yds.		yes	Ref. mound	22		1		1			1	4	1	30
316	ca. 2 R, 1 PH	T – O'Bryan 1941	6 X 3 yds.		yes		15		2				2		1	1	18
318	ca. 6 R		18 X 5 yds.	yes	yes	Ref. mound	29		3		1					1	33
319	ca. 4–6 R		6 yds. dia.	yes	yes	Ref. mound	16		1			1			1		18
327	ca. 5–10		15 X 6 yds.				18		3							1	21
332	ca. 4–8 R		13 X 7 yds.				29		1		1						31
333	ca. 4–5 R		15 X 2 yds.		yes	Ref. mound	19		1						1	1	22
334	ca. 5–6 R		18 X 3 yds.		yes	Ref. mound	10							3	3	1	24
337	ca. 3 R		10 yds. long				7									4	7
353	1 PH	E – Lancaster 1948(4)			yes		52				1	1				3	60
359	ca. 8–10 R		25 X 3 yds.	yes	yes		19	1	2	2	1		1	2			21
360	ca. 4–5 R		15 X 3 yds.	yes	yes		59	2	2	4	3			13	9	14	106
361	ca. 4–5 R		14 X 4 yds.	yes	yes		11	4	1	4	2				2		24
362				yes	yes		7									3	12
363	ca. 6–7 R		17 X 3 yds.	yes	yes							1		1			
370	ca. 20–30 R / 1+ ? PH		54 X 3 yds.	yes	yes	Ref. mound	102	37	12	24	113	1	1	4	11	5	309

Table 2 (cont.)
SLAB-BASED HOUSE SITES

Site No.	Room Estimate (R = Rooms, PH = Pithouse)	Size Of Mound (Yards)	Burned Adobe	Upright slabs	Remarks	Chapin Gray	Chapin Gray-Moccasin Var.	Chapin B/W	Piedra B/W	Reds	Cortez B/W	Mancos Gray	Corrugated	Other B/W's	Unclassified	TOTAL SHERDS
371	ca. 2 R					48		2	1	1	1				1	1	55
373	ca. 10 R	30 X 3 yds.	yes	yes		73	3	3	3	21				6	1	110
376	ca. 9-10 R	27 yds. long		yes	Ref. mound	102	2	3	3	16			1	2	4	133
386	ca. 20-25 R	70 X 5 yds.	yes	yes		127	6		9	16	1			10	8	177
387	3-4 PH ?			yes		36	5		1	1			1		2	46
389	ca. 3 R	12 yds. dia.	yes	yes		64	6	2		8			1			81
398	ca. 10-12 R	8 yds. dia.		yes		101			1	2	2		1		1	108
408	ca. 2-3 R	10 yds. dia.	yes	yes	under PII house	20		4	1	1	2		9	3	1	41
413	ca. 3-4 R	20 yds. dia.		yes		10							1	1	1	13
415	ca. 6 R	25 X 10 yds.		yes		39		2				2	2			45
417	ca. 8-10 R	24 X 7 yds.	yes	yes		27		2		3					3	35
419	ca. 8-10 R	8 X 5 yds.	yes	yes		22		1		3						26
420	ca. 2-3 R	5 X 5 yds.		yes		25			1							26
427	ca. 2 R			yes		20		1	1							22
429	ca. 3-4 R	10 X 10 yds.		yes	could be natural outcrop / could be slab pithouse	2			1					1	2	5
438	ca. 2 R	6 X 3 yds.	yes	yes		32										32
445	ca. 5-10 R	25 yds. long	yes	yes		52			1							53
449	ca. 5-10 R	15 X 5 yds.		yes		20								2		22
450	ca. 3-4 R	10 X 5 yds.		yes		5										5
455	ca. 2 R		yes	yes		43							1			44
459	ca. 1 R	2 X 2 yds.		yes		4								2		6
466	ca. 4-5 R					16	1			1						18
473	ca. 15-20 R					36		1		2						39
474	ca. 25-30 R					34				2		1	1	2		40
476	ca. 8-10 R					35		1				1	1	4	1	43
494	ca. 3-6 R	5 X 4 yds.	yes	yes		7										7
704	ca. 5-8 R	32 X 4 yds.	yes	yes		19		1	1	3						24
722	ca. 1 R	Indistinct		yes		5										5
732	ca. 4 R	14 X 5 yds.		yes		6					2					8
733	?	Indistinct	yes			27				4					3	34

POTTERY

Excavated (E) Or Tested (T) By

Table 2 (cont.)
SLAB–BASED HOUSE SITES

Site No.	Room Estimate (R = Rooms, PH = Pithouse)	Excavated (E) or Tested (T) By	Size Of Mound (Yards)	Burned Adobe	Upright Slabs	Remarks	Chapin Gray	Chapin Gray–Moccasin Var.	Chapin B/W	Piedra B/W	Reds	Cortez B/W	Mancos Gray	Corrugated	Other B/W's	Unclassified	Total Sherds
742	ca. 12-18 R		55 yds. long	yes		burial	52	4	1	2	3			1	1	2	66
745	ca. 7-10 R		20 X 10 yds.		yes		59	2	1		1			2		2	67
748	ca. 7-8 R		20 X 5 yds.		yes		7	1							2		10
754	ca. 3 R		10 X 5 yds.		yes		1										1
756	?		Indistinct		yes												
757	ca. 2-3 R		10 yds.dia.				29	1			1			2			33
759	ca. 5-6 R		15 X 5 yds.		yes		24	1			1			1			27
760	ca. 2-3 R		10 X 10 yds.				5	1		2							8
763	ca. 20-25 R		64 yds. long	yes	yes		13			1					2	1	17
764	ca. 7-8 R		23 X 4 yds.		yes		38		12					1			54
765	ca. 9-10 R		27 yds. long		yes		43										44
766	ca. 7-8 R		20 X 5 yds.		yes		30										31
769	?		30 X 10 yds.		yes	under PII house	32		1						2	1	36
772	ca. 10 R		8 X 4 yds.		yes		37							2			39
775	ca. 2-3 R			yes	yes		20				1		1				22
777	ca. 2-3 R		5 yds.dia.			could also be slab pithouse	33		2						1		36
785	?			yes		under PII house	23			1	1			6	3	3	40
786	ca. 6-8 R	T – Rohn 1958				(See table 3)											
788	1+ PH / 2 R						4							1			5
793	ca. 4-5 R		5 yds.dia.	yes	yes		69	3		6	28				2	3	111
795	ca. 10-15 R		10 yds.dia.		yes		34	3		2	3					2	44
796	ca. 3-4 R		34 X 8 yds.	yes	yes		6							1			7
846	ca. 3-4 R		5 X 5 yds.	yes	yes		4										5
849	ca. 2-3 R		3 X 3 yds.		yes		6										6
850	ca. 3-4 R		12 X 5 yds.		yes		26	2		2	3			1		1	35
851						presence under PIII house indicated by pottery	43	1		3	15			12	4	4	82
853	ca. 5-6 R	T – Lister 1956	15 X 3 yds.		yes		23				2			1		2	28
858	ca. 2-3 R		5 yds.dia.				12		1		1			1			15
861	ca. 8-10 R		26 yds. long	yes	yes		11							3			14

Table 2 (cont.)
SLAB–BASED HOUSE SITES

Site No.	Rooms Estimate (R = Rooms) (PH = Pithouse)	Excavated (E) Or Tested (T) By	Size Of Mound (Yards)	Burned Adobe	Upright Slabs	Remarks	Chapin Gray	Chapin Gray-Moccasin Var.	Chapin B/W	Piedra B/W	Reds	Cortez B/W	Mancos Gray	Corrugated	Other B/W's	Unclassified	TOTAL SHERDS
937	ca. 2 R		5 X 3 yds.		yes		2		1								3
1040	ca. 3 R		10 X 3 yds.				15				2		1				18
1046	ca. 4-6 R		15 X 4 yds.		yes												
1047	ca. 15 R		45 X 4 yds.		yes		27	6	1	1	4	1	1	1	2	3	47

NOTES:

(1) O'Bryan 1950

(2) Lancaster and Pinkley 1954

(3) O'Bryan 1950

(4) Lancaster 1968a

struction with stone slabs frequently set upright in the wall
bases as at Site 103 (O'Bryan 1950: 37. O'Bryan designates
this as "Site 102 Village"). Test excavations at Sites 111 and
786 also revealed some post-and-adobe walls without slabs and
some adobe walls with few or no posts. This would certainly
help to explain the irregular spacing of visible stone slabs
and the apparent absence of slabs at some sites. The omni-
present small burned stones had probably been studded into the
jacal or adobe walls in the manner found at Alkali Ridge (Brew
1946).

The longer mounds usually describe an arc running
east-west across a low flat ridge crest, and probably represent
contiguous surface storage and living quarters. Pithouses lie
to the south, but depressions were discernible at only four
sites prior to testing or excavation. Refuse was normally
deposited in a sheet to the south of the house, but obvious
mounds of trash occur at 21 sites.

Small mounds representing houses of less than five
rooms outnumber the larger sites, but probably housed fewer
people collectively. Most of these occur in clusters with at
least one larger site. Some are associated with refuse mounds
and one has a pithouse depression.

Chapin Gray pottery predominated in the surface
collections from these sites. Both the Chapin and Moccasin
Varieties occurred, although the latter was recorded from only
23 per cent of unexcavated sites. However, excavations in five
slab-based houses have all produced neck-banded sherds, suggesting that this variety was not as rare as the surface
collections seem to indicate. Chapin Black-on-white and Piedra
Black-on-white occurred in approximately equal numbers. Locally
made redware, Abajo Red-on-orange and Bluff Black-on-red, was
found in significant quantities only on sites of this group.
Corrugated and Mancos Black-on-white sherds appeared only when
later components were also present and apparently stemmed from
such subsequent occupations. Sherds of Cortez Black-on-white
occasionally turned up among Pueblo I assemblages.

For simplicity during the survey, each distinct house
mound was assigned a separate site number. However, the mounds
were consistently found in clusters that somewhat resembled the
plans of Site 33 in the La Plata district (Morris 1939: fig.
18) and Site 13 on Alkali Ridge (Brew 1946: fig. 27). Some of
the clusters appear to represent a single contemporaneous
settlement, while others seem to include successively occupied
house mounds and may have received contributions from all of
them.

Descriptions of five individual unexcavated sites

will help to characterize the entire group. Sketch plans for
each appear in figure 6 while sherd counts are given in table
2. Following these are brief discussions on two tested sites.

Site 742. A long low mound of small burned stones
curves slightly to form a crescent, 55 yards in length and up
to 30 inches high, across a flat ridge crest. No slabs are
showing. Sheet trash consisting of potsherds, stone chips,
burned rocks, and some burned adobe extends about 100 yards to
the south. Pithouses probably lie near the south side of the
house mound, but specific depressions are not observable. All
but one of the 66 sherds belong to a typical Pueblo I assemblage. The lone corrugated sherd may be drift from a nearby
Pueblo II mound. A flexed burial with undeformed skull and most
of a large Chapin Gray jar were salvaged from the southeast side
of the refuse area.

Site 795. This mound of burned stone and a few
pieces of burned adobe measures about 34 yards SW-NE by about 8
yards wide and rises 6 to 10 inches above ground level. Two
upright stone slabs are visible near the center. None of the
stones is large enough for masonry work; no depressions were
noted. Sheet trash extends to the south. The site probably
consists of a row of contiguous jacal houses belonging to the
large village of which Sites 786 and 793 are also a part. All
44 sherds are typical Pueblo I types.

Site 319. This is a small mound of burned stone
about 18 by 5 yards in size and 6 inches high. Part of a slab-
based jacal room at the west end has been dug out at some time
in the past. A small refuse mound lies about 10 yards to the
south. Even though only Chapin Gray and Chapin Black-on-white
sherds were found on the surface, this site's physical appearance links it to this group.

Site 1046. A low mound of fire-reddened stones,
measuring 15 yards long by 4 yards wide and 6 inches high, has
three upright stone slabs showing as parts of two cross walls.
There are no shaped building stones and no pithouse depressions.
Scattered refuse lies to the south.

Site 318. This small burned stone mound, 6 by 3
yards and 12 inches high, has one upright stone slab visible.
A pithouse depression lies south of the mound among scattered
refuse. Pueblo I sherds covered the ground surface.

While heights were estimated at the centers of the
mounds, the ends are frequently difficult to distinguish from
the natural surroundings. Experience at Site 103, 111, and 786
has shown that the houses may extend well beyond the mound
limits visible on the surface. Thus, room estimates and site
sizes should be considered as minima based on visible signs

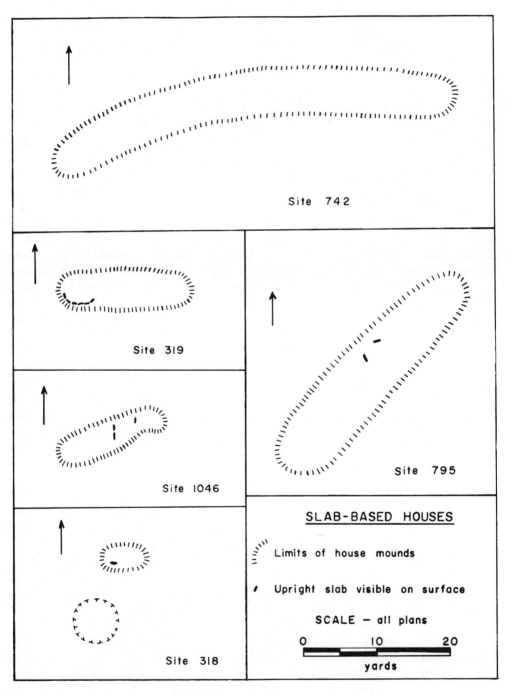

Figure 6.

only. In addition, a number of slabhouse sites were too
obscure to command attention during the survey. For example,
Sites 1046 and 1047 were both discovered about five years after
the survey in areas that had been intensively searched.

     Site 786. Had it not been for the mound formed by a
collapsing masonry shrine, the earlier remains at this site
might well have been overlooked. A limited test in 1958,
attempting to discover what this mound concealed, revealed
parts of a Pueblo I slab–house (fig. 7). Most of one large room
containing a hexagonal slab–lined firepit was cleared to floor,
about 4 inches below the old ground level. Several charred
poles of juniper and pinyon and many pieces of burned adobe
with pole impressions found on the floor indicate wattle–and–
daub construction. At least one sandstone slab leaned against
the base of the south wall. Part of a second smaller room
adjacent to its north side and probably used for storage was
also cleared.

     Once the true nature of the site was realized,
further testing to the south encountered a 7–foot deep pithouse,
one–third of which was then dug out. It had a roughly square
shape with rounded corners and a four–post roof support. One
wing wall was also exposed.

     Although the ground–level room had partly burned,
none of the charred wood could be salvaged for dating. The pithouse had not burned, but following its collapse or possible
dismemberment its depression was filled with later Pueblo I
refuse. Part of a trough metate, two broken manos, a broken
pitted hand hammer, the butt of a side–notched axe or hammer, a
sandstone saw, five hammerstones, and 65 utilized flakes came
from the pithouse fill, while one heavy grinding implement and
one hammerstone were found on its floor. The surface room
contained only a part of a trough metate. Sherd counts are
given in table 3. The 20 sherds of Mesa Verde Black-on-white
and Corrugated were found above or in the top fill of the Pueblo
I features.

     Also among the refuse filling the pithouse were 78
unworked animal bones. Nearly half (46 per cent) belong to hares
or rabbits (lagomorphs), while 40 per cent are those of
carnivores--mostly bobcat (Lynx rufus), with a few gray fox
(Urocyon cinerecargenteus) and coyote or dog (Canis sp.). There
were three artiodactyl bones, only one of which was surely
deer, and one element each of raven (Corvus corax) and rock
squirrel (Citellus variegatus). Several bones of pocket gophers
(Thomomys sp.) probably represent animals who died in their
burrows. This series is particularly notable for the complete
absence of turkey, the paucity of deer, and the high propor-

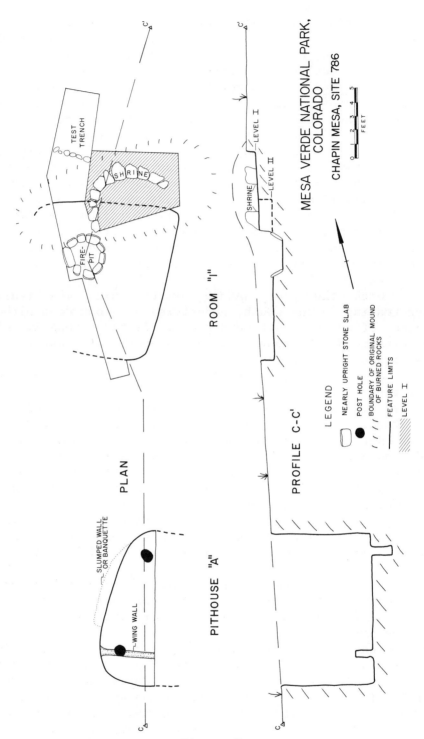

Figure 7.

Table 3

POTSHERDS FROM SITE 786

	Surface	Pithouse A, fill	Room 1, fill	Test trenches and surface	Shrine fill	Totals
Chapin B/W	1	0	0	0	0	1
Piedra B/W	1	114	4	1	2	122
Bluff B/R--Bluff Variety	0	11	0	2	1	14
Abajo R/O	0	9	0	0	0	9
Chapin Gray--						
Chapin Variety	1	50	7	6	2	66
Moccasin Variety	8	185	20	17	6	236
Body sherds	25	960	220	111	119	1435
Unclassified						
Reds	0	19	4	3	2	28
Plain sherds from B/W vessels	0	45	2	3	6	56
Black-on-white	0	18	3	1	0	22
Utility jar rims	0	0	0	0	6	6
Cortez B/W	0	2	0	0	1	3
Mancos Gray	0	0	0	1	1	2
Mesa Verde Corrugated--						
Mancos Variety	0	0	0	0	3	3
Body sherds	1	0	3	2	6	12
Mesa Verde B/W	2	0	0	0	3	5
	39	1413	263	147	158	2020

tions of rabbits and carnivores, especially bobcat. A careful look at the bones shows that a number of different individuals are represented in most cases and that many elements from one animal have not skewed the figures.

After the test, close re-examination of the ground disclosed traces of a row of above-ground rooms running east-west across the ridge for at least 20 yards, representing perhaps six to eight rooms. These rooms and the pithouse were probably associated, but when the excavated room burned, the site appears to have been abandoned. The pithouse caved in or was dismantled to salvage materials, and its depression was then filled with refuse of other Pueblo I peoples living nearby, perhaps at Sites 795 or 793. Later when the Pueblo II sites 785 and 791 were occupied, a stone masonry shrine was built atop the excavated room, whose burned remains must have been quite obvious. It does not take much imagination to envision a shrine built to ancestors who once lived on that site.

Site 111. Another test was made at Twin Trees in a partly eroded concentration of burned stones suspected of being a Basket Maker III pithouse, although the surface pottery suggested a later date. During April of 1959, J. A. Lancaster and I completely excavated two Pueblo I rooms and located two more (fig. 8). All four rooms had burned intensively causing the prehistoric occupants to abandon many objects of household use.

Floors had been slightly excavated and the natural dirt partitions formed the bases of some walls. In general, walls were built largely of plain mud about 8 inches thick, possibly with some poles imbedded in them, although no direct evidence for this was found. Walls of the larger living room (Room 2) had upright sandstone slabs built into their bases. Intense burning preserved patches of thick mud plaster. One large posthole against the west wall may have held a roof support. There was no indoor hearth. Impressions of roofing materials baked by the fire in adobe indicate the typical pattern of crisscrossing smaller and smaller elements until a thick layer of dirt could be supported.

Both Rooms 1 and 3 must have been storerooms, since both contained quantities of charred corn and beans. Whole ears of maize rested on a layer of pinyon (?) bark in the northeast part of Room 1. On the floor in Room 2, when it burned, were two plain jars (Chapin Gray--Chapin Variety), one Chapin Black-on-white bowl, one mano, two grinding stones, two hammerstones, and a chopper. Apparently one and possibly two turkeys had been trapped in the burning building and were killed when the roof fell on them.

Most household items appear to have been resting on the roofs of the buildings. Intermingled with and resting on collapsed roof debris were an Abajo Red-on-orange bowl, a dipper and a large bowl sherd of Piedra Black-on-white, two neck-banded jars (Chapin Gray--Moccasin Variety), a small shallow plain gray bowl, a very deep trough metate, five manos, three hammerstones, two choppers, two scrapers, one plane, one flake knife, three utilized flakes, and fragments of perhaps two other trough metates.

Like Site 786, this site produced a consistent ceramic assemblage (table 4). Twenty sherds of Mancos Black-on-

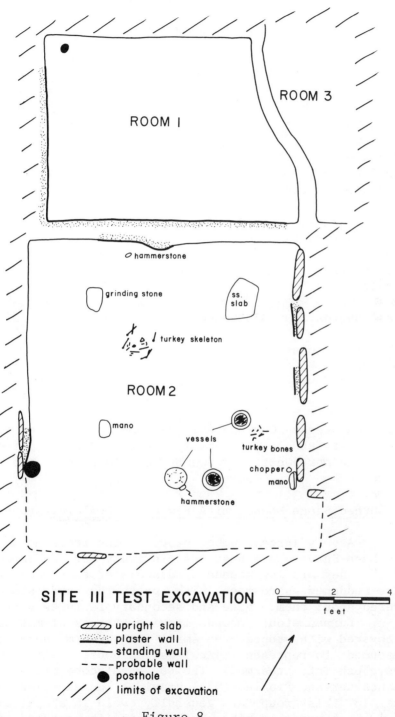

ROOM 3

ROOM I

hammerstone

grinding stone

ss. slab

turkey skeleton

ROOM 2

mano

vessels

turkey bones

chopper

mano

hammerstone

SITE III TEST EXCAVATION

0   2   4
feet

upright slab
plaster wall
standing wall
probable wall
posthole
limits of excavation

Figure 8.

Table 4

POTSHERDS FROM SITE 111

	Surface	Room 1	Room 2	Room 3	Room 4	Totals
Chapin B/W			1			1
Piedra B/W	1		12		3	16
Bluff B/R--						
Bluff Variety	5	9	3			17
La Plata Variety		2				2
Chapin Gray--						
Chapin Variety	3	4	22	1		30
Moccasin Variety	9	9	19	1	4	42
Handle	2	1	2			5
Body sherds	22	75	377	7	58	539
Unclassified						
Reds	2	4	3	1		10
Plain sherds from B/W vessels	2		9		3	14
B/W			4		2	6
Mesa Verde Corrugated	1	2	3			6
Mancos B/W		1			1	2
	47	107	455	10	71	690

white, Mesa Verde Corrugated, and some Unclassified represent Pueblo II styles that probably drifted downslope from later sites to the northwest. All twenty were found near the surface.

Burned Stone Mounds with Few or No Building Stones

A very large number of the sites recorded during the Chapin Mesa Survey are best descriptively termed "burned stone mounds." They are low mounds of discolored earth and fragments of fire-reddened sandstone with potsherds and stone chips scattered about them. Size and secondary features vary widely.
Burned stone mounds lacking traces of masonry walls and covered with stones too small for solid masonry (table 5) are assumed to represent jacal-walled houses with some small stones stuck into the mud. The post-and-adobe village at Site 16 (Lancaster and Pinkley 1954) provides an excellent example. Mounds in this group are generally ovoid in shape, averaging about 10 by 5 yards in size. Such a mound is presumed to conceal

Table 5
BURNED STONE MOUNDS WITH FEW OR NO BUILDING STONES

Site No.	Room Estimate (R=Rooms) (K=Kivas)	Size of Mound (Yards)	Burned Adobe	Upright Slabs	Chipped-edge Stones	Refuse Mound	Remarks	POTTERY: Chapin Gray	Cortez B/W	Mancos B/W	Mancos Gray	Corrugated	Bluff B/R-LaPlata Var.	Other Sherds	TOTAL SHERDS
2	ca. 3-4 R	8 x 3 yds.			yes	yes		12		2		3		2	19
3	ca. 4-5 R	8 yds.dia.						8	1	3		5		4	21
5	ca. 4-6 R	13 yds.long				yes	2 burials	8	6	7		12		6	39
6	ca. 3 R	6 x 3 yds.				yes		12	2	2	1	15		9	41
9	ca. 2-3 R	5 yds.dia.						1		8	1	17		14	41
10	ca. 2-3 R	5 yds.dia.						8			3	3		6	20
12	ca. 3-4 R	8 x 5 yds.				yes		5	3	7	1	11		8	35
14	ca. 2-3 R	6 yds.dia.	yes					16		2		3		7	28
15	ca. 4-7 R	10 x 6 yds.				yes		2	1	9		11		11	34
16	ca. 4-6 R 1 K			yes			Lancaster & Pinkley 1954								
17	ca. 3-4 R	10 x 3 yds.			yes			5		5		4		3	17
21	ca. 4-6 R	13 x 9 yds.	yes					9		2		1		4	16
24	ca. 2 R	3 yds.dia.						2		2	1	8		9	22
25	ca. 3-4 R	10 x 3 yds.						7	3			17		5	32
28	ca. 3-4 R	5 yds.dia.						14				2		1	17
29	ca. 3-4 R	5 yds.dia.			yes			8		1				1	10
30	ca. 4-6 R	8 x 5 yds.		yes		yes	large stones on surface	3	1	7		11		9	31
37	ca. 2-3 R	3 yds.dia.						4				1		1	6
40		Indefinite						4	2					2	8
41	ca. 2-3 R	3 yds.dia.					pottery bowl & pitcher	11	1	1		3		5	21
43	ca. 2-3 R	6 x 5 yds.						6		1		9			16
44	ca. 3-4 R	8 x 4 yds.				yes		7		13		13		5	38
47	?							5			3			4	12
48	ca. 4-5 R	15 yds.long				yes			3	12		4		2	21
49	ca. 3-4 R	6 yds.long						2	7	3		9		7	28
50	ca. 8-10 R 1 K?	11 x 6 yds.				yes		6	6	29		11		9	61
51	?							5		1		2		5	13
53	ca. 5-6 R	20 yds.long				yes?		2		13		3		8	26
54		ea. mound 7 yds.dia.					Tested by Lancaster 1941 3 circular mounds	22	15	42	7	82		43	211
56	?	Indefinite						1		5		4		3	13
61	?	Indefinite				yes?		2		9		5		7	23
66								5		1		1		1	8

Table 5 (cont.)
BURNED STONE MOUNDS WITH FEW OR NO BUILDING STONES

Site No.	Room Estimate (R=Rooms) (K=Kivas)	Size of Mound (Yards)	Burned Adobe	Upright Slabs	Chipped-edge Stones	Refuse Mound	Remarks	POTTERY — Chapin Gray	Cortez B/W	Mancos B/W	Mancos Gray	Corrugated	Bluff B/R-LaPlata Var.	Other Sherds	TOTAL SHERDS
67	ca. 3-4 R	5 yds.dia.						5				1			6
70	?						Tested in 1950 – postholes & hearth	12			1	1		3	17
83	?	Indefinite						4				1		1	6
86	ca. 5-6 R	10 x 6 yds.						7		1		6		8	22
88	?	Indefinite						8				6		4	18
89	ca. 5-6 R	10 x 6 yds.						3				1		1	5
94	?	Indefinite				yes		4		4		8		7	23
97		Indefinite						10				3		1	14
98		Indefinite						2	1			6		5	14
102	2 R / 1 K						O'Bryan 1950– T-R Dates A.D. 947+ 1 burial								
123	?	Indefinite				yes		15	1	3				2	21
126	ca. 6-10 R	20 x 20 yds.						13		17	2	19		36	87
136	ca. 3-4 R	5 x 5 yds.						20		1		3		6	30
139	ca. 5-6 R	10 x 8 yds.						7	1	6	1	3		6	24
144	ca. 3-4 R	5 x 5 yds.				yes		5	1	3		6		3	18
146	ca. 3-4 R	5 yds.dia.						10		4		2		1	17
147	ca. 5-6 R	10 x 10 yds.								13		7		4	24
148	ca. 6-8 R	15 yds.dia.						13		2		2		3	20
150	ca. 3-4 R	5 x 5 yds.				yes		2		10		4		7	23
153	ca. 3-5 R	10 x 5 yds.				yes		9		3	1	7		5	25
156	ca. 2 R	5 x 3 yds.						4	1	2		4		5	16
157	ca. 3-5 R	10 x 5 yds.						5		2		3		7	17
162	ca. 2-3 R	4 yds.dia.								1		5		11	17
163	ca. 2 R	5 x 3 yds.				yes		5		4		5		5	19
164	ca. 3-5 R	10 x 5 yds.						2	2	4		6		3	17
167	ca. 4-6 R	10 x 10 yds.						6	2	1		3		6	18
172	ca. 3 R	8 x 3 yds.						4				1		3	8
176	?	Indefinite						3						2	5
179	ca. 2-4 R	7 x 4 yds.						15				3		1	19
182	ca. 3-5 R	10 x 5 yds.						5		2	2	3		1	13
183	?	Indefinite								1				5	
190	ca. 3-4 R	10 x 2 yds.						1		3		3		2	9

Table 5 (cont.)
BURNED STONE MOUNDS WITH FEW OR NO BUILDING STONES

Site No.	Room Estimate (R=Rooms)(K=Kivas)	Size of Mound (Yards)	Burned Adobe	Upright Slabs	Chipped-edge Stones	Refuse Mound	Remarks	Chapin Gray	Cortez B/W	Mancos B/W	Mancos Gray	Corrugated	Bluff B/R-LaPlata Var.	Other Sherds	TOTAL SHERDS
191	ca. 3–5 R	10 x 5 yds.						4		7		11		1	12
192	ca. 6–10 R	17 x 5 yds.				yes		11		1		4		8	19
195	?	Indefinite						5	1			2			7
199	ca. 2–3 R	8 x 3 yds.						1	1	1		9		2	23
205	ca. 2–3 R	5 x 5 yds.						5				5		2	14
206	ca. 2–3 R	5 x 5 yds.						1			1	1	1	2	4
208	ca. 3–5 R	10 x 5 yds.					slab firepit	5		1	1	2		3	11
212	ca. 3–5 R	10 x 5 yds.						12		1				1	14
213	ca. 2–3 R	5 x 5 yds.						12				1		1	14
222	ca. 3–5 R	10 x 5 yds.						29		1		2		1	33
227	ca. 2–3 R	6 x 4 yds.						21		1	1	1		1	24
231	ca. 4–6 R	15 x 5 yds.				yes		5				2		2	9
232	ca. 2–3 R	5 x 5 yds.				yes			11	12		7		16	48
239	1 K?	10 x 10 yds.						3		5		9		12	29
240	ca. 3–4 R	8 x 5 yds.						14				1			15
243	ca. 3–4 R	8 x 7 yds.						5		2		2		7	16
245	ca. 3–5 R	10 x 5 yds.						3		2		1		6	12
247	ca. 3–4 R	8 x 5 yds.						10		1		1		3	16
256	ca. 3–4 R	8 x 8 yds.				yes	slab firepit?	3		2		11	1	5	23
258	ca. 1–2 R	4 x 4 yds.						5	2			2		2	10
268	ca. 2–3 R	7 x 5 yds.				yes	Tested by Lancaster 1952		2	2		2		6	10
284	ca. 3–5 R	10 x 7 yds.		yes				2				7		2	11
293	ca. 2–3 R	5 x 5 yds.						1		3		2			6
299	?	5 yds.dia.	yes	yes		yes	under later house	26	30	104	32	71	1	50	314
301	ca. 2–3 R	11 x 5 yds.	yes					8				1			9
304	ca. 3–4 R	6 x 5 yds.				yes		7		2		3		7	19
306	ca. 2–3 R	Indefinite				yes		4		2		6		8	20
309	ca. 1–2 R	5 x 5 yds.						3		2		6		9	20
311	ca. 2–3 R	10 x 5 yds.		yes		yes	Poss. BMIII component	19	1			5		4	29
313	ca. 3–4 R	10 x 6 yds.						14	2	5		6		3	30
314	ca. 3–5 R	5 yds. dia.						14		5	2	9		6	36
315	ca. 2–3 R	11 x 2 yds.										5			5
324	ca. 4–5 R	7 x 5 yds.						9		2		1			12
326	ca. 2–3 R	3 yds.dia.					2 "megalithic" slabs	6			1	2		2	11
330	ca. 1–2 R	3 yds.dia.						2							2

Table 5 (cont.)
BURNED STONE MOUNDS WITH FEW OR NO BUILDING STONES

Site No.	Room Estimate (R=Rooms) (K=Kivas)	Size of Mound (Yards)	Burned Adobe	Upright Slabs	Chipped-edge Stones	Refuse Mound	Remarks	POTTERY: Chapin Gray	Cortez B/W	Mancos B/W	Mancos Gray	Corrugated	Bluff B/R-LaPlata Var.	Other Sherds	TOTAL SHERDS
336	ca. 4-5 R	12 x 5 yds.						36			1	1		2	40
337	?	18 x 3 yds.		yes		yes	Began as PI house	10	1		2	3		8	24
345	ca. 4-5 R	11 x 5 yds.				yes		7		11		26	1	17	62
351	ca. 1-2 R	4 yds.dia.						7		2		4		2	15
355	ca. 2	4 x 4 yds.		yes						5	2	10		8	25
356	ca. 1-2 R	3 yds.dia.						5	3	3	2	9		8	30
372	ca. 4-8 R	4 yds. dia.					Possible PI component Possibly 2 units	52			2	10		7	71
381	ca. 2-4 R	6 x 6 yds.						6		4		11		4	25
390	ca. 4-6 R	10 x 8 yds.						39		1		4		4	48
393	ca. 3-4 R	10 x 5 yds.					1 masonry wall outline BMIII pottery	11				1		1	13
403	ca. 2-3 R	5 yds.dia.						2				2		4	8
406	ca. 3-4 R	10 yds.dia.						1		1		1		2	5
410	ca. 2-3 R	5 yds.dia.					metate	18	1		2	3		2	26
436	ca. 2-3 R	8 x 8 yds.						7	1					2	10
439	ca. 2-3 R	5 yds.dia.						3		2	1			15	21
448	ca. 3-4 R	Indefinite						12		1	1	9		12	35
451	ca. 2-3 R	5 yds.dia.										1			1
460	ca. 1-2 R	5 yds.dia.						13	2		3	2		2	22
468	ca. 1-2 R	Indefinite			yes			11		1		3		1	16
469	ca. 1-2 R	5 yds.dia.						1				1			2
471	ca. 1-2 R	Indefinite						1		1		3			5
479	ca. 1-2 R	Indefinite					BMIII pottery	16			1	1		2	20
483	ca. 3-4 R	10 yds.dia.						29				8		6	43
495	?	50 yds.dia.			yes			7	3			1		5	16
497	ca. 3-4 R	Indefinite						4				6		1	11
498	ca. 3-4 R	Indefinite					slab firepit					2		4	6
708	ca. 2-3 R	8 yds.dia.						6				1		5	12
713	?	Indefinite						9		1		2		2	14
741	ca. 4-6 R?	15 yds.dia.						10				6		3	19
753	ca. 3-4 R?	15 yds.dia.						4				3			7
755	ca. 1-2 R?	5 yds.dia.						6		3		2		2	13
758	ca. 3-4 R	11 x 6 yds.						10	1		1			6	18
767	ca. 5-6 R	15 x 10 yds.							2	4		13		13	32

Table 5 (cont.)
BURNED STONE MOUNDS WITH FEW OR NO BUILDING STONES

Site No.	Room Estimate (R=Rooms)(K=Kivas)	Size of Mound (Yards)	Burned Adobe	Upright Slabs	Chipped-edge Stones	Refuse Mound	Remarks	Chapin Gray	Cortez B/W	Mancos B/W	Mancos Gray	Corrugated	Bluff B/R-LaPlata Var.	Other Sherds	TOTAL SHERDS
776	ca. 3-4 R	10 yds.dia.						14		3		6		7	30
778	ca. 2-3 R	Indefinite			yes			8				1		1	10
785	ca. 2-3 R	5 yds.dia.					San Jose point base	26		2		6		6	40
791	ca. 2-3 R	10 x 5 yds.						7		1		3		3	13
794	ca. 2-3 R	10 x 5 yds.						15				2		2	20
806	cca. 2 R	5 yds.dia.						2						2	4
813							Prob. began during PI	24		1	3	2		11	40
814	ca. 7-10 R	5 yds.dia.						10	3	6	2	3		2	18
815	ca. 2-4 R	10 yds.dia.			yes			20	12	5	1	8		22	60
816	?	10 yds.dia.		yes			Prob. part of 815	16			9	7	1	14	63
817	ca. 5-6 R	10 yds.dia.			yes			16	6	7	3	5	2	17	49
818	ca. 5-6 R	?	yes		yes	yes	Prob. under later house	14		21	7	20	1	22	92
823	?				yes	yes		22	2	27	1	31		51	135
824	ca. 4-8 R / 1 K	12 x 6 yds.	yes				1 kiva depression	11	1	14	1	14	6	24	71
825	ca. 5-10 R / 1 K	15 x 10 yds.	yes	yes			1 kiva depression	6		15		16		17	54
827	ca. 3-4 R	Indefinite	yes					6	1	4		11		12	34
829	ca. 3-4 R	Indefinite						37		2	2	4		18	63
841	ca. 2-3 R	10 yds.dia.						6		1	1	6		3	17
862	ca. 3-4 R	5 yds. long						6				2		1	9
886	ca. 2-3 R	5 yds.dia.					1 kiva depression	7	5	6	2	4		12	36
923	5 R / 1 K	10 x 5 yds.						1							1
942	ca. 2 R	Indefinite						7		1				3	11

(Columns Chapin Gray through Bluff B/R-LaPlata Var. and Other Sherds are grouped under POTTERY.)

approximately three to five average-sized rooms. The larger
mounds may measure as much as 20 by 20 yards and might contain
as many as ten rooms in an L-shaped arrangement. Crude earth-
walled kivas form a part of both excavated sites, but kiva
depressions show faintly at only six of the unexcavated sites.
Heights of the mounds reach 6 to 18 inches.

Typical surface collections of potsherds include
Chapin Gray and Mesa Verde Corrugated body sherds, Cortez
Black-on-white, Mancos Black-on-white, and Bluff Black-on-red--
La Plata Variety. Most other sherds are unclassifiable plains
or unpainted parts of painted vessels. Red sherds of any kind
are very rare.

Two sites of this group have been excavated. Site 16
(Lancaster and Pinkley 1954) contained at least five components
one of which was a wattle-and-daub house of about four to six
rooms arranged in an "L" to the north of an earth-sided kiva.
Later house construction obliterated the central portion of the
jacal building and confused the pottery associations here. The
pueblo component at Site 102 (O'Bryan 1950) is a two-room house
built of mud walls containing many small stones. An earth-
sided kiva lies to the south. Tree-ring dates indicate this
house was built no earlier than A. D. 947. In 1952 Lancaster
tested Site 268, but found no house remains.

The four individual site descriptions following cover
most of the range of variation observed in this group.

Site 232. This very small mound measures only about
5 yards square and could contain only two to three rooms.
There are no building-size stones and no kiva depressions. A
small refuse mound, possibly 1 foot deep, lies 20 yards to the
southwest. Eleven sherds of Cortez Black-on-white, 12 Mancos
Black-on-white, 1 Mancos Gray, 7 corrugated, 1 Bluff Black-on-
red--La Plata Variety, and 16 unclassified sherds were gathered
from the surface. This mound is typical of most habitation
sites yielding early Pueblo II pottery.

Site 356. All that remains of this site is a 3-yard-
square faint mound of burned stones with potsherds scattered
down a rapidly eroding slope to the southwest. No traces of a
kiva depression, refuse mound, or building-size stones can be
seen. One to two rooms may once have stood here. The extremely
small size of this site recalls the field houses of much later
date. However, it has no clear association with field areas,
nor is it remote from contemporary dwellings as are the field
houses. Instead, Site 356 seems to belong to a scattered
community of several small house sites. It must also be
realized that a portion of the assumed wattle-and-daub building
could have been completely obliterated through the leveling

processes of the last 1000 years and that only a fraction of it may now be visible on the ground surface. Finally, the many sherds around the mound represent occupational refuse. The 30 collected potsherds include 3 Cortez Black-on-white, 3 Mancos Black-on-white, 5 Chapin Gray, 2 Mancos Gray, 9 corrugated, and 8 unclassified.

Site 825. This mound has some attributes in common with the sites showing chipped-edge building stones. There is a faint kiva depression, several building-size stones--none of them shaped, however--on the surface, and surface pottery more commonly expected from a masonry pueblo. The house mound itself measures about 15 by 10 yards and could cover anywhere from five to ten rooms. There are two slabs standing on edge and some tiny pieces of burned adobe. It is not hard to imagine this as a transitional house anticipating the developments in late Pueblo II house sites, which are so abundant in this Far View Locality. The surface pottery collection contains 15 Mancos Black-on-white, 16 corrugated, 5 Chapin Gray, 1 Abajo Red-on-orange, and 16 unclassified sherds.

Site 25. A low mound about 10 yards long and 3 wide, standing less than a foot high, covers approximately three or four rooms presumably built of wattle-and-daub. There are no signs of building-size stones, a kiva depression, or a refuse heap. This site is located on the west side of a low ridge in an area of sagebrush where the woodland had burned off sometime during the last century. The 32 potsherds collected from the surface were classified as 3 Cortez Black-on-white, 17 corrugated, 7 Chapin Gray, and 5 unclassified. Sherds and other refuse are scattered for over 15 yards to the southwest.

Miscellaneous Burned Stone Mounds and Other Sites

Because of the nondistinctive surface appearance of all unexcavated burned stone mounds from late Basket Maker III through early Pueblo II, we cannot expect to place satisfactorily every such site in one of the preceding groups. All unassigned burned stone mounds as well as a few additional later ruins are listed as miscellaneous sites in table 6, where a special column is devoted to their probable stage in terms of the Pecos Classification. Ceramics, and to some extent the physical appearance of the sites, governed the Pecos designations. For descriptive purposes, miscellaneous sites are discussed here by sub-groupings determined by these same criteria.

Table 6
MISCELLANEOUS SITES

Site No.	Room Estimate (R=Rooms) (PH=Pithouse)	Size of Mound (Yards)	Prob. Date	Remarks	Chapin Gray	Chapin Gray-Moccasin Var.	Chapin B/W	Piedra B/W	Reds	Cortez B/W	Mancos Gray	Corrugated	Other B/W's	Unclassified	TOTAL SHERDS
19			BMIII-PI		19		3							1	23
23		7 x 4 yds.	BMIII-PI		7		1							2	10
32		5 x 4 yds.	?	Line of large unshaped stones	3									1	4
36/39			BMIII-PI		7/8		2/1								9/9
42			BMIII-PI		33	2			1						36
57	ca. 3-4 R	7 x 5 yds.	PI	3 stone concentrations	20						1	2	1	2	26
62	?		PI		16		2	2						4	24
63			PI		12			1				2		1	16
65			BMIII-PI		17										17
69	ca. 2-3 R	3 yds.dia.	PI			4				6					10
71	?	10 x 4 yds.	PI-PII	Some upright stones											None
81			PI		13									2	15
85			BMIII-PI		7							1			8
87			BMIII-PI		14		1								15
91	ca. 2-3 R	10 yds.dia.	PI		19							2			21
92			BMIII-PI		17		1						4	2	24
93			PII		12							2		2	16
96			BMIII-PI		12					2	1			1	16
100		6 yds.dia.	BMIII-PI	Slab on edge	17		3					6		3	29
122			PII		8									1	9
138		5 x 5 yds.	BMIII-PI		28								2		30
140		20 x 5 yds.	PI-PII		16		1					2		3	22
141		5 x 5 yds.	BMIII-PI		24		1								25
142			BMIII-PI		10		1							2	13
152		5 x 5 yds.	BMIII-PI		24							1			25
155			PI		13									3	16
158		10 x 5 yds.	PI		8		1	2						1	12
160			BMIII-PI		17		1	1							19
161		5 x 3 yds.	PI-PII		8									1	9
165		10 x 5 yds.	PI-PII		5								4		9
168		10 x 10 yds.	PI-PII	2 upright slabs	2		1					5	4	8	20
171		5 x 3 yds.	PI		16		1			1				1	19
173		10 x 5 yds.	PI-PII		4					1					5
174					4										4
177			?		12									5	17
178			BMIII-PI		8			1							9

Table 6 (cont.)
MISCELLANEOUS SITES

Site No.	Room Estimate (R=Rooms)(PH=Pithouse)	Size of Mound (Yards)	Prob. Date	Remarks	Chapin Gray	Chapin Gray-Moccasin Var.	Chapin B/W	Piedra B/W	Reds	Cortez B/W	Mancos Gray	Corrugated	Other B/W's	Unclassified	TOTAL SHERDS
181		15 x 5 yds.	PI-PII		24		1							1	26
184			BMIII-PI		14		1								15
186		10 x 10 yds.	BMIII-PI		10										10
188			PI		1		1					1			3
189		7 x 3 yds.	PI-PII		8							1			9
194		10 x 10 yds.	PI-PII		6							1			7
196		5 x 3 yds.	PI-PII		10		1					1	1	1	14
197		10 x 5 yds.	PI-PII		12		2							1	15
211			BMIII-PI		19									2	21
214			PI-PII		12		1					1		2	16
215			PI-PII		14								1		15
216		5 x 3 yds.	PI		10		1					1			12
217		10 x 5 yds.	PI		14		2								16
218		10 x 10 yds.	PI		15		2							1	18
219			BMIII-PI		12	1									13
220		5 x 5 yds.	PI		26		2								28
221		5 x 5 yds.	PI		23									1	24
223			BMIII-PI		12		3								15
228		5 x 3 yds.	PI		8		2								10
237			?		10		1					1			12
255		5 x 5 yds.	PI		17		1							1	19
257		13 x 6 yds.	PI		18		1						1	2	22
265		7 x 5 yds.	?	Tested by Lancaster 1952	2										2
267			BMIII-PI	Slab lining	3		1								4
279	1 PH or shrine	2 yds.dia.	BMIII-PI	Poss. slab-lined firepit	26		1						1	6	34
282		10 x 5 yds.	PI-PII		13										13
289			PI?		12										12
290	1 PH?		BMIII?	Tested by Lancaster 1952											None
292	1 PH?		BMIII?	Tested by Lancaster 1952											None
305		4 x 4 yds.	PI		7								1	3	11
307		5 x 3 yds.	PI-PII		14								1	1	16
317		7 x 5 yds.	PI		13		1								14
321			PI		17										17
322			PI		12		1								13
323			PI		18										18

Table 6 (cont.)
MISCELLANEOUS SITES

Site No.	Room Estimate (R=Rooms)(PH=Pithouse)	Size of Mound (Yards)	Prob. Date	Remarks	Chapin Gray	Chapin Gray-Moccasin Var.	Chapin B/W	Piedra B/W	Reds	Cortez B/W	Mancos Gray	Corrugated	Other B/W's	Unclassified	Total Sherds
329			PI		18		5								23
331		15 x 5 yds.	PI		19		2								21
338		6 yds.dia.	BMIII-PI		19		1								20
339		2 yds.dia.	BMIII-PI		2										2
341		8 x 2 yds.	PII	Chipped-edge stones; Burial; Plain gray jar	19						3			4	26
344			PI-PII		8		1	2				1	2	3	17
346			BMIII-PI		20		1								21
349			?	Flat-topped metate	31		2					1	1	2	37
357		3 yds.dia.	BMIII-PI		17										17
358		3 yds.dia.	BMIII-PI		16									1	17
365			BMIII-PI		4				2			1			7
368			PI		60							5		6	71
374		5 x 3 yds.	BMIII-PI		45			1				1			47
375		10 x 6 yds.	BMIII-PI		61			1				1	1		64
377		12 yds.long	PI-PII	1 upright slab	85					1	1	5	1	5	98
378		8 x 8 yds.	PI-PII		48			2	1			1		5	57
379		6 yds.dia.	BMIII-PI		61			1				1			63
380		6 x 6 yds.	BMIII-PI		32			3							35
384		10 yds.dia.	PII	Lancaster & Abel 1968	4		1	1				5	4	7	22
391		5 yds.dia.	?		50					1		1		3	55
396		12 x 6 yds.	BMIII-PI		26							1			27
399			BMIII-PI	Poss. slab-lined	13										13
400		8 yds.dia.	?			1									1
407		20 x 10 yds.	?												None
409		20 x 10 yds.	?		15						3	7		1	26
411		5 x 5 yds.	PI-PII		39			1			1	3			44
418		5 x 5 yds.	?		32		1	1				1	2	4	41
422		20 yds.dia.	?		9									1	10
423		8 yds.dia.	PI		18										18
424		5 yds.dia.	?		6								3	2	11
425			?		30		1		1			3	1	4	40
430		5 x 5 yds.	PI		1				1			2		2	6
431		10 x 10 yds.	?		28				1			1	2		32
432		8 yds.dia.	BMIII-PI		6			1			1	2		4	14
437		10 x 10 yds.	BMIII-PI		28			1			1	2		2	34

Table 6 (cont.)
MISCELLANEOUS SITES

Site No.	Room Estimate (R=Rooms) (PH=Pithouse)	Size of Mound (Yards)	Prob. Date	Remarks	POTTERY — Chapin Gray	Chapin Gray-Moccasin Var.	Chapin B/W	Piedra B/W	Reds	Cortez B/W	Mancos Gray	Corrugated	Other B/W's	Unclassified	TOTAL SHERDS
444			?												None
447			?		33		1					1	1	2	38
456		5 yds. dia.	PI-PII		33	1	2						1	1	38
461		10 yds. dia.	PI		8							1		1	10
462		10 yds. dia.	PI		35							1		5	41
470		5 yds. dia.	BMIII-PI		30							1	1		32
477		10 yds. dia.	PI		20							1		3	24
478		10 yds. dia.	PI		26	1			1			1		1	30
480		10 yds. dia.	PI		3			1							4
481		10 yds. dia.	?		4		1					1			6
482			BMIII-PI	Upright slabs											None
485		12 yds. dia.	BMIII-PI		13									2	15
486			?		26		1							1	28
488			BMIII-PI		8									2	10
489			BMIII-PI		15		1					1	1	4	22
490			BMIII-PI		4										4
491		10 yds. dia.	BMIII-PI		14		1			1	2	7	11	14	50
496		10 yds. dia.	BMIII-PI		1										1
705		10 yds. dia.	PI		2	1	1					1			5
707		10 yds. dia.	BMIII-PI		5					1		1			7
709		5 yds. dia.	PI-PII		30		2	1				6		4	43
711			BMIII-PI	3 rock clusters	27		1								28
716		5 yds. dia.	?		4		1								5
723		5 yds. dia.	BMIII-PI		8								2		10
724		8 yds. dia.	BMIII-PI		19		2								21
729			?		3		1					1	1		6
730		8 yds. dia.	?		11		1								12
737			BMIII-PI		9		1					1			11
738			BMIII-PI		22		1							1	24
739	ca. 4 R	40 yds. dia.	PII		4		1					2			7
740		10 yds. dia.	BMIII-PI		10							2	1	1	14
746		5 yds. dia.	BMIII-PI		13		1		1			1		2	18
752		10 x 5 yds.	BMIII-PI		7									2	9
762		20 x 10 yds.	BMIII-PI	Upright slabs										1	1
768		15 yds. dia.	BMIII-PI		31	1								1	33
770			?												None

Table 6 (cont.)
MISCELLANEOUS SITES

Site No.	Room Estimate (R=Rooms, PH=Pithouse)	Size of Mound (Yards)	Prob. Date	Remarks	POTTERY — Chapin Gray	Chapin Gray-Moccasin Var.	Chapin B/W	Piedra B/W	Reds	Cortez B/W	Mancos Gray	Corrugated	Other B/W's	Unclassified	TOTAL SHERDS
774		10 yds.dia.	?		34								1		35
797		5 yds.dia.	PI	Upright slabs?	6				1						7
798		5 yds.dia.	?												None
799		5 yds.dia.	?												None
801		8 x 5 yds.	?	Tested by Rohn 1958											None
838	? R, 1 K		PII	"Megalithic" slabs	7					1	2	11	6		27
839	ca. 4 R		PII	"Megalithic" slabs	1					1		8	9		19
845	ca. 3-4 R, 1 K		PII	"Megalithic" slabs	4						1	14	8		27
855		5 yds.dia.	BMIII-PI		12			1							13
859		5 yds.dia.	BMIII-PI		13							1		3	17
860		5 yds.dia.	BMIII-PI		5							1			6
882		10 x 5 yds.	PII												None
883	ca. 2-3 R		PII	"Megalithic" slabs	1							5	2	7	15
885	ca. 3 R, 1 K		PII	Upright slabs	1							6	5		12
887		6 yds.dia.	?		1							1	1	2	5
889		10 yds.dia.	?						4			1			5
904	ca. 3-5 R	10 x 10 yds.	PII		6							14	24	56	100
905		10 yds.dia.	PII		1					9	5	3	23	16	60
939		10 yds.dia.	BMIII-PI		1										1
940		10 yds.dia.	BMIII-PI		23				2				2		27
941			BMIII-PI		37			1					4		42
1035		5 x 3 yds.	BMIII-PI	Mano fragment	4								1		5
1036		4 yds.dia.	BMIII-PI		3										3
1039		3 yds.dia.	?												None

Basket Maker   III–Pueblo I Sites. The 66 sites
designated in table 6 as BMIII–PI could not be interpreted
clearly as either Basket Maker III pithouse sites or Pueblo I
slab-based houses.   This is not to say that none of them
represents one or the other, or that they are all transitional
although some must be.   None of these sites has been excavated
or tested.   All consist of unmounded clusters or low mounds of
fire-reddened stones ranging from about 2 yards to 10 yards in
diameter.   Only two are larger than this. Potsherds, none
distinctive enough to help cultural placement, stone chips, and
some burned adobe may be found.   There are no signs of masonry
building stones or of depressions to mark the locations of pithouses.   The true nature of each of these sites will be
revealed only by excavation.

Pueblo I Sites. There are 36 sites listed as PI in
table 6, none of them with either the long narrow mound or
upright sandstone slabs.   Instead they vary from scattered
traces of burned stones to distinct mounds up to 12 inches high
but never more than 15 yards long.   Again, none has been
excavated or tested.   The one unifying feature is the presence
in all their surface collections of sherds of Piedra Black-on-
white, neck-banded gray ware, and the red types.   The conscien-
tious reader will observe that some of the sites in table 2
appear to duplicate some in this category, but I must plead
that visual differences apparent to the on-the-spot viewer do
not always reproduce in the considerably abbreviated tables
covering many sites.

Pueblo I–Pueblo II Sites. A third sub-group consists
of 21 sites designated as PI–PII. These two are scattered areas
of burned stones or distinct small mounds, but they each
yielded sherds of corrugated pottery and Cortez or Mancos
Black-on-whites. Many of them also had upright sandstone slabs.
Aside from the fact that it is extremely difficult to call any
of them either Pueblo I or early Pueblo II, many or all of
these sites may be transitional between the two.

Pueblo II Sites. There are nine areas with scattered
burned stones labelled PII.   They do not have the distinct
mounds that usually produce Cortez and Mancos Black-on-white's,
Mancos Gray, and corrugated sherds.

Other Sites. Of the remaining 31 sites in table 6,
23 are burned stone mounds with ambiguous or anomalous sherd
collections, or none at all. Several have been damaged by later
activities, such as the digging of the Far View Ditch, or by
modern road building.   In general, they are simply hard to
explain.   The last eight sites deserve individual mention since
they do not fit any of the more generalized sub-groupings.

Site 400 is a mound of large unshaped sandstone blocks, now standing 2 to 3 feet high and about 8 yards in diameter. It is situated along a low bedrock rim with a possible kiva depression below. Recent quarrying of rock has damaged the site slightly. This could be a small masonry house and kiva or a ceremonial structure like Site 397 and its affiliates. Only one Chapin Gray sherd was found.

Site 486 is a large depression about 12 yards across surrounded by a rim of burned stone and some chipped-edge building blocks. It is quite probable that a kiva lies underground, but no trace of any above-ground structure has been located. The Pueblo I pottery found there may have drifted from other sites.

Site 384 may be the same kind of site as it consists of a circular wall of unshaped stone masonry about 10 yards in diameter. A small group of burned stones and potsherds about 25 yards south may be refuse. The pottery is all Pueblo II.

Site 279 is marked by several upright sandstone slabs in a rough D-shape among a cluster of crude unshaped stones about 2 yards across and 12 inches high. Two more slabs 10 yards south possibly represent a firepit. The general location and appearance suggest a ceremonial structure like Site 276 and 278, but considerable early pottery keeps open the possibility of its being a slab-lined pithouse like Site 283.

Site 887. A series of large unshaped sandstone blocks set on edge forms a rough circle about 5 or 6 yards across. The tallest stones stand about two feet high. There are no fallen stones and no refuse. It is located on a slope near the bottom of Navaho Canyon.

Site 1039 is a low mound of burned stone measuring about 3 yards in diameter located on the crest of a mesa-top ridge. There are no obvious building materials visible and no depressions of any kind. A limited test made at the time of survey revealed charcoal and burned stone to a depth of 12 inches below the present ground surface. No sherds were seen on the surface or in the test, and one stone chip was collected. It is interesting to speculate that this could be a non-ceramic pithouse.

Site 391 was completely excavated in the fall of 1954 by J. A. Lancaster and Leland J. Abel in order to determine what kind of ruin lay beneath this small burned stone mound. In this case, the results proved as perplexing as the unexcavated surface aspect (Lancaster and Abel 1968). The whole area of the site was carefully trowelled along the former ground level, but only a charred section of a log, pieces of burned adobe with casts of poles and small brush, and two possible postholes were encountered. A 2½-foot deep test beneath this

level revealed no further cultural material. The 55 sherds from
the   excavation and   the   surface collection   included 50 Chapin
Gray and one   each of corrugated and Mancos Black-on-white.   If
any structure   once stood   here, it   must have been a temporary
shelter built of brush--a campsite or field house. Although not
likely, there   is always the possibility that this material was
dumped here by the occupants of another site nearby.

     Site 801 is   one of the most interesting sites in the
whole survey because extensive   testing produced   no   evidence
either of a structure or of ceramics. About   one-third   of   an
area of scattered   rocks   and   darkened   soil around 5 yards in
diameter was trowelled in September 1958 to the probable original ground level.   In addition a partially slab-lined hearth 27
inches across, located at the center of the area, was excavated.
Sterile ground   underlay the trowelled zone.   The total collection   consisted of   one large   side-notched point, two bases of
unnotched points or knives, and seven stone chips.   Contents of
the hearth   closely   resemble   conditions   at   Site   261, which
appears to   have been a shrine, and Site 801 may also belong in
this category.   Or, it could be   a briefly used campsite either
of non-ceramic   peoples, dating   before, during, or   after   the
Puebloan occupation of   Mesa Verde, or of   pottery-using people
who simply failed to break any pots while there. The one nearly
complete   artifact   belongs   to   a   group   that   has been found
associated with Chapin Mesa sites ranging from Basket Maker III
through Pueblo III.

Burned Stone Mounds with Chipped-edge Building Stones

     Burned stone mounds that average slightly larger than
those   of the previous group, with chipped-edge building stones
visible   in wall   outlines or   loose in the rubble, belong to a
distinct group of sites (table 7). They represent small masonry
pueblos   of about   five to   seven rooms, located along   the low
ridge crests of the   mesa top.   The mounds   are generally ovoid
in shape, sometimes   L-shaped, about   15 by 8 yards in size and
standing around 1 foot high.   Larger mounds   run up to 40 yards
long and stand up to 2½ feet high.

     The distinctive chipped-edge building stones serve as
a kind of marker for these sites.   In   order   to reduce selected
sandstone blocks   to   a nearly uniform width, the   prehistoric
Indian   masons   chipped   bifacially   the   two opposed long   and
narrow sides, much   as   they   would sharpen the edge of a stone
knife blade or projectile point. This produced a kind of ragged
wedge-shape   on   the stone   faces that would normally appear in

Table 7

BURNED STONE MOUNDS WITH CHIPPED-EDGE BUILDING STONES

Site No.	Est. No. Rooms	Kiva Depressions	Size of Mound (yards)	Chipped-edge Stones	Single-coursed Masonry	Refuse Mound	Remarks	Chapin Gray – All Others	Chapin Gray – Mummy Lake Var.	Mancos Gray	Cortez B/W	Mancos B/W	Mesa Verde B/W – McElmo Var.	Mesa Verde B/W – All Others	Mesa Verde Corrug. – Mancos Var.	Mesa Verde Corrug. – Mesa Verde Var.	Mesa Verde Corrug. – Indet.	Other Sherds	Total Sherds
4	ca. 8-12	2-3	25 x 5 yds.	yes	yes	yes	Upright slabs?; bone awl; Tested	32	2		2	9			8		26	22	101
8	ca. 4-6		10 yds. long	yes		yes		2	1	1		6			9		15	17	51
16	4	1		yes		yes	Lancaster & Pinkley 1954												
18	ca. 10	1	10 x 10 yds.	yes		yes	Part of human femur. Broken 2-hand manos.	2		1	3	12		1	1		11	14	45
31	ca. 5-6	1	11 x 5 yds.	?		yes		4			14	24			5		12	21	80
59	2	1		yes		yes	Tested by Lancaster	32			13	6			13		24	16	104
73	ca. 5-6		10 x 5 yds.	yes		yes		9			3	7			7		15	12	53
80	ca. 3-4	1	10 yds. long	yes		yes	Tested 1952-burial, burned pit, ladle.	1		1	2	17	1	1	1		1	9	32
82	ca. 3-4	?	10 yds.+ long	yes		yes		13			6	22	8	1	17	1	12	16	89
120	ca. 8-16	1?	15 x 5 yds.	yes		yes		1			1	14			3		7	19	55
124	ca. 3-4		5 yds. diam.	yes		yes		17	1	3	3	1					5	12	41
125	ca. 7-10	2-3	20 x 6 yds.	yes		yes	Tested by O'Bryan	9		16	20	8		4	2		1	16	72
127	ca. 6-10		20 x 10 yds.	yes		yes		10		1	4	15	3		13		31	27	107
128	ca. 7-12	1	23 x 15 yds.	yes		yes		8		2	2	2	1		5		8	21	47
129	ca. 2				yes	yes		8		1	1	6			1		5	7	30
130	ca. 5-8	1?	15 x 5 yds.	yes		yes		10		2	1	5		1	4		10	4	36
132	ca. 8-12	1-2?	35 x 10 yds.	yes		yes		9		7	19	51		1	5		4	30	126
133	ca. 10-15	1	30 x 12 yds.	yes		yes		12		6	7	36			5		5	26	97
135	ca. 3-4		10 x 5 yds.	yes		yes		20		7	4	1						9	41
143	ca. 2		5 x 3 yds.	yes		yes		9			1	4			1		4	5	24
151	ca. 4		10 x 3 yds.	yes		yes	1 upright slab	8			3	22		12	3		3	5	36
200						yes		1				13	11	·	8	6	22	31	111
201	ca. 8-10	1	13 x 8 yds.	yes		yes	2 burials					4			2		8	2	17
207	ca. 3-5		10 x 5 yds.	yes		yes		4			3	6		1			1	4	14
210	ca. 2-3		5 x 5 yds.	yes		yes		3					2				2	2	11
226	ca. 4-8		12 x 7 yds.	yes		yes	roughly squared stones			2		23		1	2		6	5	39
229	ca. 3-4		8 x 8 yds.	yes		yes		10				7			1		6	7	23
230	ca. 3		10 x 2 yds.	yes				3			1	2		1				2	15
234	ca. 5		10 x 7 yds.	yes		yes						9	2		1		5	14	33
235	ca. 4-8		15 x 10 yds.	yes		yes						9					2	9	20

Table 7 (cont.)
BURNED STONE MOUNDS WITH CHIPPED-EDGE BUILDING STONES

								POTTERY											
								Chapin Gray					Mesa Verde B/W		Mesa Verde Corrug.				
Site No.	Est. No. Rooms	Kiva Depressions	Size of Mound (yards)	Chipped-edge Stones	Single-coursed Masonry	Refuse Mound	Remarks	All Others	Mummy Lake Var.	Mancos Gray	Cortez B/W	Mancos B/W	McElmo Var.	All Others	Mancos Var.	Mesa Verde Var.	Indet.	Other Sherds	TOTAL SHERDS
236	ca. 3-5		11 x 5 yds.	yes								1	1				8	2	12
238	ca. 2		10 x 5 yds.					3			1				6		27	4	41
244	ca. 4-6		12 x 7 yds.	yes		yes	upright slabs	6			4	20					2	11	43
252	ca. 3-5		10 x 6 yds.				roughly squared stones					1			2		3	4	10
262	ca. 2-3		6 x 4 yds.	yes				1				2					3		6
263	ca. 3-5	1	10 x 10 yds.	yes				36							1			2	39
269	ca. 10	1	12 x 8 yds.	yes		yes	upright slabs	1				10			4		5	7	27
275	ca. 4	1	9 x 7 yds.	yes				2				7			4		4	15	32
281	ca. 4-5		12 x 5 yds.	yes		yes		16									3	9	28
286	ca. 4-8	1	12 x 10 yds.	yes		yes	upright slabs	1			3	12			1		6	10	33
287	ca. 10		13 x 12 yds.	yes			upright slabs				4	8			7		4	13	36
294	ca. 1-2		4 x 4 yds.	yes				1			1	9			3		11	4	29
296	ca. 10-12	1	14 x 10 yds.	yes		yes					7	18			1		2	5	33
298	ca. 2-3		5 x 5 yds.	yes			upright slabs								1		1		2
299	?	?	?	yes	yes	yes	under later house	25	1	32	30	104	2	3	32		39	46	314
303	ca. 15-20	1	20 x 20 yds.	yes		yes	Tested by Abel & Bradley 1952. Point	3				23	2	1			6	11	46
308	ca. 2-3		5 yds. diam.	yes		yes		4				1			3		8	3	19
312	ca. 3-5	1	14 x 9 yds.	yes		yes		4			2	3			3		8	6	26
335	ca. 8	1	13 x 6 yds.	yes		yes		8				2		1			3	6	20
340	ca. 6-10		16 x 5 yds.	yes				4			1				2				7
342	ca. 2-3		5 x 5 yds.	yes				6				1					4	2	13
347	ca. 2-3		5 yds. diam.	yes		yes		7									2	1	10
348	ca. 4		6 x 5 yds.	yes		yes		8											8
350	ca. 2-3		5 yds. diam.	yes				8		3		1						2	14
367	ca. 3-4		10 x 5 yds.					12				1	1		3		6	4	27
369	ca. 1-2	1	10 x 5 yds.					18		1	1	13			11		14	27	85
382	ca. 2-4		6 yds. diam.	yes				12				1			4		2	5	24
385	ca. 15	1	40 yds. long	yes				9				16	1		10		12	29	77
401	ca. 4-5		Indefinite	yes				21			1	7			5	1	9	7	51
402	ca. 2-3		5 x 5 yds.	yes				5						1	1		3	8	18
404	ca. 4-6		12 yds. diam.	yes				14	1	1		10			3		11	5	45
408	small		30 x 20 yds.	yes			upright slabs	20		1	2	1			4		5	8	41
421	ca. 2-3		8 x 5 yds.	yes				9									3	2	14
426	ca. 3-4		8 yds. diam.	yes				14		3	2				3		8	2	32

Table 7 (cont.)

BURNED STONE MOUNDS WITH CHIPPED-EDGE BUILDING STONES

Site No.	Est. No. Rooms	Kiva Depressions	Size of Mound (yards)	Chipped-edge Stones	Single-coursed Masonry	Refuse Mound	Remarks	Chapin Gray: All Others	Chapin Gray: Mummy Lake Var.	Mancos Gray	Cortez B/W	Mancos B/W	Mesa Verde B/W: McElmo Var.	Mesa Verde B/W: All Others	Mesa Verde Corrug.: Mancos Var.	Mesa Verde Corrug.: Mesa Verde Var.	Mesa Verde Corrug.: Indet.	Other Sherds	Total Sherds
428	ca. 6-10	1	20 yds. diam.	yes				16		1		9		1	16		12	16	71
440	ca. 2+		6 x 5 yds.	yes				4		1		1	1	1	2	3	6	3	22
446	ca. 2-5	1?	Indefinite	yes				20			1							2	22
452	ca. 2		5 yds. diam.	yes				1											1
453	ca. 3-4	1	8 yds. diam.	yes				12		2			1				2	2	18
454	ca. 5-6		10 yds. diam.	yes				2							3		2	7	18
458	ca. 4-6		10 yds. diam.	yes				3		2		3	1		2		2	3	12
463	ca. 3-4		10 yds. diam.	yes				12		1		10	1		4		5		29
464	ca. 6-8		20 x 15 yds.	yes				4									21	26	67
465	?		Indefinite	yes			point	4				1					1	1	5
472	?		Indefinite	yes				1		1		4			2		2	3	5
475	ca. 2-3	1 at 486	13 x 4 yds.	yes				12				3					7		29
487	ca. 5-10		Indefinite	yes				29		4	2	1			1		8	15	62
492	ca. 3-4		10 yds. diam.	yes				1				1					1	9	3
706	ca. 5-6		15 yds. diam.	yes				6		5	2		1		1	2	1		23
710	ca. 10-20		50 x 20 yds.	yes			2 units	43		4		7			3		10	6	70
743	ca. 3-4		12 x 6 yds.	yes			upright slab	33				30			2	1	1	8	44
744	ca. 2-3		12 yds. diam.	yes		yes	under later house	39		1		2						6	46
747	ca. 2-3	1	4 yds. diam.	yes		yes	under later house	7				3	5	11	1		6	23	61
751	?		?	yes		yes		3		3		5	2	2	7		6	15	74
769	ca. 2	1	8 x 5 yds.	yes			upright slabs	32			6	1	1		1		5	2	36
779	ca. 3-4		10 yds. diam.	yes				3									16		15
781	ca. 2	2	11 x 5 yds.	yes				9		1	2				8		9	23	64
783	ca. 5-6	1	5 x 4 yds.	yes		yes		18				1	2		2		2	2	32
802	ca. 2	1	11 x 9 yds.	yes								1							4
803	ca. 3-4		10 yds. diam.	yes				3		1							1		
804	ca. 3-4		6 x 6 yds.	yes				1						1			1		5
805	ca. 2		5 yds. diam.	yes				12		1				1	1		4	4	9
807	ca. 2-4			yes		yes				10				2	1		4	1	30
808		1			yes	yes	under later house / Far View House / Fewkes 1917 / later home added												
809	10			yes	yes	yes	pipe shrine house / Fewkes 1923												

Table 7 (cont.)
BURNED STONE MOUNDS WITH CHIPPED-EDGE BUILDING STONES

Site No.	Est. No. Rooms	Kiva Depressions	Size of Mound (yards)	Chipped-edge Stones	Single-coursed Masonry	Refuse Mound	Remarks	Total Sherds	Other Sherds	Indet.	MV Corrug. Mesa Verde Var.	MV Corrug. Mancos Var.	MV B/W All Others	MV B/W McElmo Var.	Mancos B/W	Cortez B/W	Mancos Gray	Chapin Gray Mummy Lake Var.	Chapin Gray All Others
810	16	2		yes	yes		Far View Tower; Fewkes 1923	42	6	6		2			2		9		17
811	ca. 10-15		22 x 4 yds.	yes		yes		43	10	2		3			4	1	6		17
812	ca. 2-4		5 yds. diam.	yes				60	22	7		1			6	3	1		20
815	ca. 5-6	?	10 yds. diam.	yes				92	18	6		14	2	4	21	6	7		14
818	?			yes		yes	under later house	62	16	9	1	7		1	7	3	5		13
819	ca. 8-10	?	25 x 10 yds.	yes		yes		69	17	7	2	2	8	9	14	3	5		3
820	?	?	?			yes	under later house	135	30	20		9	9	13	27	2	1		22
823	?		?	yes		yes	under later house	69	16	14	2	4			16	6	3		10
826	ca. 3-5	?	10 yds. diam.					111	21	8		5	12	20	32		1		16
828	?		?	yes		yes	under later house	48	16	7		1			3		4		4
830	?		Indefinite	yes				19	16	5	1	2			3		1		4
831	ca. 6-8		16 x 5 yds.	yes		yes	upright slabs	68	4	3	1	8			24		11		16
832	ca. 4-6		10 x 10 yds.	yes				91	17	14		3			14		5		8
834	ca. 5-6		14 x 8 yds.	yes		yes	upright slabs	39	38	3		4	3	1	7	2			3
836	ca. 7-10		20 yds. diam.	yes		yes		53	12	8	3	3			15		3		3
837	ca. 3-6	1	12 x 12 yds.	yes		yes	under later house	192	23	2		16	29	38	64	9			3
840	?	?	5 x 5 yds.	yes		yes		47	23	21		4	2	1	7			2	
843	ca. 4	1	10 yds. long	yes		yes	roughly squared stones	23	10	9		2			5		3		7
865	ca. 4-5	1	?	yes	yes	yes	Lister 1966	112	25	10	2	8	6	4	44	5	1		7
866	?	2	5 x 5 yds.	yes			under later house	62	21	21		5	1	1	12				1
867	?	1	10 x 5 yds.		yes			45	16	7		4			10				8
868	ca. 2-4		10 yds. diam.					26	7	9		4							2
869	ca. 3-4		10 x 10 yds.	yes				23	4	8		2			4				
870	ca. 3-4		?	yes				85	16	13	3	4	1	5	8	6	6		3
871	ca. 3-4	?	15 x 10 yds.	yes		yes	under later house	104	33	9		2	15	4	26	9	8		10
872	?	?	13 x 6 yds.	yes				61	13	2		4	4	1	32				18
873	ca. 6-8	1		yes								2			8				
874	ca. 4-5	1		yes															
875	17	3	Indefinite	yes	yes	yes	Lister 1965	23	7	3		1	1	1			3		6
876	?			yes	yes	yes		95	19	8		1	1	3	48	5			
908	?	1		yes		yes	point	9	3	1			1	1	5	11			1
1058	ca. 4-8		18 x 4 yds.	yes								1			5		3		

the finished wall surface. Masonry walls built with chipped-edge stones were normally a single stone thick (single-coursed) so that both of the modified edges of each stone would show on opposite sides of the same wall.

Kiva depressions and refuse mounds are commonly reported for these sites. Quite likely, not all kivas left visible depressions following their collapse and filling, but about one-third of the unexcavated sites possessed marked hollows. Trash mounds, on the other hand, would hardly be concealed by natural deposition, so their presence at about one-half of these sites indicates their actual popularity.

House mounds, kiva depressions, and refuse mounds normally stand quite apart from one another in a line from north to south. This produces an observable layout distinct from that found in later sites where kivas are partly enclosed by the house mounds.

The associated ceramic assemblages consist of Mancos Black-on-white, Cortez Black-on-white, Mesa Verde Corrugated--Mancos Variety, and Chapin Gray including the Mummy Lake Variety. Mancos Gray and Mesa Verde Black-on-white frequently show up where there is other evidence of multiple components.

Five sites in this group have been excavated and four tested by various persons in the past. J. W. Fewkes excavated Sites 809 (Pipe Shrine House) and 810 (Far View Tower) (Fewkes 1923); Site 16 was dug by J. A. Lancaster in 1950 (Lancaster and Pinkley 1954); and the University of Colorado field school from 1954 to 1956 exposed Sites 875 and 866 (Lister 1965 and 1966).

At Site 16, four single-coursed, chipped-edge stone masonry rooms and a masonry-lined kiva lie beneath a later structure. Similar rooms at Site 875 were mostly obscured by a much larger house site of later date, and an earthen-walled kiva was found filled with trash. Two separate houses of this same construction, both with kivas, had been built one atop the other at Site 866.

Nine rooms of Pipe Shrine House (Site 809) were constructed of chipped-edge blocks laid one stone thick (rooms 1 through 9, fig. 13). Subsequent inhabitants of the site added more rooms using a different masonry style but also continued to use the original group, probably remodeling the kiva. Far View Tower (Site 810) was built on top of the remains of a 16-room pueblo of chipped-edge masonry that probably had two kivas. One of these was remodeled for the later use in association with the tower.

Three of the four tests also revealed single-coursed masonry walls of chipped-edge stones. The fourth, in the Site

80 trash mound, entailed excavation of an adult male burial with deformed skull but no offerings, resting on his left side in a tightly flexed position, with his head toward the west (fig. 9). Further testing at the edge of this same refuse heap exposed a rectangular pit containing a small scoop-shaped dipper (Lancaster 1968b). This very unusual piece of pottery was painted in the style of Mancos Black-on-white using white paint on a black background.

Eight of the sites included in this group represent large pecked-face masonry buildings overlying earlier components, among which are traces of chipped-edge stone houses with appropriate pottery types present in the total site collection. Since four of the five excavated chipped-edge masonry sites were found beneath later structures, it becomes probable that many other large rubble mounds of later date also conceal house sites of this group. Six sites known to include chipped-edge masonry houses belong to the Far View Group; the other two lie on opposite sides of Cliff Canyon.

Site 4. A mound of burned stones and fallen building blocks about 25 yards long and 5 yards wide marks this site. It stands about 1 foot above the surrounding ground except at the east end where it reaches a height of about 2 feet. Several outlines of single-coursed, chipped-edge stone masonry walls are visible on the higher part of the mound, indicating a double row of rooms in that section at least. Numerous sandstone building blocks with edges chipped bifacially are scattered about on the surface. The presence of one kiva has been verified by a test hole, while the site layout suggests the presence of one or two others (fig. 10). A distinct refuse mound, about 10 yards in diameter, lies 25 yards to the southwest.

The 101 potsherds gathered from the surface include 9 Mancos Black-on-white, 2 Cortez Black-on-white, 8 Mesa Verde Corrugated--Mancos Variety, 26 indeterminate corrugated, 34 Chapin Gray, two of which belong to Mummy Lake Variety, and 22 unclassified.

Site 82. This is a complex arrangement of mounds, depressions, and wall outlines, most of which can be attributed to Pueblo III occupation. Extending westward for 10 yards from the northwest corner of the complex is a low mound with several chipped-edge stones on its surface. A small refuse mound yielding characteristic pottery is located to the south but separate from the main trash heap along the southeast side of the site. No separate kiva depression could be seen, but it is possible that the later occupants remodeled the earlier kiva, as had been done at several other sites (cf. Sites 809, 810,

875).

Figure 9. Burial from Site 80.

Site 127. This site consists solely of a low mound measuring about 20 by 10 yards in size, situated on the west side of a low ridge crest (fig. 10). Several chipped-edge building stones are visible on the surface, although no wall outlines can be traced. There is a small refuse mound about 15 yards south of the house mound, but no depression remains from any possible kiva.

The 107 potsherds gathered from the surface were classified as follows: 15 Mancos Black-on-white, 4 Cortez Black-on-white, 13 Mesa Verde Corrugated--Mancos Variety, 31 indeterminate corrugated, 10 Chapin Gray, and 27 unclassified. Seven sherds of Mesa Verde Black-on-white cannot be explained logically.

This site may once have consisted of six to ten one-story rooms. It is one of a large cluster of contemporaneous dwellings.

Site 201. What may once have been an eight- to ten-room house is now concealed under a rubble mound about 13 by 8 yards in size and presently standing up to 2 feet high. A shallow depression directly south of the center of the house mound probably represents a kiva, and a trash mound 10 yards in diameter lies just south of that (fig. 10). Although no chipped-edge stones are visible now, the many building stones in the rubble of the mound indicate masonry walls, and the layout of house and kiva closely agree with that of the other sites in this group.

The surface pottery collection numbered 4 Mancos Black-on-white, 2 Mesa Verde Corrugated--Mancos Variety, 8 indeterminate corrugated, 1 Chapin Gray, and 2 unclassified. Two restorable vessels, a Mesa Verde Black-on-white--McElmo Variety pitcher and half of a Sosi Black-on-white bowl, were excavated as offerings for a burial found eroding out of the south end of the refuse dump. An adult woman with deformed skull lay on her back with her knees drawn up into a semi-flexed position, her head pointing toward the east (fig. 11). The pitcher rested on her chest and the bowl at her feet. Nearby, but not associated, was the skeleton of an infant, also on its back, but with legs extended. The baby's left foot lay

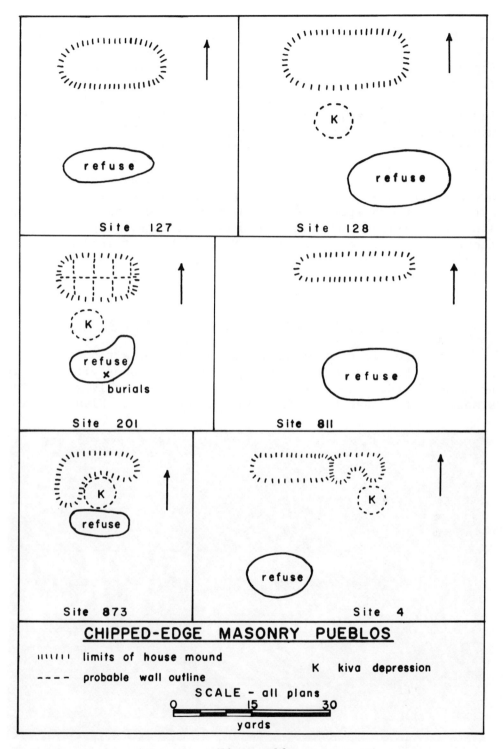

Figure 10.

in the bowl of a small, crude Mancos Black-on-white dipper
whose handle was missing. Both burials were excavated in
September 1952 by J. A. Lancaster, J. M. Pinkley, and Leland
J. Abel.

      <u>Site 744</u>. This is a small rubble mound about 4 yards
in diameter, possibly covering the remains of two to three
masonry-walled rooms. Some chipped-edge building blocks are
visible on the surface. This house was built on the southeast
edge of a large slab-based jacal house site that had apparently
fallen into ruin (Site 742). Since the large earlier house
occupied the low ridge top, its rubble and debris have almost
surrounded the smaller masonry building. Therefore, refuse and
sherd collections from the two sites are thoroughly mixed. In
fact, a burial exposed near Site 744 contained a pottery
offering that almost certainly earmarks the person as a former
inhabitant of Site 742.

Rubble Mounds with Pecked-face Building Stones

      The most obvious sites on the mesa top consist of
relatively high mounds of shaped building stones with equally
pronounced rubbish heaps, both mounds generally supporting
stands of big sagebrush (<u>Artemisia tridentata</u>). Kiva locations

Figure 11. Burial from Site 201.

are easily visible as depressions within or against the mounds. Wall outlines or even sections of standing walls are commonly observed features.

Partially because greater detail is evident in these sites, but also because they vary so greatly from one to the next, it is difficult to describe many consistent features that apply to all sites. Perhaps the best guides for recognizing them are the rock-pile appearance of the fallen building blocks and the position of kiva depressions partly enclosed by arms of the rubble mound. The former seems to result from the collapse of solid masonry walls, some undoubtedly two stories high, and many probably double-coursed (two stones thick). The latter appears to represent a real change in relative position of rooms and kivas, from the separateness noted in the previously described groups, to a partial incorporation of kivas into the room blocks, as is characteristic of the cliff dwellings.

Pecked-face building stones, whose exposed faces have been pock-marked by the pecking away of uneven spots with small hand-held stone hammers, are virtually diagnostic when they can be observed, although most of the stone blocks have only been roughly trimmed. In general the mounds are not only higher but cover more ground than any others. Refuse mounds, usually located toward the south, are discernible at over half the sites including all the larger ones. Some trash dumps abut the south ends of the buildings, completing enclosure of the kivas. Round towers were recorded at 14 sites and may be present, but not visible on the surface, at some others.

Typical pottery assemblages at these sites suggest various ceramic styles were changing during the time of occupation. Many of these pueblos overlay or were outgrowths of earlier houses, so that many incongruously early types, such as Cortez Black-on-white and Mancos Gray, often appear. Mancos Black-on-white dominates the painted wares, but is closely followed by the beginnings of Mesa Verde Black-on-white, usually classified as McElmo Variety. In several collections, McElmo Variety sherds outnumber those of Mancos Black-on-white. A few sherds of the Mesa Verde Variety of Mesa Verde Black-on-white occur consistently except at those sites that appear to be somewhat earlier. Both varieties of Mesa Verde Corrugated are common, the Mancos Variety predominating at one site and the Mesa Verde Variety at another. A few sherds of Chapin Gray (probably Mummy Lake Variety) and various reds also occur consistently, the latter acquired through trade or apparently from slab-house sites where red pottery was once made locally.

Eight sites in this group have been completely excavated. Five were excavated by Fewkes from 1916 through 1922,

but were only partially described or superficially mentioned in
his brief reports of explorations for those years, appearing in
the Smithsonian Miscellaneous Collections. Where possible, I
will present additional information on them. Sun Point Pueblo
(Site 7) is thoroughly reported by Lancaster and Van Cleave
(1954), but the ravaging of its walls for building materials by
later cliff dwellers limits our knowledge of it. Sites 499 and
875 were excavated in 1954 to 1956 by Robert Lister of the
University of Colorado, and reports on them provide our best
published data (Lister 1964; 1965).

A larger number of sites in this group (table 8) will
be individually mentioned to help give a more complete picture
of them. Excavated sites are considered first.

Site 808 (Far View House). Fewkes' separate paper on
this site (1917) covers the general aspects of architecture
fairly well and includes quite a few illustrations. During
stabilization work there in recent years, however, J. A.
Lancaster disclosed a fifth kiva in the east half of the court.
This kiva had been completely filled with refuse dumped through
its central roof hatchway. Its features are consistent with
the other four kivas: ventilator tunnel, masonry deflector,
circular firepit, sipapu, banquette, and six pilasters. The
above-floor ventilators in this and three of the other kivas
were found to have replaced older ventilators that passed
beneath the kiva floors to openings near the firepits, as in
typical kivas at Chaco Canyon.

Site 119 (Unit House). O'Bryan (1950: 137-140) quotes
an excerpt from Ralph Linton's unpublished manuscript "The
Small Open Ruins of the Mesa Verde," describing work at this
site in 1919 under the overall direction of Fewkes. The original ground plan was not included, however, so I have redrawn
it to provide comparison with others (fig. 12).

Site 809 (Pipe Shrine House). Since no ground plan
was presented in the only published record of this site (Fewkes
1923), one is given here in figure 13. Fewkes observed
that the northern double row of rooms (numbered 1 through 9)
was "built later than the others and constructed of poorer
masonry than those of the south side." Actually, these nine
rooms formed the original house block of the pueblo and were
built while single-coursed masonry with chipped-edge stones was
in vogue. Later occupants added the east, south, and west
wings to this unit using pecked-face stones in both single-
coursed and double-coursed walls. The kiva was also remodeled
at this time and in its final form contained six pilasters (not
eight as Fewkes states) resting on a narrow banquette, a sub-
floor ventilator tunnel resembling those in the Chaco Canyon,

Table 8
RUBBLE MOUNDS WITH PECKED-FACE BUILDING STONES

Site No.	Est. No. Rooms	Kiva Depressions	Size of Mound (yards)	Pecked-face Stones	Double-coursed Masonry	Refuse Mound	Remarks	Chapin Gray	Mancos B/W	McElmo Var.	Mesa Verde Var. (B/W)	Indet. (B/W)	Mancos Var. (Corrug.)	Mesa Verde Var. (Corrug.)	Indet. (Corrug.)	Other Sherds	TOTAL SHERDS
7	ca. 20	1		yes	yes		Sun Point Pueblo Lancaster and Van Cleave 1954; Tower.	2	1	6	6			2	14	13	44
72	ca. 4	1	9 x 7 yds.	yes	yes	?	2 "megalithic" slabs			8	4	7		1	22	6	48
74	ca. 10-12	1	24 x 10 yds.		yes	?	many "megalithic" slabs	1	17	9	6	4			19	20	76
75	ca. 8-10	?	16 yds. diam.		yes	?											
79	ca. 5		12 x 11 yds.	yes													
82	ca. 8-10	1	20 x 12 yds.	yes	yes	yes	Tower	13	22	1	9	1	17	6	12	23	89
119	3	1		yes	yes		Linton 1919; O'Bryan 1950. T-R date - A.D. 1190. "Megalithic" slabs.										
149	ca. 5-8	1	23 x 10 yds.	yes		yes		1	22	2	1	3	4		7	17	53
200	ca. 20-30	1	20 x 20 yds.	yes		yes	2 burials	8	13	11	2	2	8	12	22	31	111
202	ca. 2		8 x 5 yds.														
203	ca. 2		10 x 5 yds.														
204	ca. 3-4	?	9 x 6 yds.			?	Tower?	2	2	2	1	1				10	31
241	ca. 5-6		10 x 8 yds.														
299	ca. 20-30	1	32 x 32 yds.			yes	Tower; 2 burials.	26	104	2	37	1	71	9	6	108	314
303	ca. 15-20	1	24 x 20 yds.			yes	point	3	23	2	9	8	1		5	11	46
325	ca. 25-30	1	25 x 20 yds.			yes			15	2		7	1		4	9	32
328	ca. 20-25	1	25 x 15 yds.			yes			6			2				9	20
499	12	2		yes	yes	yes	Lister 1964										
703	ca. 10-15	1	30 x 20 yds.	yes	yes	yes		2	4	21	9	2		12		7	86
728	ca. 3-4	1	10 x 8 yds.	yes	yes	yes	Tower	7	23	9	12	11	7	1		9	72
747	ca. 20-25	3	20 x 15 yds.	yes	yes	yes	Tower	3	7	5		14				23	61
751	ca. 12-15	1	15 x 15 yds.						30	2						24	74
773	ca. 20-25	2	20 x 18 yds.	yes		yes	Tower		18	21					6	11	75
782	ca. 40-50	2	30 x 20 yds.	yes		yes	Tower		8	17	54			1		9	107
790	ca. 7-8	1	12 x 10 yds.	yes	yes	yes	Megalithic House Fewkes 1923; "Megaliths"	1	6	1			4			6	24
808	ca. 50	5		yes	yes	yes	Far View House Fewkes 1916										
809	22	1	46 x 37 yds.	yes	yes	yes	Pipe Shrine House Fewkes 1923; Tower	14	21	4	1	1	14	1	6	31	92
818	ca. 10-15	1	30 x 20 yds.	yes		yes											

Table 8 (cont.)
RUBBLE MOUNDS WITH PECKED-FACE BUILDING STONES

Site No.	Est. No. Rooms	Kiva Depressions	Size of Mound (yards)	Pecked-face Stones	Double-coursed Masonry	Refuse Mound	Remarks	Chapin Gray	Mancos B/W	Mesa Verde B/W McElmo Var.	Mesa Verde B/W Mesa Verde Var.	Mesa Verde B/W Indet.	Mesa Verde Corrug. Mancos Var.	Mesa Verde Corrug. Mesa Verde Var.	Mesa Verde Corrug. Indet.	Other Sherds	TOTAL SHERDS
820	ca. 30-40	5	40 x 25 yds.	yes	yes	yes	Tower; excavated by Lister 1970	3	14	9	8		2	1	7	25	69
821	ca. 30-40	5	45 x 20 yds.	yes	yes	yes		8	48	15	4	3	7		19	59	163
822	ca. 2-4	?	8 yds. diam.			yes		16	4	2	2	5	1		28	35	93
823	ca. 20	1	25 x 25 yds.			yes		22	27	13	4	5	9	2	20	33	135
828	ca. 10-15	2	15 x 15 yds.			yes		10	32	20	7	5	5	2	8	22	111
835	14	1	16 x 16 yds.	yes	yes	yes	One Clan House	1	12	14	4	13		1	7	20	72
840	ca. 25-40	2	36 x 18 yds.	yes	yes	yes	Fewkes 1923; B/W mug	5	64	38	19	10	16	3	2	35	192
851	ca. 10-12	1	20 x 15 yds.				Tower	44		2					12	24	82
856	ca. 20-25	2	26 x 15 yds.			yes		1	30	30	20		11	2	3	14	111
857	ca. 7-8	1	12 x 10 yds.			yes		4	5	8	5	5				6	33
864	ca. 7-9	1-2	14 yds. across					7		4		5				15	31
867	ca. 10-15	1	40 x 10 yds.			yes		3	44	5	2	13	4	3	6	32	112
872	ca. 10-12	1	20 x 20 yds.			yes			26	20		6	17			16	85
875	15	1	30 yds. diam.	yes	yes	yes	Lister 1965										
881	ca. 10-15	1	20 x 20 yds.					3		4	2		3	2		3	17
888	ca. 9-12	2	30 x 20 yds.			yes			14	5				5	25	9	58
902	ca. 5	1	10 yds. diam.					1		5	3		3		4	3	19
906	ca. 20	2	30 x 20 yds.	yes		yes	Tower		25		8	2	3	5		11	54
907	ca. 75	5	100 x 30 yds.	yes		yes	Tower		22	4	24	8	3	3	11	13	88
919	ca. 2-3	1	10 x 10 yds.					1				4			14	1	20
920	ca. 8-10	1	15 yds. diam.					2		7	2	3		2	24	3	43
932	ca. 7-9	1	11 yds. diam.					3	6	6	3	1			13	11	43
933	ca. 6-8	1	15 x 15 yds.	yes				1	2	4	2	6	1	14	10	9	49
1909	ca. 4-6	1	9 x 9 yds.	yes			Poss. field house; point							14			

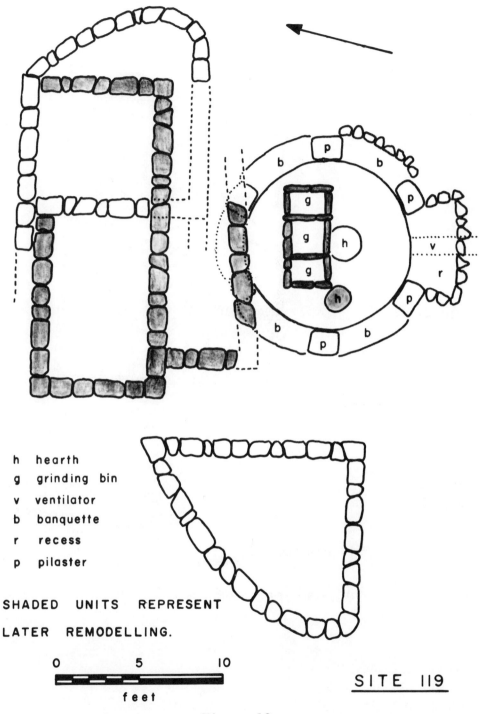

h   hearth
g   grinding bin
v   ventilator
b   banquette
r   recess
p   pilaster

SHADED UNITS REPRESENT
LATER REMODELLING.

0   5   10
feet

SITE 119

Figure 12.

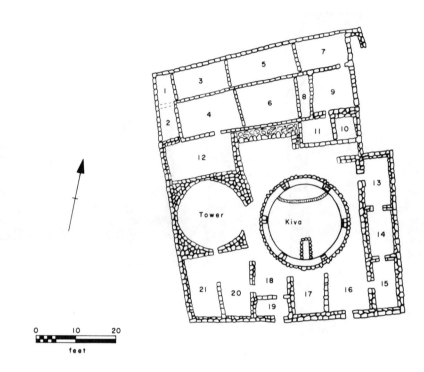

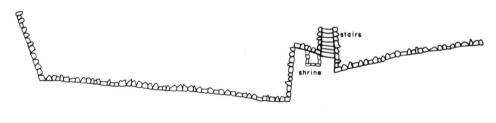

SITE 809 — PIPE SHRINE HOUSE

Figure 13.

and the shrine described by Fewkes, but no recess. Just south
of the building, a flight of steps leads through a long
retaining wall to the refuse mound.

    Site 835 (One Clan House). Fewkes (1923: 102-105)
devotes nearly one whole page to the description of this site
with two excellent photographs. Figure 14 is a ground plan of
One Clan House made in 1962 after the kiva had been reduced to
a rough hole in the ground. The kiva features and size have
been dubbed in with dashed lines from the photographs and from
Fewkes' unusually complete description of this structure.

    Some room walls are single-coursed (room 11) while
others are double-coursed (rooms 2 and 3). Rather rough squared
stones were used in both. Very few building blocks display
pecked faces. A rather large refuse mound, about 75 feet in
diameter, adjoins the south side of the house. During the
survey, a complete mug and a large bowl sherd of Mesa Verde
Black-on-white--McElmo Variety were collected from this mound
along with a small sherd of Tusayan Polychrome. Other sherds
collected from the surface at this time include 1 Cortez Black-
on-white; 12 Mancos Black-on-white, 2 with organic paint; 14
McElmo Variety of Mesa Verde Black-on-white plus 4 Mesa Verde
Variety and 13 indeterminate sherds; 1 Chapin Gray; 1 Mancos
Gray; 8 Mesa Verde Corrugated, with 1 rim of Mesa Verde Variety; and 18 unclassified sherds.

    Site 790 (Megalithic House). Here too, it is desir-
able to present a recently drawn ground plan (fig. 15). While
parts of the kiva are still open to view, it would be necessary
to re-excavate it in order to show all its details. The
"Cyclopean walls" mentioned and illustrated by Fewkes (1923:
110) are restricted to only two rooms (6 and 7), while all other
walls were constructed of roughly squared blocks, some with
pecked faces, laid in single-coursed masonry. Similar "megaliths" are recorded at only two other sites in this group. A
low refuse mound, covering an area about the size of the building, abuts its south side. The two dozen sherds gathered from
the dump during the Archaeological Site Survey include one
Cortez Black-on-white, six Mancos Black-on-white, one McElmo
Variety of Mesa Verde Black-on-white, one Chapin Gray, one
Mancos Gray, four Mesa Verde Corrugated--Mancos Variety and six
indeterminate sherds, and four unclassified.

    Perhaps the best way to convey an adequate impression
of the layout of these sites is to present the field sketches
of several of them (fig. 16). The typical horseshoe shape of
the "unit type" pueblo, as seen at Site 818, holds for Sites
200, 703, 751, 851, 857, 864, 872, 902, 906, and with a slight

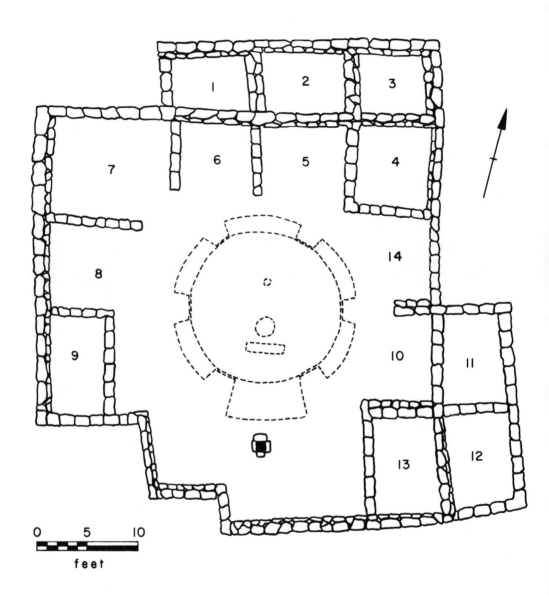

SITE 835 — ONE CLAN HOUSE

Figure 14.

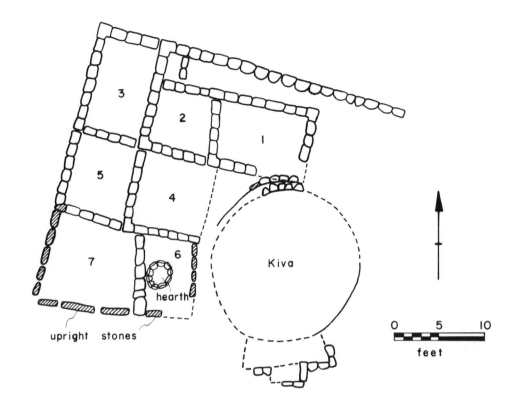

SITE 790 — MEGALITHIC HOUSE

Figure 15.

variation for 303 and 881. Completely enclosed single kivas characterize Sites 82, 809, 823, 835, 875, 920, and 932. The presence of two or more kivas results in adaptations of these basic plans.

Site 818. A 30 by 20 yard rubble mound is arranged in a horseshoe around a pronounced kiva depression (fig. 16). A refuse heap of the same size adjoins the south extending arms of the house mound. While the layout is typical, single-coursed masonry walls built of chipped-edge sandstone blocks show through the mound surface on both the east and west sides. The surface pottery assemblage contains 20 Mancos Black-on-white, 6 Cortez Black-on-white, 7 Mancos Gray, 14 Mesa Verde Corrugated-- Mancos Variety, 6 indeterminate corrugated, 14 Chapin Gray, and 19 unclassified. Six Mesa Verde Black-on-white sherds could represent drift from later sites uphill to the north, the intensive use of the whole area by Pueblo III people living in nearby houses, or possibly the somewhat transitional nature of this particular site. Excavation might possibly reveal two or more superimposed houses.

This mound is situated in the center of the level south-sloping Far View locality among pinyon, juniper, and woody brush. It shares some features with both major kinds of sites in that locality.

Site 840 (fig. 16) has the form of a double-horseshoe or capital "E" with two kiva depressions between the projecting arms flanking a tower at the end of the central arm. Portions of double-coursed pecked-face masonry walls are visible in the house mound. A large refuse heap closes the open ends of the horseshoe.

Site 867 has three kiva depressions along the south side of an elongated rubble mound, the central part of which must have accumulated from the collapse of a two-story building (fig. 16). An arm of the house mound projects between two of the kivas. The westernmost wing of the mound and the western kiva appear to be parts of an older chipped-edge masonry house. A separate trash mound lies toward the southwest.

Site 821 is one of four early Pueblo III sites with five kivas. Its plan suggests that it grew by accretion from a simple "unit type" pueblo. In its final appearance (fig. 16), the massive central part of the building stood at least two stories high. The large trash mound seems to be a continuation toward the south of the main mound, an effect that may result from later parts of the structure having been built over adjacent rubbish. Double-coursed pecked-face masonry wall outlines show, but none indicates a tower.

Site 299 is a site of long occupation, possibly beginning as early as Pueblo I. The latest component consisted of two broad wings of presumably one-story pecked-face masonry rooms and a detached tower unit largely surrounding a kiva (fig. 16). A second kiva depression and a small mound at the west end may represent holdovers from an earlier component.

In April 1953 Lancaster and Abel excavated two burials from the south edge of the large trash dump. One was a fragmentary infant skeleton with whom the bowl of an unslipped Mancos Black-on-white dipper had been placed. The second was a badly disturbed adult with deformed skull lying on its right side with legs flexed. Part of a Mancos Gray jar lay under the pelvis.

Site 200. Lancaster and Abel excavated two burials during September of 1952 from the refuse heap of this typically horseshoe-shaped "unit-type" pueblo (see table 8 for additional details). Both were adult males, one badly disturbed but accompanied by an unbroken jar of Chapin Gray--Mummy Lake Variety. The other had a deformed skull and rested in a flexed position on his right side (fig. 17). His grave offerings con-

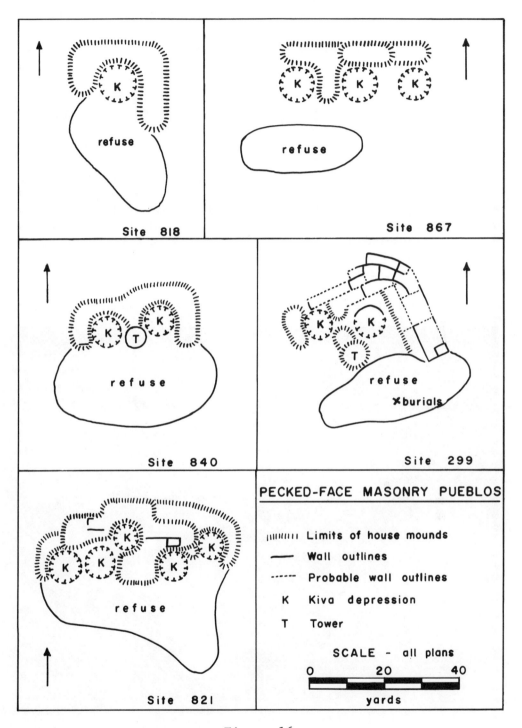

Figure 16.

sisted of a small corrugated jar, a Mancos Black-on-white bird
effigy pot (fig. 92) containing a yellowish-white granular
substance that appears to be corn meal, and a cache of worked
and unworked objects (fig. 93) that had originally filled a
coiled basket. Items in the cache are described in Chapter V.

   Site 828. The house mound of this site follows a
typical horseshoe plan around a kiva depression with an additional wing of rubble and a second kiva depression adjacent to
the east side of the horseshoe. In May 1950 a ditching machine
working on the Mancos River water pipeline unearthed an infant
burial with a small plain dipper from the west edge of the
trash heap. A second, adult skeleton was also exposed, which J.
A. Lancaster then excavated. The body lay on its right side
with legs drawn up into a flexed position. Mourners had placed
a Mancos Black-on-white pitcher, decorated in organic paint, by
the face and a Mancos Black-on-white bowl with corrugated
exterior at the feet.

   One interesting cluster of sites (fig. 18) varies

Figure 17. Burial from Site 200.

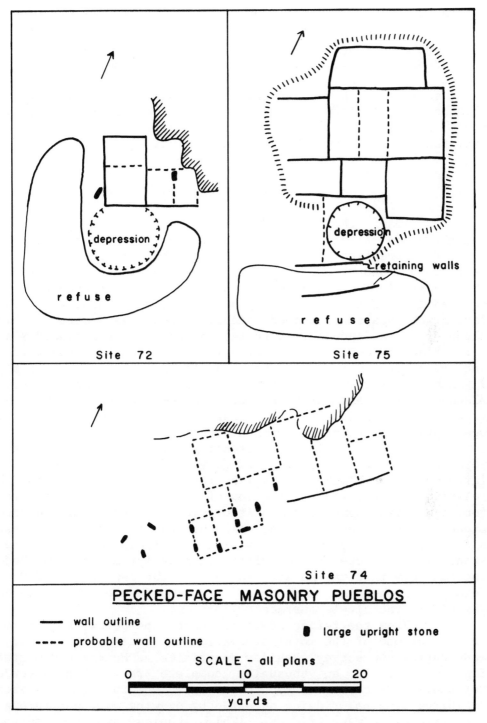

Site 72

Site 75

depression

depression

retaining walls

refuse

refuse

Site 74

PECKED-FACE MASONRY PUEBLOS

——— wall outline

▌ large upright stone

---- probable wall outline

SCALE - all plans

0   10   20

yards

Figure 18.

considerably from the generalities of ground plan stated above. They are located in the general vicinity of Square Tower House, and probably belong to a single settlement. Several other sites (202, 203, 204, 241, 919, and 1909) without kivas and with only two to six rooms, may or may not belong in this group. Small size, scarcity of kivas, and low trash mounds are suggestive of some seasonally-occupied field houses (see Chapter III), but their situations and the relatively large sherd collections from them raise enough doubts to merit inclusion here.

Talus Sites

Among the more difficult sites to decipher are those built on the talus slopes in the canyons, often against the base of a vertical cliff. Piles of rubble indicate that all were once masonry-walled buildings. Several possess distinct kiva depressions. In general, their builders employed roughly squared and unshaped building stones but occasionally pecked-face or chipped-edge stones occur. Refuse was scattered down slope from the houses. Ceramics at most sites included Mesa Verde Black-on-white--both varieties, Mancos Black-on-white, and Mesa Verde Corrugated--both varieties. Eight sites (table 9) had earlier pottery assemblages with predominantly Mancos Black-on-white and Mesa Verde Corrugated--Mancos Variety. The great bulk of these sites lie toward the north end of the mesa. Descriptions of several representative sites follow.

Site 508. This interesting site was built on the point between two forks of Cliff Canyon (fig. 19). A series of large sandstone blocks had fallen from the cliff and retained a relatively level spot at the top of the talus where a group of four to seven rooms were built of single-coursed chipped-edge stone masonry. Two retaining walls helped to support the east side. No kiva depression is visible. Between two large sandstone blocks close to the cliff is a wall remnant of pecked-face masonry that may be associated with the few sherds of Mesa Verde Black-on-white and Mesa Verde Corrugated--Mesa Verde Variety in the site's surface collection.

From the refuse scattered downslope below the earlier house came one of the more informative collections of pottery made during the survey. Besides quantities of Mancos and Cortez Black-on-white's, an unusually complete range of Mesa Verde Corrugated--Mancos Variety turned up. Numerous large sherds exhibited diagonal ridging accented by drawing a finger through the troughs between ridges. This technique appeared on the exterior of one Mancos Black-on-white bowl sherd.

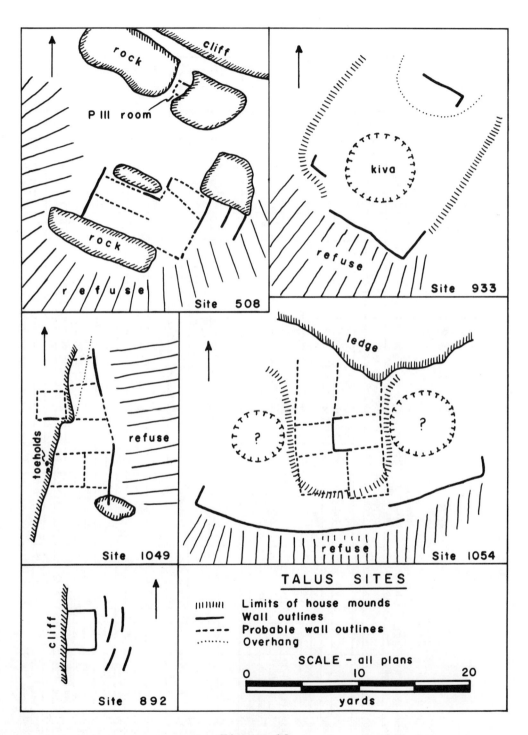

Figure 19.

Table 9
TALUS SITES

POTTERY columns are grouped as follows: "Mesa Verde B/W" comprises McElmo Var., Mesa Verde Var., and Indet.; "Mesa Verde Corrug." comprises Mancos Var. and Mesa Verde Var.

Site No.	Est. No. Rooms	Kiva Depressions	Size of Mound (yards)	Shaped building stones	Refuse area	Remarks	Chapin Gray	Mancos B/W	McElmo Var.	Mesa Verde Var. (B/W)	Indet. (B/W)	Mancos Var. (Corrug.)	Mesa Verde Var. (Corrug.)	Indet.	Other sherds	TOTAL SHERDS
508	ca. 4-7		13 x 6 yds.	Chipped-edge	yes	Later room with pecked stones.	3	73	8	5	1	31	3	6	14	144
527			20 x 10 yds.				1		2		2			3	8	16
531	ca. 10-20		20 x 8 yds.	Unshaped	yes	Storage room in cliff.					1		1			4
620					yes	Burial in trash slope.				15	6		5	6	6	38
623	2?	1	7 x 5 yds.	Unshaped	yes	Storage room in cliff.					1					1
720	ca. 2-3		40 yds. diam.		yes	Stone axe. Tower.				35			4	25	6	70
891	ca. 20-30	1	75 x 15 yds.		yes	Storage room in cliff.	1	10			5			9	4	29
892	ca. 1		4 x 3 yds.	Pecked-face	yes	Stone phallus.	3	2	7	3			3	6	7	40
893			15 yds. diam.	Unshaped	yes	Stone axe.		2		6	2			8	4	22
894				Unshaped								3		3	5	13
895			30 yds. diam.				8	7	1					36	8	60
896	ca. 10+		18 x 10 yds.	Unshaped	yes	"Megalithic" slabs.		29	16		2	2	2	8	6	65
897	ca. 8-10	1		Unshaped	yes	Stone axe. "Megalithic" slabs.	3	15	8	2	3	3		2	18	41
898			6 x 6 yds.	Unshaped		"Megalithic" slabs. Tower.		24	2			1		1		56
910	ca. 5-6	1	14 x 6 yds.					2	1		5				6	11
911	ca. 8		20 x 10 yds.		yes		1	8			4	4		7		29
912	ca. 10	1	12 x 10 yds.	Unshaped	yes	"Megalithic" slabs.		20	8	12	6	4		9	9	68
913	ca. 7		22 x 14 yds.			"Megalithic" slabs. 1 terrace.		18	2	2		1		16	29	69
914	ca. 12	1	10 x 10 yds.	Unshaped	yes	"Megalithic" slabs.		32	11	13		1		2	13	76
915	ca. 3-5		15 x 10 yds.	Pecked-face	yes	"Megalithic" slabs.		9	27	51	2		2	3	6	104
922	ca. 6-8	1	15 yds. diam.	Unshaped	yes		3	7				1		1	12	21
924	ca. 10	1	10 x 8 yds.					11	1		1	2		33	14	66
925	ca. 1-2		10 yds. diam.	Unshaped							1			1	4	7
926	ca. 1-2		11 yds. diam.	Unshaped												
932	ca. 7-9	1	15 x 15 yds.	Pecked-face	yes	Chipped knife.		6	6	3	3	3	14	10	11	43
933	ca. 6-8	1	15 yds. long				1	2	4	12	3	1			9	49
969														7	1	9
986	ca. 10-12	1	15 x 15 yds.					1	5	14		1	4	17	4	48
1049	ca. 5-6		15 x 5 yds.		yes				4	1			5	13	4	30

Table 9 (cont.)
TALUS SITES

Site No.	Est. No. Rooms	Kiva Depressions	Size of Mound (yards)	Shaped building stones	Refuse area	Remarks	POTTERY Chapin Gray	Mancos B/W	Mesa Verde B/W McElmo Var.	Mesa Verde B/W Mesa Verde Var.	Mesa Verde B/W Indet.	Mesa Verde Corrug. Mancos Var.	Mesa Verde Corrug. Mesa Verde Var.	Mesa Verde Corrug. Indet.	Other sherds	TOTAL SHERDS
1054	ca. 6-8	2?	10 x 10 yds.	Pecked-face	yes	Grooved stone hammer.			2	7	2		3	4	2	20
1064	ca. 1		3 x 2 yds.	Unshaped		Hammerstones.										
1065	ca. 1-2		6 x 3 yds.	Unshaped												
1068	ca. 1-2	1?														

Site 933. The remains of six to eight rooms built around a kiva (fig. 19) stand on the south-facing talus slope of a V-shaped canyon tributary to the west side of Soda Canyon. Walls of roughly-squared stone blocks have collapsed into a heap of rubble. An overhanging rock on the upslope side shelters one of the walls. Refuse is scattered downslope on the south to the ravine bottom where a long series of check-dams is located. The series of sandstone ledges above the ruin can be rather easily negotiated.

This site seems too elaborate to be a field house. Its kiva and refuse indicate a substantial period of occupation, yet its situation suggests an association with the nearby farming terraces. Ceramics indicate a temporal overlap with early Pueblo III mesa-top houses and with the cliff dwellings.

Site 986. This talus pueblo of posibly 10 or 12 rooms built around one kiva was constructed of large roughly shaped sandstone blocks. Its downslope side, facing south, was terraced by a series of crude retaining walls over which the refuse was cast. There is a close resemblance in plan and ceramic content to mesa-top pueblos built of pecked-face stone masonry.

Site 896. A mound of rubble measuring about 18 by 10 yards is located on a relatively gentle portion of the slope facing east into Soda Canyon. Building stones were roughly shaped but not dressed. Large rocks on edge formed the base of a number of walls. A refuse area, about 20 yards in diameter, lies to the south at the same elevation, rather than downslope. There is no cliff or sandstone ledge nearby. At least 10 rooms can be seen from the wall outlines. The sherd collection resembles those from pecked-face masonry sites on the mesa top.

Site 892. Seemingly one large room, about 8 by 10 yards in size, was built against a low cliff face on the west side of Soda Canyon. The masonry walls once incorporated several stones with pecked-faces. A level platform was provided by a series of short retaining walls on the downslope (east) side (fig. 19), where refuse was also dumped.

Site 1049. A rubble mound representing five to six rooms was set against a sandstone ledge and partly under a small overhang at its north end (fig. 19). Walls seem to have been built of rough block masonry. A rough retaining wall extends across the downslope side east of the mound, and refuse is scattered down the slope beyond. A small fragment of wall indicates the former presence of one room on top of the low ledge. There is no sign of a kiva depression, but Cedar Tree Tower (Site 397) is less than 100 yards upslope. No pottery was found on the surface.

Site 1054. This 4-foot-high rubble mound with several wall outlines showing probably represents six to eight one-story rooms. Walls were apparently both single-coursed and double-coursed of unshaped sandstone blocks with some pecked faces. Two rough retaining walls stand up to 3 feet high in places and set off two kiva depressions, one on either side of the house mound (fig. 19). An irregular low sandstone ledge borders the north, upslope side of the site, and very thin sheet trash is scattered downslope. Pottery type counts for all of these sites are given in table 9.

Cliff Dwellings

All masonry-walled buildings situated in the many scattered shallow rock shelters of the vertical sandstone cliffs are customarily referred to as cliff dwellings and are the primary reason for Mesa Verde's widespread fame. These numerous sites exhibit remarkable uniformity in construction and in the artifact remains usually found associated with them.

Cliff dweller masonry generally involved setting roughly shaped locally-derived sandstone blocks into a pink to brown mud mortar, then chinking most joints with small sandstone spalls. Nearly all dressed stone faces show signs of pecking although only a minority are dressed at all. Single-coursed walls (one stone thick) predominate, but double-coursed walls (two stones thick) appear consistently in sections of the larger ruins. In small shelters and under low ledges, the stone walls rise to the natural ceiling, while many buildings within the larger overhangs were roofed in much the same manner as they would have been in the open on the mesa top. Reasonably accurate room counts and estimates are obtainable because of excellent preservation in the shelters.

Not all of these so-called cliff dwellings served as habitations, however. Fire Temple, Site 520, near the head of Fewkes Canyon, belongs with a group of other structures that probably functioned ceremonially. At least two other sites, 553 and 536, were clearly field houses and are discussed with that group. There is a good possibility that several more belong in this category also. The remaining cliff sites are listed in table 10.

Forty-three of these ruins consist of a single room while 27 others have only two rooms (fig. 20). In many cases their builders simply took advantage of a room-size space by walling it shut, while others perched them on virtually inaccessible ledges (fig. 21). Most of these can best be

Table 10
CLIFF DWELLINGS

Pottery column group: the **Indet.** and **Mesa Verde Var.** columns fall under the heading **Mesa Verde Corrug.**

Site No.	Site Cluster	Room Count	Kivas	Excavated (E) or Tested (T) by	Pecked-face Masonry	"Megalithic" Slabs	Refuse Mound or Area	Remarks	Mesa Verde B/W	Mesa Verde Var.	Indet.	Mancos B/W	Chapin Gray	Other types	TOTAL SHERDS
501	C-F	7-8	1										1		1
502	C-F	4	1?											1	1
504	C-F	15-18	2					Storage only	10	2	8	1		2	23
505	C-F	2	0			yes	yes	Pictographs	4		4			1	9
506	C-F	9	1							1	3				4
507	C-F	5	0						14	3	6	73	3	45	144
508	C-F	1	0	T-Nusbaum 1926			yes	Burial	33	6	18	1	4	9	71
509	C-F	10	1					Fallen cave roof	39				2	5	46
510	C-F	2	1						2	2	10			3	17
511	C-F	3-4	1			yes	yes	Storage only							
512	C-F	1	0			yes	yes	Chipped-edge masonry	10	2	13	3	1	9	38
514	C-F	38+	4			yes		Chipped-edge masonry							
515	B H	11	3		yes		yes	Incised plaster designs	5		16	2	1	6	30
516	B H	2	0												
517	C-F	6	0		yes			Poss. field house	1	1	1		1	4	8
518	596?	1	0					Fallen cave roof	4						4
519	C-F	5	0	E-Nusbaum 1926				Bldg. materials "robbed"							
520	C-F	0	1	Fewkes (1916a; 1921);				Fire Temple	1		1	1		1	4
521	C-F	4	2	Cassidy (1960)				Wall painting							
522	C-F	20	3	Fewkes (1916a; 1921)	yes	yes	yes	New Fire House							
523	C-F	52-55	6	Fewkes (1916a; 1921)	yes	yes	yes	Oak Tree House							
524	C-F	12	2	Fewkes (1916a; 1921)	yes	yes	yes	Mummy House							
526	C-F	1	0												
528	STH	5+	?		yes	yes		Tree House							
529	STH	13-15	2					Alcove House; Burial							
530	STH	1	0					Storage only							
532	UNC	2	0					Storage only							
533	UNC	1-2	1		yes		yes		9		11				20
534	?	8	1		yes		yes				1				1
535	MNC	20-22	3						29	6	23		8	11	77
537	MNC	1	0					Storage only							
538	MNC	2	0					Pictograph	5		4		2	3	14
539	SqT	1	0					Storage only							

Table 10 (cont.)
CLIFF DWELLINGS

Site No.	Site Cluster (see key)	Room Count	Kivas	Excavated (E) or Tested (T) by	Pecked-face Masonry	"Megalithic" Slabs	Refuse Mound or Area	Remarks	Mesa Verde B/W	Mesa Verde Var.	Indet.	Mancos B/W	Chapin Gray	Other types	TOTAL SHERDS
540	?	2	0												
541	USC	14+	1		yes			Chipped-edge masonry	89	20	15	7	2	28	161
542	USC	12–13	1		yes		yes	Wall painting	17	6	18			7	48
543	USC	2	0				yes	Storage only	7	3	13	1		3	27
544	USC	7–10	1–2		yes	yes		Pictograph							
545	USC	1	0												
546	USC	4–5	0												
547	USC	1	0					Rock Fall							
548	USC	3–5	0		yes	yes		Storage only							
549	PKH	2	0												
550	PKH	4	0												
551	PKH	2	0												
552	PKH	4	0												
554	?	3	0							2					2
555	PKH	1	0							7					7
556	PKH	1	0												
557	PKH	13	2	Nordenskiöld (1893); Fewkes (1921)				Painted Kiva House	13	1	14	11	2	13	54
558	USC	2	0				yes	Pictograph	1						1
559	USC	2	0												
560	USC	5	0												
561	USC	3	0												
562	?	1	0												
563	UNC	5	0												
564	UNC	1	0												
565	UNC	1	0												
566	UNC	1	0										1		1
567	UNC	1	0												
568	UNC	4	0								1				1
569	SC	2–3	0												
570	SC	2+	0		yes		yes	Roof partly caved in							
571	SC	1	0												
572	SC	5–6	1												
573	SC	3	0		yes			Pictographs	2	1	2				5
574	SC	1	0		yes										

Table 10 (cont.)
CLIFF DWELLINGS

Site No.	Site Cluster (see key)	Room Count	Kivas	Excavated (E) or Tested (T) by	Pecked-face Masonry	"Megalithic" Slabs	Refuse Mound or Area	Remarks	Mesa Verde B/W	Mesa Verde Var.	Indet.	Mancos B/W	Chapin Gray	Other types	TOTAL SHERDS
575	SC	2	0		yes			Pictographs	10		13			4	27
576	SC	1	1		yes		yes	Pictographs	1	5	30			2	38
577	MNC	5+	1												
578	MNC	2	0												
579	MNC	2	0					Large rock fall on upper ledge	2	1	8			2	13
580	MNC	8	1		yes		yes	Pictograph	1					1	2
581	MNC	5+	1												
582	MNC	6	0					Pictograph							
583	MNC	4-5	0												
584	MNC	4	0												
585	MNC	2	0												
586	MNC	3	0		yes		yes	Pictograph		2	5				7
587	MNC	3-4	0				yes		1	1	2	2		1	7
588	MNC	6	0												
589	MNC	4	0								4			1	1
590	MNC	2	0			yes									4
591	MNC	6	0												
592	MNC	1	0												
593	596	4	1												
594	596	2	0		yes		yes	Pictographs	5		6		1		12
595	596	9	0		yes										
596	596	1	0				?								
597	596	0	1		yes										
598	596	4	0												
599	5-6	3	0												
600	5-6	5	0												
601	5-6	1	0												
602	5-6	1	0												
603	5-6	2	0												
604	5-6	1	0					Pictographs			1				1
605	5-6	1	0												
606	5-6	1	0												
607	5-6	1	0												
608	5-6	2	0					Pictographs			1	1			2
609	5-6	4	0												

Table 10 (cont.)
CLIFF DWELLINGS

Site No.	Site Cluster (see key)	Room Count	Kivas	Excavated (E) or Tested (T) by	Pecked-face Masonry	"Megalithic" Slabs	Refuse Mound or Area	Remarks	Mesa Verde B/W	Mesa Verde Corrug. Var.	Mesa Verde Corrug. Indet.	Mancos B/W	Chapin Gray	Other types	Total Sherds
610	596	1	0						1					1	1
612	B H	3	0			yes					1			3	3
613	B H	3	0		yes	yes								2	4
614	B H	3	0												
615	B H	44	2	E-Nusbaum 1910	yes		yes	Balcony House, Turkey pens	18	6	33			8	65
616	B H	2	1					Pictograph						1	1
617	B H	1	0												
618	B H	3	0												
619	C-F	14	1?				yes	Grinding bins	10	2	16		1	5	34
621	B H?	1	0				yes	Notched stone axe	5	1	2			2	10
622	B H?	6	0		yes		yes				2			2	4
624	C-F	11–14	0	Nordenskiöld (1893)											
625	C-F	220	23	Fewkes (1911)	yes		yes	Cliff Palace; wall painting	56	11	23	12	2	31	135
626	C-F	30	4		yes		yes	Sunset House; Turkey pens.		1	1			1	2
627	C-F	5	1		yes		yes	Pictographs.	4	5	6	2	3	3	19
628	C-F	10–12	1		yes		yes		20	4	5	3		4	34
629	C-F	16	2		yes		yes	Swallow's Nest							
630	C-F	1	0				yes		17		30		2	8	64
631	C-F	6	1												
632	C-F	1	0						2	1	5				8
633	C-F	3	0						10	1	9			4	24
634	C-F	17	2						7	1	10			4	22
635	C-F	13	1												
636	C-F	5–6	1?												
640	STH	114	8	Nordenskiöld (1893); Fewkes (1909)	yes		yes	Spruce Tree House; Wall paintings; grinding bins							
641	STH	9	0		yes										
642	STH	1	0												
643	STH	2	0			yes		Bark bucket							
644	STH	1	0												
645	STH	1–2	0												
646	SqT		0												
647	SqT	24	4		yes		yes	Little Long House	20	2	14	1	1	7	45
648	SqT	11	1						2	1	9	1	1	2	15

Table 10 (cont.)
CLIFF DWELLINGS

Site No.	Site Cluster (see key)	Room Count	Kivas	Excavated (E) or Tested (T) by	Pecked-face Masonry	"Megalithic" Slabs	Refuse Mound or Area	Remarks	POTTERY Mesa Verde B/W	Mesa Verde Corrug. Mesa Verde Var.	Mesa Verde Corrug. Indet.	Mancos B/W	Chapin Gray	Other types	TOTAL SHERDS
649	SqT	1	0												
650	SqT	70+	7	Fewkes (1920)	yes		yes	Square Tower House	6		6		2	6	20
651	STH	1	0												
652	STH	1	1												
653	STH	1	0												
654	STH	1	0												
655	?	1	0					Burial							
656	?	2?	0												
657	?	2	0												
660	596	2	0												
662	SqT	3	0		yes		yes								
1050	PKH	1	0		yes										
1051	PKH		0												
1063	B H	2	0												

KEY TO SITE CLUSTERS:

C-F	Cliff-Fewkes Canyon
STH	Spruce Tree House
SqT	Square Tower House
B H	Balcony House
MNC	Middle Navaho Canyon
USC	Upper Soda Canyon
PKH	Painted Kiva House
596	Site 596
S C	Spruce Canyon
UNC	Upper Navaho Canyon
5-6	Sites 599-609
?	Unassigned

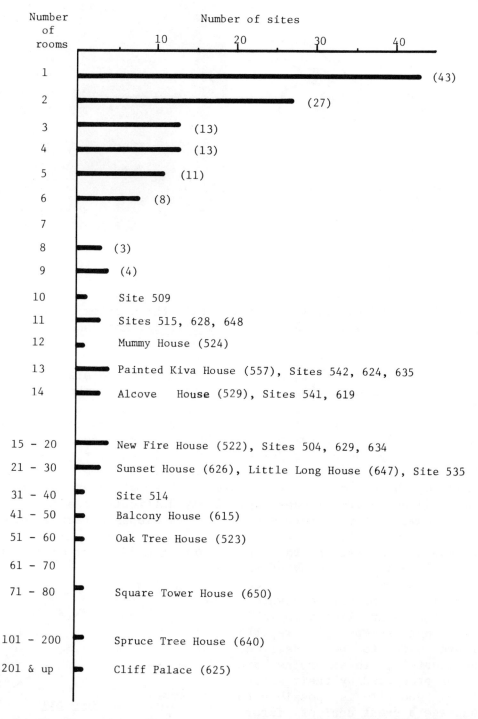

Figure 20. Plot of cliff dwelling sites according to their room counts.

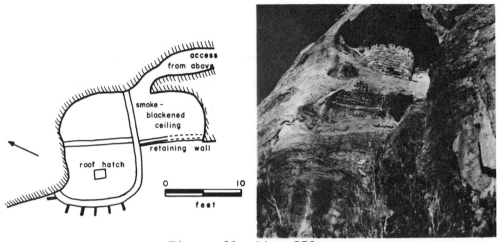

Figure 21. Site 578.

explained as storehouses, where even predatory rodents would find the sheltered foodstuffs hard to reach. They tend to be located near larger houses, although some appear to have been set closer to the fields. In general, these sites should not properly be tabulated as cliff <u>dwellings</u>, nor should their distribution be treated as indicative of actual occupation areas.

Forty-five ruins contain from three to six rooms and occasionally a kiva (fig. 22). Together with a number of the two-room structures, these sites probably represent small habitations, similar in size to those represented by burned stone mounds with few or no building stones. Buildings this size probably housed a single household each, together with much of their stored provisions. Once again, some of them may only have been seasonally occupied. These sites are generally located on narrow ledges, relatively difficult of access, and have some scattered refuse on the talus slopes directly below.

Only 32 of the cliff houses contain eight or more rooms, and only six of these have more than 30 rooms each. The five largest and many of the smaller ones have been completely or mostly excavated (references are listed in table 10), but skimpy site reports leave much to be desired. Fortunately, these ruins have been preserved by their situation, and it is possible to salvage a great deal of information about their architecture

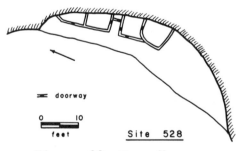

Figure 22. Tree House.

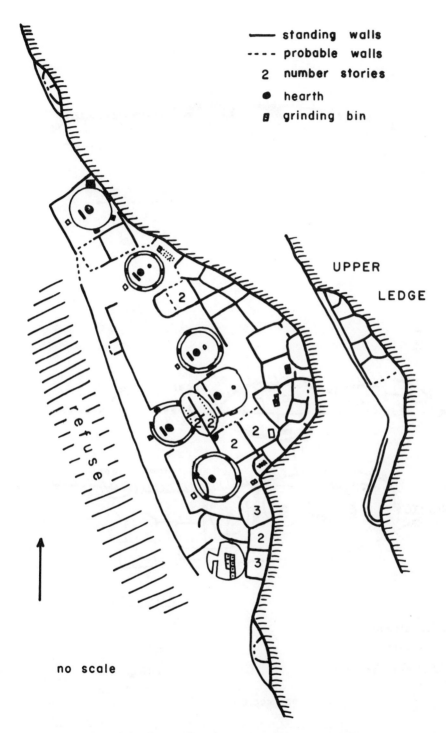

standing walls
probable walls
2   number stories
hearth
grinding bin

UPPER
LEDGE

refuse

no scale

Figure 23. Oak Tree House, Site 523.

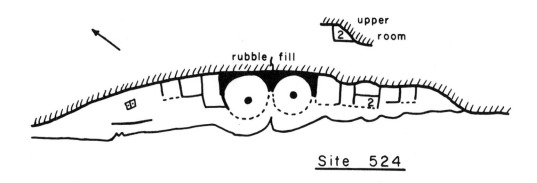

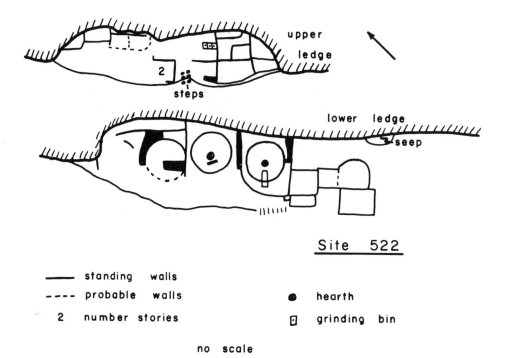

Figure 24. New Fire House, Site 522, and Mummy House, Site 524.

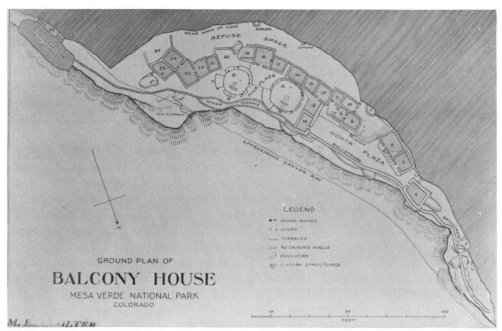

GROUND PLAN OF
BALCONY HOUSE
MESA VERDE NATIONAL PARK
COLORADO

Figure 25. Photograph of ground plan for Balcony House, Site 615.

at least.

Individual reports with ground plans have been published for Spruce Tree House (Site 640) (Fewkes 1909) and Cliff Palace (Site 625) (Fewkes 1911). A report on the work in Square Tower House (Site 650) with descriptions of the intact kiva roofs is available, but without any plan (Fewkes 1920). References to Oak Tree House (Site 523), Mummy House (Site 524), and New Fire House (Site 522) appear in more than one place (Fewkes 1916a, 1921, 1922, and 1923), but revised ground plans for each of them are presented in figures 23 and 24. Painted Kiva House (Site 557) has been reported by two workers (Nordenskiöld 1893; Fewkes 1922). Several other sites, some of them excavated, are discussed below.

Site 615 (Balcony House). In 1910 the School of American Research assigned J. L. Nusbaum to excavate Balcony House. Two kivas and 27 ground-floor rooms, many of which were two-stories high, plus a system of retaining walls across the front of the cave were uncovered and stabilized (fig. 25). The rooms were arranged to set off two courtyards in front and an open space at the back of the cave. The two kivas occupy most of the south court. A protective parapet wall borders the outer side of the smaller north court, which its users had slightly enlarged by pecking away part of a large boulder. Communication between the two courtyards was limited to a narrow passageway against the cave's back wall.

Pecked-face stones were commonly used in masonry walls both one and two stones thick. Several complete room roofs and other normally perishable features, such as the fine balcony for which the ruin was named, are still well preserved (fig. 26). Both kivas contain most of the features typical of late Pueblo III, although some factor caused an interesting adjustment in their orientation.

As any visitor to Balcony House soon discovers, access to the dwelling was restricted to two difficult routes. The main trail led from the base of the cliff about 100 yards to the south up a set of toeholds to a narrow ledge on which stood a two-story tower (Site 617). Once past the tower, it traversed the length of this ledge to a narrow crevice between the cliff and a large detached portion of it. This the Balconyites had walled up with masonry leaving only a crawl space that could easily be guarded by one defender. The second route ascended an irregularly sloping portion of cliff below the south block of rooms and would have required both hands and feet to negotiate. It would seem quite likely that burdens were either lowered or raised into Balcony House with the use of ropes.

Water was close at hand, for a good spring ran into the back of the cave while another occupied a second overhang directly beneath the northernmost part of the ruin. On this same lower level and below the center of the ruin are the remains of dry-laid masonry walls that apparently once served as turkey pens. Consolidated masses of turkey droppings are

Figure 26. View of Balcony House, Site 615, from an airplane.

jumbled among the fallen sandstone blocks.

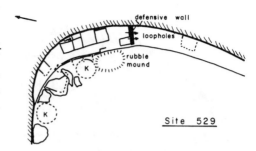

Fig. 27. Alcove House, Site 529.

Site 529 (Alcove
House).   This is   a   masonry
pueblo built on two levels in a
small cave   at   the head of a
rincon in Spruce Tree Canyon
(fig. 27). The upper ledge has
the remains of   seven   rooms
protected by a   thick defensive
wall and one additional room
outside (south of) the wall. The lower ledge contains the
remains of two kivas, three rooms--two of which once rested
partly on the roof of the central kiva--and a large pile of
rubble that may have resulted from the collapse of two or more
additional rooms.   Two   loopholes in the thirty-inch-thick
defensive wall commanded a view of the ledge to the south,
which provided the only access to the upper rooms besides lad-
ders from the roofs of rooms below. The skeleton of an adult
male, accompanied by two pottery vessels, was excavated about
70 yards west at the cliff base. He had a deformed skull and
lay on his right side in a tightly flexed position.   Both
vessels were of Mesa Verde Black-on-white: one a bowl of the
McElmo Variety, and the other a mug of the Mesa Verde Variety.
          Site 626 (Sunset House). A cliff dwelling on two
ledges   occupies a cave 250 feet long, 40 feet deep, and about
60 feet high in the east wall of Cliff Canyon (fig. 28). The
low and narrow south portion of the upper ledge contains eight
rooms and a set of two grinding bins, and was reached only by
crawling across a now collapsed platform from the north end of
the ledge. The north portion is
wider and less sheltered by the
overhang and contains two kivas
and   four   rooms,   one of which
had been built on top of one of
the kivas.   One kiva had five
pilasters, instead of the customary six. This entire upper
ledge could only have   been
entered along this same level
from the north where the ledge
pinches down to a width of less
than one foot at one point.

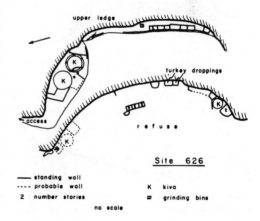

Fig. 28. Sunset House, Site 626.

          Buildings   in   the
lower main part of the cave are
divided into three groups, two

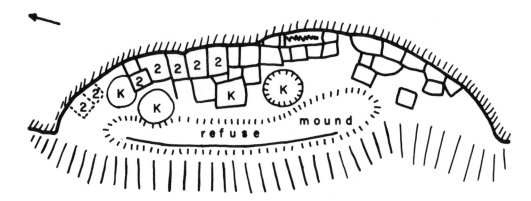

Site   514

Figure 29.

rooms and a kiva at the north end, three two-story rooms in the front center, and seven rooms and one kiva at the south end. Three dry-wall enclosures at the back of the cave contain massed turkey droppings indicating their use as turkey pens. The total room count reaches at least 30 with four kivas.

Walls were built in the same manner as in Balcony House. Rubbish was dumped down the slope in front of the cave. Water may have been available within the site if a weak seep at the back of the shelter had been developed.

Site 514. Located in the east side of Cliff Canyon north of Cliff Palace is a large pueblo in poor condition with at least 38 rooms and four kivas in a cave about 100 yards long with a high sloping overhang (fig. 29). Typical masonry of roughly shaped sandstone blocks in many cases topped large upright stones ("megaliths") set in as wall bases. Both chipped-edge and pecked-face stones were also occasionally used. Many rooms stood two stories high and many were obviously for storage. Three kivas were circular in plan with banquettes and pilasters, but the fourth was rectangular with at least a banquette. A long low mound, presumably of refuse, extends across most of the front of the shelter.

Site 515. This well-preserved   cliff dwelling of 11 rooms and three kivas is

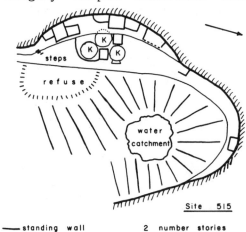

standing wall   2   number stories
probable wall   K   kiva
                no scale
Figure 30. Site 515.

located on two levels in a small canyon head north of Balcony House (fig. 30). There are seven dwelling rooms on the upper ledge and three kivas and four rooms, only one of which seems to have been for storage, on the lower level. Again roughly shaped blocks, chipped-edge and pecked-face stones were all used in building walls. All three kivas are circular and appear to have had six pilasters. A complex design of lines was incised into the plaster of one of them. Refuse was dumped down the slope from the ruin. Directly beneath the pour-off at the bottom of the canyon head is a water catchment that may either be naturally or artificially formed.

     Site 647 (Little Long House). There are at least 24 rooms and four kivas in this ruin built on two ledges (figs. 31 and 32) located in Navaho Canyon around the corner of cliff to the west of Square Tower House. The kivas and rooms in the lower section, when built up, provided access to the long low upper ledge, along which the bulk of the rooms were arranged. At the extreme north end of the shelter are stains indicating where rainwater runs off. In the floor of the upper ledge directly under these stains are a series of depressions pecked

Figure 31. Little Long House, Site 647.

into the bedrock, apparently to
trap some of the water passing
by here.

Site 528 (Tree
House). This small dwelling of
four average-size rooms and one
small storage compartment (fig.
22) is situated on a high
ledge, accessible only by
climbing down from above and
located a short distance south
of Spruce Tree House. Heavily
smoked fallen rocks in the
small cave directly below may
conceal the remains of several
more structures. The upper
group of rooms is still perfectly preserved. Their walls
are single-coursed with only a
few pecked-face stones. Large
upright slabs provide the wall
bases for one room. Several
fine perishable artifacts are
reported from this site.

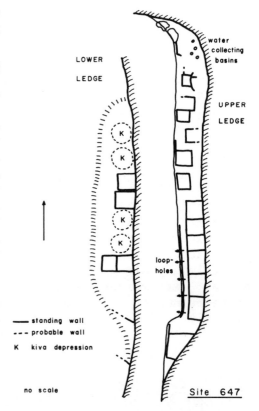

Figure 32.
Little Long House, Site 647.

III

NON-HABITATION SITES

Farming Terraces and Check-dams

The farming terrace systems of Chapin Mesa have already been described (Rohn 1963b). Table 11 gives a listing of all sites surveyed as farming terrace locations. Each site usually consists of a series of rough stone walls laid across the ravines and tributary canyons through which rainwater runs off the mesa top into the deeper canyons. These check-dams slowed down the rushing water, thereby capturing and holding much of the sediment load that was being carried away. The resultant terrace offered to the farmer relatively loose soil, containing some decaying vegetal matter, as well as greater assurance of adequate moisture for his crops.

Check-dams were built with the rough pieces of sandstone readily available on the slopes of the ravines. They were apparently started quite low and added to periodically as the sediments accumulated behind them. Conceivably one person or just a few could construct them quickly and easily, but once a substantial series was functioning, these same workers would be kept busy maintaining them. Since the great majority of check-dams recorded in the survey have partially washed out, we can imagine some of the problems the prehistoric farmer had to face.

Over 900 stone check-dams have so far been counted on Chapin Mesa. Of course we cannot tell how many have been completely washed away or buried beneath sediments, or how many dams might have been built of perishable materials such as logs and brush. In any event the 900 recorded terraces would provide some 20 to 30 acres of top quality farmland. They are found in almost every drainage that would not produce a large head of runoff water (fig. 33).

True hillside terraces were also tried in order to take advantage of sheet wash on some of the talus slopes. Although only two separate series were recorded by the survey, there is a distinct possibility that more existed formerly and

Table 11

FARMING TERRACES AND CHECK–DAMS

Site No.	Number of Terraces	Remarks
134	20	
166	17	14 in one draw; 3 in another.
169	1	One large slab dam about 20 yds. SE from ruin.
246	11	Assoc. field house 248.
366	12	
392	3	Hillside terraces.
395	62?	Cliff Dweller Dams (Stewart 1940).
457	29–41	Assoc. field houses 394 & 981.
717	Ca.22	
718	Ca.68	
719	Ca.24	Assoc. Talus Site 720 and field house 721.
727	Ca.57	Assoc. field houses 725 and 726.
736	17	
749	17	
750	4	
761	3	
780	42	Assoc. field house 536.
800	Ca.55	Assoc. field house 789.
844	Ca.40	
854	5	
877	17+	Assoc. field house 1908.
878	17+	
890	36	Assoc. field house 900.
901	10	Little Soda Canyon.
909	2	Little Soda Canyon; Upright slabs.
921	3	Little Soda Canyon.
927	16	Little Soda Canyon.
928	8	Little Soda Canyon.

Table 11 (cont.)

FARMING TERRACES AND CHECK-DAMS

Site No.	Number of Terraces	Remarks
929	5	Little Soda Canyon.
930	4	Little Soda Canyon.
931	1 or 2	Hillside terraces.
934	29+	(Stewart 1940); assoc. Talus Site 933, and field house 553.
935	25	
936	23	Assoc. field house 852.
938	9	
944	32	
946	8+	
947	13+	
948	3+	Not counted. Assoc. field house 714.
980	20	Assoc. field house 434.
982	32	
988	11+	South of Park boundary on Ute Reservation
989	33	
991	7	
997	14	
998	8-10	
1055	35	Assoc. Talus Site 1054.

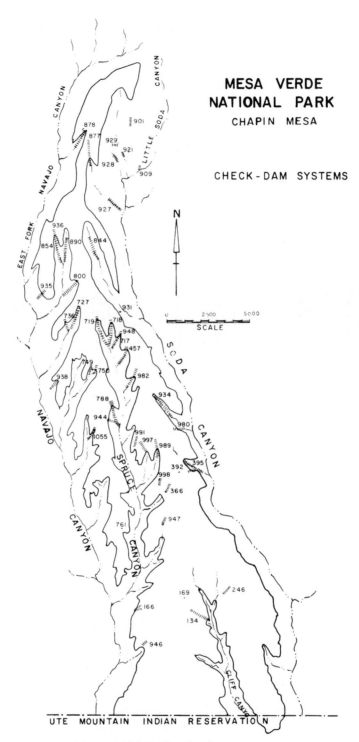

Figure 33. Check-dam systems.

that they have been thoroughly concealed by the dense brushy growth so common on the talus slopes.

As it is impossible to date the construction and use of check-dam systems directly, it is necessary to rely on associations. Several systems include one or more field houses that consistently yield ceramic assemblages ranging in date from late Pueblo II through Pueblo III. This would agree with the use of rough stone masonry and the increased focus toward the canyons, as opposed to the flat mesa tops, that seem to be taking place during those phases. In addition, several series of farming terraces are associated exclusively with an extensive settlement of late Pueblo II and early Pueblo III house sites on the wide alluvial benches near the bottom of Little Soda Canyon. Habitation sites belonging to either earlier or later stages are entirely absent from this locality. If farming terraces were in use anywhere on Chapin Mesa prior to late Pueblo II, they may have been built of perishable materials and so are not now recognizable.

Check-dams occur in series of from 3 to more than 60 in a single wash. One system may have controlled an entire ravine or only a portion of one. Descriptions of several of the more fully recorded individual systems will help to illustrate the general patterns of occurrence.

Site 800 (fig. 34) is a series of 43 visible dams in a V-shaped canyon with a relatively constant 20 per cent grade leading into the east side of Navaho Canyon north of the head of Spruce Canyon. Most have been badly eroded and are discernible only as butt ends or unnaturally piled large blocks of sandstone in the stream channel. Suitable stone was readily available from the canyon sides, and several boulders too large to be lifted were apparently warped into a usable position. Outcropping bedrock was utilized for footings or side anchors of many dams. Spaces between the large blocks were chinked with smaller stones, some of which had been fire-reddened indicating a source somewhere outside the canyon.

The dams are remarkably alike, averaging 5 to 6 yards long with a maximum length of 9 yards. Most are presently represented by two to three masonry courses standing 1½ to 2 feet high. One complete dam shows six courses 40 inches in height. Uniform spacing of the recognizable dams at 4 to 6 yards strongly suggests that at least 12 additional walls have been completely washed out, and that originally there were at least 55 dams of virtually identical size, spacing, and construction. These would have furnished about 1/3 acre of farm land.

Leading away from the west end of dam 9, counting

from the upper end, and
following the contour for at
least 6 yards along the side
slope is a low lateral wall
supporting a narrow hillside
terrace. Three courses are
visible in one place. At the
far end, the wall is lost
among the moving talus, so
that its total original length
is not discernible on the
surface. There may have been
several more such features on
both slopes that would have
increased the site's tillable
acreage. In addition to
utilizing sheet runoff down
the slopes, these terraces
would receive some overflow
from the dams to which they
were attached.

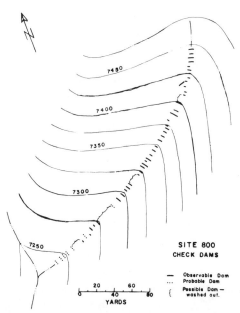

Figure 34. Site 800 check-dams.

No habitation sites lie near this ravine, indicating
that the farmers travelled some distance to their fields. On
the ridge crest about 200 yards to the north stands a two-room
masonry structure (Site 789) lacking traces of a kiva or refuse dump. This building was probably used only during the cultivation season. Thirteen potsherds from the surface are all classifiable as early Pueblo III (table 12).

This system of terraces, and the field house, appear to represent the work of a single economic group-- family, household, etc.--who terraced the entire draw as a unit. Even though 250 to 300 yards of stone walls had to be built, it must be remembered that building stones were readily available, the stones were laid without mortar, and that initial dam heights probably never exceeded three

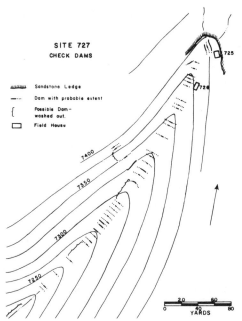

Figure 35. Site 727 check-dams.

to four courses. While construction was simple and fast, it
quite likely spanned several years.

Site 727 (fig. 35) lies in a narrow V-shaped canyon
leading southwestward at about 20 per cent grade into the
east side of Navaho Canyon. Beginning at a low pour-off from
the mesa top, 42 dams were recorded, representing about one
acre of tillable ground. One of two pour-off channels, adjacent
to Site 725 and with a 55 per cent incline, was terraced with
three or possibly five stone dams about 10 to 12 yards in
length. Below, in the main channel, 34 dams were counted
ranging from 4 to about 20 yards apart. Only remnants are still
visible, but the completed terraces must have measured 8 to 15
yards across. The presence of nine additional dams is suggested
by unusual breaks in slope, vegetation, and jumbled stones.

A portion of the west slope also revealed signs of
terracing. One lateral dam extended the area of a stream bottom
terrace near the head of the draw, while a separate series of
hillside terraces ran at least 45 yards up the west side. Four
dams are actually visible and could be traced for about 15
yards each; possibly two more are badly disrupted; and several
others may once have existed nearer the mesa rim. These dams
are located on a 30 per cent slope, down which there are no
distinct runoff channels. Other portions of the slope may also
have been terraced.

Immediately above the low pour-off at the head of the
draw is a broad slightly sloping (10 per cent) area covering
about an acre and one-half. It is strewn with loose stones,
some of which lie in rough alignments. Whether or not this
area was terraced with stone dams, or even with brush dams held
in place with stones, it was almost certainly farmed together
with the terraces at Site 727.

Two field houses are associated with this farming
system. Both lie in the upper end of the draw, immediately
adjacent to terraces. Site 725 contains about three masonry
rooms built against the outcropping sandstone ledge at the
south end of the uppermost dam. Site 726 also had about three
masonry rooms, but was located in the bottom of the draw
against the base of the east talus slope. Neither house had a
kiva depression nor a refuse deposit. Twenty potsherds found at
the two sites were all typical of sherds found in late Pueblo
III cliff dwellings. The nearest clusters of contemporary
houses lie from one to three miles to the south.

Site 134 consists of 20 stone dams in a shallow wash
on the mesa top just west of Cliff Canyon. The terraces average
about 13 by 10 yards and furnished close to one-half acre of
farmable ground. Slopes here approximate 10 per cent and

Table 12
FIELD HOUSES

Site No.	Est. No. of rooms	Size	Situation	Assoc. dams	Chapin Gray	Mancos B/W	Mesa Verde B/W	M.V. Corr.: Mancos Var.	M.V. Corr.: M.V. Var.	M.V. Corr.: Indet.	Other types	Total
76	1	4 x 12 yds.	against ledge		2	2	2		1	2	2	5
77	1	4 x 4 yds.	against ledge		1	1	2			3	7	7
79	5	11 x 11 yds.			1	2	35		1	1	4	49
169	3	15 x 10 yds.					1		2	2	1	9
170	?	15 x 5 yds.			4	2				10	5	5
202	2	8 x 5 yds.			3	2	7			1	1	28
203	?	10 x 5 yds.					3		1	10	3	8
241	5-6	10 x 8 yds.		246			8			4	5	22
248	?	7 x 7 yds.	steep slope	395			7				1	16
394	3	20 x 10 yds.	slope	980	1	1					1	1
434	2	?					2			12	1	14
441a	2	5 x 5 yds.								3	1	7
441b	1	?										
484	2-3	3 x 4 yds.			1	1	4		2	7	5	19
493	2	?			4	4				1	2	7
500	2				1	1	3			4	2	10
536	3-4	?	under ledge	780	7		1			1	2	3
553	3		under ledge	934	1		2					1
714	2	3 x 4 yds.	against ledge	948		1				12	6	28
721	1	6 x 8 yds.	steep slope	719	1		1		3	12	1	1
725	3		vale bottom	727			3	1		2	2	15
726	3	8 x 8 yds.	steep slope	727	1		1			8	4	11
789	2	3 x 3 yds.		800								13
852	1	5 x 5 yds.		936	1				2	1	1	1
862	?	5 x 5 yds.			6				1	9	1	9
863	1?	3 x 3 yds.	slope					1				12
880	1											1
884	Ca. 4	8 x 8 yds.	slope		3	15	1	2	1	14	13	49
899	1	5 x 5 yds.	against ledge	890	2	2		1		5	4	13
900	1	4 x 4 yds.	slope			10				12	13	36
903	1	5 x 5 yds.	slope		2	1	1			17	5	26
917	1	5 x 5 yds.	slope									
918	9	(Luebben, Rohn, and Givens 1962)-395										
981	1	(Rohn 1963)										
1032	1	5 x 5 yds.			2		1			3	3	9
1041	7-8	16 x 10 yds.	against ledge	877	1	4	4		2	4	3	18
1057	1	3 x 3 yds.										0
1908	?	5 x 4 yds.										0

all the surrounding area would have been tillable without
terracing.

Occupants of the large cliff dwellings in nearby
Cliff Canyon undoubtedly farmed this area, although terracing
could have been started earlier. Pueblo II sites are clustered
on the low ridge just west of the draw.

Field Houses

Near many of the terrace systems are remains of small
seasonally occupied "farmhouses" (table 12). These sites are
distinguished by their small size, generally only one to three
rooms, by the lack of evidence for kivas or occupational
refuse, and by their obvious association with farming terrace
systems. They were usually built of roughly squared sandstone
blocks, a Pueblo III trait, and produce almost exclusively
Pueblo III pottery. At least two small cliff dwellings fall
into this category, and many sites listed under various
categories in the preceding chapter may in reality belong here.

The only two field house sites excavated on Chapin
Mesa to date are both exceptional to this generalized picture.
Site 981 (Luebben, Rohn, and Givens 1962) consists of nine
rooms--three large spaces with hearths and six smaller rooms
probably used for storage. Architecture and pottery indicate
contemporaneity with the late Pueblo III cliff dwellings, and
the site is clearly associated with a large farming terrace
system of more than 60 check-dams (Site 395) near Cedar Tree
Tower. The great storage capacity of Site 981 supports
Woodbury's belief that harvests would be stored in field houses
to be transported home at leisure (Woodbury 1961: 14).

Site 1032 (fig. 36), excavated in 1958 near the Park
first aid station, contained the remains of a brush shelter or
windbreak, closed on only three sides, with use surfaces in
front of the open side (Rohn 1963b: 447-448). I have classed
this as a field house because of its clearly temporary nature,
although associated fields cannot definitely be identified.
The surrounding mesa top consists of residually formed soils
with poor agricultural potential. The 14 check-dams (Site 947)
in the draw to the east were all built of stone masonry typical
of a later date than indicated by pottery from this structure.
However, it is possible that this same draw was originally
terraced with non-durable materials that were later replaced by
the stone walls. The structure could also have temporarily
sheltered a small hunting party or group of travelers, but its
associated pottery--Cortez Black-on-white and Mancos Gray--

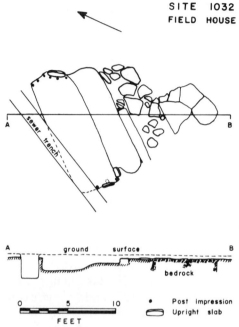

SITE 1032
FIELD HOUSE

Fig. 36. Site 1032 field house.

clearly indicates use by early Pueblo II people.

Site 553, Corn Cob House, is a three-room masonry cliff dwelling built under the shelter of an overhanging ledge in a ravine bottom at the lower end of a series of more than 30 check-dams (Site 934) located north of Cedar Tree Tower. It has all the characteristics of a typical field house and is excellently preserved in a small cave. One Mesa Verde Black-on-white--Mesa Verde Variety potsherd has been used to chink one of the walls. Evidence of trash and kivas is lacking.

Site 880 is a one-room masonry structure, about 3 yards square, built of rough sandstone blocks, located among the collection ditches of the Mummy Lake water system. In this position it probably provided temporary shelter for persons working on or tending the waterworks. A single sherd of Mesa Verde Corrugated--Mesa Verde Variety was picked off the surface.

Only those sites for which the evidence seems clear are classed as field houses. As yet, too little is known for adequate distinctions to be made between these seasonal shelters and year-round habitations from surface indications alone. Thus, many other sites probably also served as field houses, but their recognition awaits excavation.

Reservoirs and Ditches

There is definite evidence that at least the later Pueblo inhabitants of Chapin Mesa tried to manage their domestic water supply (Rohn 1963b). In addition to the numerous runoff checks creating farming patches in the drainage courses, they constructed reservoirs to trap and hold rainwater and ditches to conduct it from one place to another. The bulk of this effort seems to have been directed toward improving the availability of water for drinking, cooking, construction, and so forth rather than for crop irrigation purposes.

        In   a   land without   permanent   streams or ponds--the
Mancos   River   to   the   south   is   several   miles away--springs
provide the only source of water that can be relied upon at all
times   of   the   year.   Many such   springs and seeps are evident
today   (fig. 37),   although most   of   them   would   require some
cleaning   and   development   in   order to hold the moisture that
comes   out   of   the   sandstone.   Others may have existed in the
past,   but   are now so   choked   with debris   and vegetation that
their   former   productivity   could   only   be determined   by
excavation.

        Chapin   Mesa's springs are fed from the small propor-
tion   of rainfall that is not immediately lost through evapora-
tion and   runoff, but that soaks into the ground and percolates
through the   porous sandstones of the Mesaverde formation until
it   meets a non-porous   bed   of shale.   This ground   water then
flows along   the top of the shale until intersected by a canyon
side, at which point it reappears in a spring or seep.

        Artificial reservoirs represent an   attempt to add to
the   water supply   by salvaging some   of   the normally unusable
runoff.   Not   only   would   semi-permanent ponds be formed,   but
moisture   soaking   through the bottoms and sides would increase
the total amount of ground water.

        In   several   instances,   the   Indians   on Chapin Mesa
built reservoirs   as   if   they understood that nearby   springs
would profit from a local increase in ground water. At the head
of Fewkes Canyon   stands   part of a stone wall 2 to 4 feet high
and   at least   30 feet long now (Site 26).   All indications are
that the wall once was longer and supported a dirt bank to hold
the   water   collected   in   the natural drainage area   above it.
Within 100 yards downstream from the dam and at the base of the
main   pour-off into the canyon is a weak spring.   Regardless of
whether   or   not   the   reservoir   held   water all year long,   a
significant portion of the runoff water it collected would soak
into   its bare sandstone floor and reappear at this spring.   It
is   impossible   to   speculate   on   whether   or   not the   Indians
comprehended the hydrological principles involved, but they may
well   have realized   that a reservoir   built in that particular
spot would cause greater flow from the spring below it.   Such a
phenomenon may have belonged to their repertory of magic, which
might   account   for   the presence   of the pecked series of five
concentric   circles   around   a   dot   (Site 27) on   the   exposed
bedrock surface a short distance downstream from the dam.

        A   similar   situation once existed in the small   wash
above Little Long House (Site 647).   The location of an old dam
about   50   feet back   from the pour-off   is currently marked by

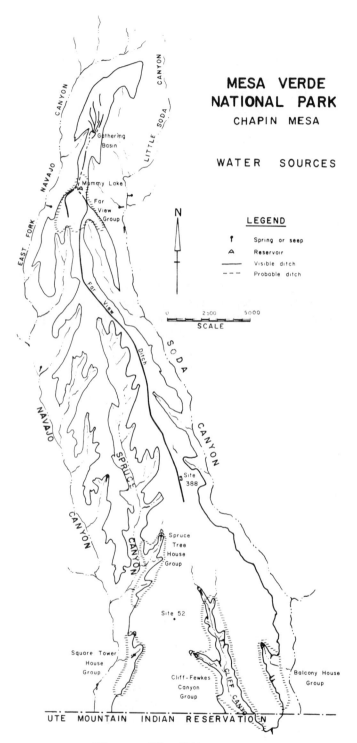

Figure 37. Water sources.

only a few crudely shaped sandstone blocks arranged in a rough
wall. Near the cliff edge is a small but deep natural hollow
in which water stands for some time after a rainstorm. That it
too was used by the prehistoric peoples is shown by a series of
steps out into the bedrock facilitating access to the trapped
water (Nordenskiöld 1893: 73). Moisture from both of these
tanks would have entered the bedrock to reappear at the base of
the cliff, although today there is such a large accumulation of
rock, soil, and brush that any water flowing out would be
immediately dispersed.

    As if this were not sufficient, seven basins were
pecked into the bedrock floor on the upper ledge in Little Long
House at a place 30 feet from the pour-off, where sheet runoff
from heavy rains runs down the cliff face and across the floor
of the ledge. Only one of the basins could hold very much
water, so their utility is open to question. From largest to
smallest, the sizes are as follows:

Diameter	Depth
24"	12"
14"	6½"
14"	4"
9"	3¼"
7"	4"
8½"	2"
4"	1½"

They were arranged in a rough triangle about midway between the
cliff face and the ledge rim. Without these basins, all of the
water passing over this spot would have been lost down the
canyon.

    This kind of reservoir-spring relationship may also
have once been present at the head of Spruce Tree Canyon.
Workmen who constructed a dam there in the 1930's to catch
runoff above the spring in the canyon head claimed they built
over the remnants of an older dam that could have been
prehistoric. Unfortunately, there are no written records or
descriptions of this earlier dam.

    A different arrangement was followed at Site 689, a

cliff house built in a horseshoe-shaped cave at the head of a
short tributary to Pool Canyon. Here a stone dam was laid up
across the canyon bottom in front of the ruin, forming a basin
about 50 feet in diameter. Although the center of the dam has
washed out, both ends remain intact.

The pool of water that frequently stands in the head
of the canyon below Site 515 may have either an artificial or a
natural origin that only excavation can reveal. Two pools
beneath pour-offs in the head of Pool Canyon probably were
formed naturally, but they certainly supplied the needs of
people living nearby.

By far the most spectacular water management system
on Chapin Mesa centered around Mummy Lake near Far View House.
Mummy Lake itself (Site 833) is a circular depression roughly
90 feet in diameter formed by a high artificial bank on its
south and east sides (fig. 38). The interior of the depression
is lined with a stone masonry wall everywhere but at the inlet.
Excavations in 1969 by David A. Breternitz of the University of
Colorado revealed a second stone wall supports the earth bank
on the exterior and a set of stone steps leads through the
center of the south interior wall.

Water entered the reservoir at its southwest corner
through an intake channel that completely changed its direction
of flow. This caused deposition of silts in the inlet, rather
than in the tank where dredging
would have been hampered by the
presence of the water body.

Other components of
the Mummy Lake water system are
the catchment area (Site 1075),
the main feeder ditch (Site
1074), and the Far View Ditch
(Site 1059). In the 25-acre
catchment area, a series of
ditches and diversions
deflected runoff from its
natural southeastward course
toward the south along the main
ridge of the mesa. The col-
lecting ditches converged in a
shallow natural drainage head
that was converted into a
gathering basin by the
construction of a stone bank
across its low southeastern
end. From this gathering basin,

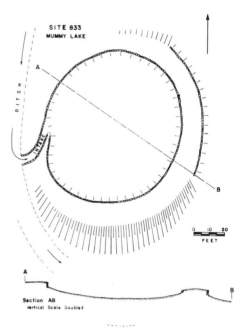

Figure 38. Mummy Lake, Site 833.

the water then passed into the main feeder ditch for the one-half mile trip to Mummy Lake (fig. 39).

Just before reaching the reservoir, water could be diverted from the main feeder ditch into a distributary ditch leading to a series of farming terraces in a ravine to the southwest. This is the only clear case on Chapin Mesa where water was conducted to fields. The National Geographic Magazine for February 1964 (vol. 125; no. 2: 192–193) contains a painting by Peter V. Bianchi showing the entire system as it might have looked when in operation.

The Far View Ditch seems to have been a later addition to the system. It was attached to the end of the feeder ditch, not to a spillway from Mummy Lake. It detoured around the houses of the Far View group and ran down the main ridge of the mesa for at least four miles (fig. 45). Along most of this course, it had a broad shallow cross section, where dirt had been excavated and then heaped along either one or both banks. A series of measurements taken by Stewart (1940) shows an average width of about 30 feet with a range from 23 feet to nearly 44 feet. At present the center measures from 6 to 18 inches below the banks, but in the past it was somewhat deeper. The profile in a trench cut across it for a Park water line revealed an original depth of about 3 feet, indicating that at times a considerable volume of water must have rushed down the channel.

In one spot near Far View House, the ditch runs along the very edge of the mesa top. Here a bank of stones has been heaped along the edge to provide a stronger border than was needed elsewhere. In at least two other locations, the course of the ditch had to be diverted from natural drainages. A stone bank was again employed in one of these places south of Pipe Shrine House.

Several rows of stones lying across the ditch at various locations may represent diversion sites to turn water into systems of check-dams or into small storage basins. Site 388, located on the east bank of the ditch between Cedar Tree Tower and Spruce Tree House, could be such a storage unit.

Excavation of Site 388 revealed a thick-walled masonry rectangle about 22½ feet long and 14 feet wide with a 6½-foot opening in its west side facing the ditch. The wall averaged 3 feet thick, was faced with sandstone blocks on both faces and filled with rubble, and stood an average of 8 to 15 inches high. The total amount of stone contained in the fill around the wall would have sufficed to raise it only about 6 inches more. While building materials may have been robbed for later uses, there was no evidence for this and no later house

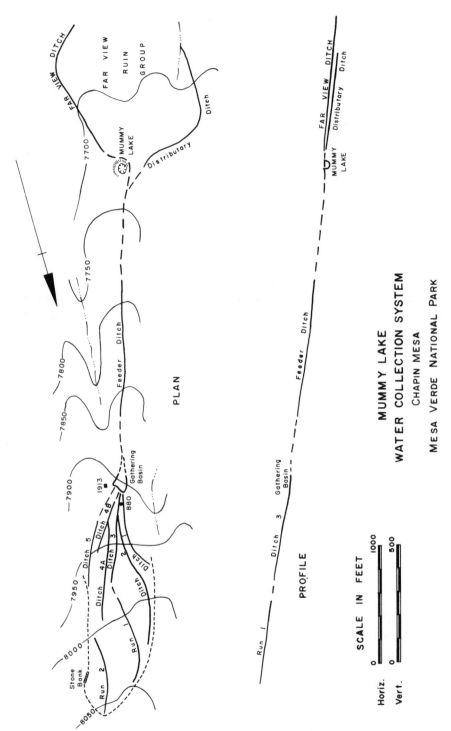

Figure 39. Mummy Lake water collection system.

sites   closeby where the materials could have been conveniently
used.   Apparently then, Site 388's walls never stood higher
than   about   20 inches and served either to retain water, or
earth for a platform. The presence of a row of stones across
the ditch, coinciding with the opening in the west wall,
suggests that water was stored here, but the nearest contemporary house sites lie near the bottom of Soda Canyon about
one-half mile to the east.   The few sherds found in the fill in
and around the structure appear to have washed in from surrounding Pueblo I sites. Lack of a trash deposit indicates Site
388 did not function as a habitation.

Although Stewart suggested that the Far View Ditch
provided irrigation water for several systems of farming
terraces, I believe this was at most only a secondary function.
The largest concentration of check-dams around the head of
Spruce Canyon could easily have been watered by the ditch if
several short distributary canals were dug, but no traces of
any have been found.   Even the two terrace systems mapped by
Stewart have no spillways leading to their draws.   Furthermore,
all of these draws caught sufficient quantities of runoff water
to irrigate the terraces contained in them. Therefore, it seems
more likely that water was channeled from the wetter northern
end of Chapin Mesa to its broader drier middle regions
primarily for domestic use.

Mummy Lake never fed water into the Far View Ditch,
since the bottom of its intake channel, and its only opening,
is 3 feet higher than the present bottom of the depression.
When first built, this difference was about 12 feet, indicating
that the reservoir could have held up to half a million gallons
of water. Furthermore, there is no presently visible connection
between Mummy Lake and the ditch, as implied by Stewart. If the
reservoir once got full, surplus water could have been diverted
out the end of the feeder ditch into a swale that now leads
directly into the upper end of the Far View Ditch. Thus, in the
system's final form, water could be directed either into Mummy
Lake or into the Far View Ditch. All water transported by the
Far View Ditch had to come directly out of the collection
system and feeder ditch.

Unfortunately, we do not know how far south the Far
View Ditch actually ran. It is traceable now to the vicinity of
Spruce Tree House, at least four miles from its start, but any
possible further extension to the south has been obliterated by
borrow pits and road construction dating from the early days of
development of the Mesa Verde for public use. Water spilling
out of the present end of the ditch would flow into both the
head of the west fork of Cliff Canyon and the head of Spruce

Tree Canyon, but if the ditch did extend to the south, and I
think it did, all of its water would have entered Cliff Canyon
or its tributary Fewkes Canyon.

Several lines of evidence help to date the construction of the water system. A test pit into the east bank of
Mummy Lake revealed two separate building periods. First, the
interior was retained by a low masonry wall while the exterior
sloping surface of the bank was covered with a layer of sandstone blocks packed together in a kind of rough pavement.
Subsequent remodelers raised the interior masonry wall and
built a similar one along the exterior side of the bank.
Recovery of the following sherds from the dirt fill on top of
the earlier stone riprapping, but between the two walls of the
later construction, means that the vessels represented must
have been broken and discarded prior to the additon of the
upper part of the bank.

Mancos Black-on-white--Mancos Variety	-12
Mesa Verde Black-on-white--indeterminate variety	- 1
Chapin Gray, body sherds	- 2
Mancos Gray, body sherds	- 1
Mesa Verde Corrugated--indeterminate variety	- 3
Unclassified--plain sherds from decorated vessels	-14
Unclassified--plain	-16
Unclassified--black-on-white	- 3
	——
Total	52

This would indicate that the upper bank could not have been
added earlier than late Pueblo II, and that the lower bank was
possibly built during Pueblo II. This also agrees with the
"sudden" appearance of a profusion of house sites during Pueblo
II around Mummy Lake.

A rough date for the construction of the Far View
Ditch may be derived from its relationships to various sites
by which it passes. It cuts through the Pueblo I Sites 386,
389, and 1047, but it skirts the entire Mummy Lake group. Had

these latter houses been empty, the short easy route down the
main ridge could have been followed instead of the precarious
mesa rim, a route that also required crossing a natural
drainage channel. Finally, Site 388 with typical Pueblo III
masonry, rests on the east bank. All of this helps to establish
a time placement between early Pueblo II and late Pueblo III. I
would guess that the Far View Ditch was constructed during
early Pueblo III.

SHRINES

The 14 sites treated under this heading represent
only those that could be called shrines with some degree of
certainty. Technically, a shrine is any structure, natural
formation, or place held in some degree of sacred esteem. This
means that some unusual rock formation where a legendary event
took place can be as important a shrine as a purposely-built
structure. In fact most artificial shrines are constructed to
commemorate a particular place or feature.

Archaeologically, only special structures or artificial embellishments at sacred places can even be considered,
and these may vary greatly. Thus, my primary criteria for
identifying shrines of the prehistoric Chapin Mesa Indians
center around the gross similarities to historic Pueblo shrines
described in some of the older ethnographies (Fewkes 1906;
Stevenson 1904; Mindeleff 1891; and Fewkes 1898). Actually most
or all of the larger sites covered in the succeeding section
and some of the pictograph locations may also have been
shrines, but it is desirable to separate the somewhat more
speculative items from the relatively clearer cases.

Site 999. (fig. 40). This rectangular slab-lined box
was completely excavated in 1958 and found to be in almost
perfect condition. The enclosed space measures exactly 4 feet
in length, averages about 16 inches wide, and is outlined on
both long sides and one end by sandstone slabs standing upright
to a height of around 10 inches above a slab bottom. A tilted
stone at the remaining end may have slumped from an originally
vertical position. Since the stone lining projects about 4
inches above the present ground surface, the net result is a
shallow pit.

The primary content is a large chipped-edge building
stone--of the sort used in stone masonry during the latter half
of Pueblo II, apparently in the A.D. 1000's--around which the
upright slabs seem to have been closely fitted. Whatever this
building stone may have symbolized, it does appear to have been

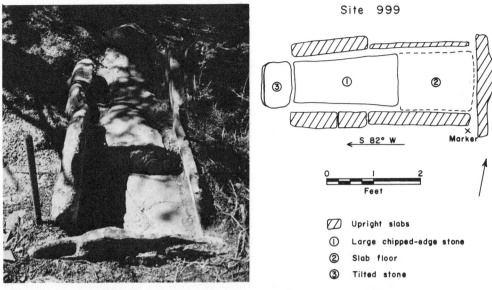

Figure 40.   Slab box shrine, Site 999.

the significant feature of this shrine.

Aside from the sandy soil deposited there by wind and water, the remaining space contained at least 163 small unshaped slabs of sandstone averaging about 2 to 4 inches in diameter. Seven pieces were clearly fire—altered. Such an accumulation is attributable to human activity for the fol-lowing reasons: 1) natural outcrops or deposits where small slabs are found contain many pieces broken from softer portions of the sandstone mass, the majority of which lack tabular shape and range widely in size; 2) collection of so many small slabs would require scouring a large area of the mesa top, and selecting only a certain kind of piece; 3) fire—altered stones are found only on the ground surface where they have been exposed to forest fire, or in the debris of human habitations (all seven burned pieces lay beneath the surface); and 4) no trace of burning could be seen within the box, indicating that the seven slabs must have been altered by fire before their deposition in the shrine. This is in keeping with the "stones, concretions, and other oddly shaped substances" Fewkes observed in many Hopi shrines (Fewkes 1906: 350).

This site is situated on the east edge of a low ridge crest running southeasterly from Sun Point Pueblo (Site 7) to the rim of Cliff Canyon above House of Many Windows (Site 635). The closest habitation sites of any period, including these two, lie about 250 yards distant; only one is upslope. There is no obvious topographic feature at this point other than the low ridge, but a second shrine (Site 11) rests on this same ridge

145 yards to the southeast.

Shrines resemble pictographs when the archaeologist faces the problem of dating them. Fortunately, though, the presence of the chipped-edge building stone provides an early time limit of about A.D. 1000 when stones of this type came into use in masonry. If the stone was shaped especially for inclusion in this feature, the shrine was probably built sometime between A.D. 1000 and 1100 while such blocks were in fashion. If the stone had been gathered from some house in ruins (such as Site 8) in the course of salvaging building materials, its construction would most likely fall between A.D. 1100 and 1300. The only sherd in the vicinity, found 2 feet east, belongs to Mesa Verde Corrugated--Mancos Variety, favoring the earlier placement, but this fragment could conceivably have drifted the 250 yards downslope from Site 8.

Site 261. Eight upright sandstone slabs form a straight-sided ovoid, measuring about 6 by 4 feet. It is situated on the east side of a low ridge crest trending northeast-southwest toward the east side of Cliff Canyon north of Cliff Palace (Site 625). A small test in one corner revealed quantities of charcoal and black soil, with a heavy concentration of small unshaped, but fire-altered sandstone slabs and spalls from 3 to 9 inches below the present ground surface. The bottom of the pit consisted of unburned native soil. Again the presence of so many stone slabs and spalls, as well as the evidence of burning, must be the work of men, but the absence of white ash and of baking in the surrounding earth suggest incomplete combustion, quite different from the expected characteristics of a typical cooking firepit.

Again, the nearest habitation sites of any period lie 200 or more yards away, and none is in a position to serve as a source for the 19 potsherds gathered from the surface of the slope southeast of the site. Nine Chapin Gray body sherds, nine Mancos Gray, and one corrugated suggest an early Pueblo II date, but association is at best tenuous.

Site 1056. Five fire-reddened upright sandstone slabs form about three-quarters of an ovoid approximately 40 inches in diameter. The signs of burning, the lack of association with any other site, and its situation at the termination of an almost imperceptible ridge pointing southwestward toward the east side of Navaho Canyon, all closely resemble characteristics at Site 261.

Site 842. This isolated slab-lined pit, far removed from the nearest house site (more than 600 yards), is situated on the steep narrow ridge dropping into the west side of Soda Canyon from the Far View Ruin group. Small sandstone slabs set on edge outline an area 6 by 3½ feet, filled with about 6 inches of ash. Three Chapin Gray body sherds and one plain red may or may not be associated with this site. Here again, isolation, situation, size, and form resemble the other shrines, although the possibility it represents an isolated hearth cannot be excluded.

Site 99. A cluster of several large stones, one partly on edge, located on the crest of a low ridge sloping toward the southeast, is faintly suggestive of Sites 999 and 261. There are several house sites in the vicinity, but this group of stones does not appear to be associated with any of them.

Site 11 (fig. 41). Most of the recorded shrines were built above ground of rough stone masonry without mortar. Site 11 is one of the best preserved of these and represents a form that might be called an alcove, niche, or vault. The opening faces east and is capped by a large sandstone slab supported on two crude piles of rough stones that form the sides. The back and most of the superstructure above the lintel seem to have fallen down.

Total length across the front (east side) is 58 inches; total depth or width was once about 40 inches. The overall standing height above ground is 26 inches, but the open niche measures only 16 inches wide by 10 inches high.

This shrine is situated on the same low ridge crest as Site 999, but only about 105 yards northwest of House of Many Windows (Site 635). There is no associated habitation site or refuse, and a single plain jar sherd was collected 9 yards east. The edges of several stones seem to have been roughly chipped in a manner similar to that seen on chipped-edge building stones, possibly indicating a late Pueblo II time placement.

Site 1911. A pile of rough sandstone blocks that appear to have fallen from a low niche-like shrine, similar in appearance to Site 11, is located atop a break in slope along the crest of a narrow ridge running southeast toward the rim of Soda Canyon north of the Far View Ruin Group. The situation affords an excellent view of Soda Canyon to the south. The original size of the shrine may have been about

Figure 41.
Alcove shrine, Site 11.

3 by 2 feet, and it may have stood close to 3 feet high.

Site 291. This is one of three U-shaped dry masonry structures, built on bedrock sandstone outcrops along ridge crests nearing the canyon rims. Site 291 is 66 inches long, 42 inches wide, and stands 30 inches high. None of the stones is shaped or dressed. The opening on the north end is flanked by a small upright sandstone slab. About 5 yards to the southwest, in a crevice between two large chunks of bedrock, are traces of a hearth, possibly associated with the shrine.

The 21 sherds collected from the surrounding surface do not appear to have drifted downhill from the three Basket Maker III-Pueblo I sites located from 70 to 160 yards upslope, unless it were the two Chapin Black-on-white and five Chapin Gray fragments. The remaining sherds (1 Cortez Black-on-white; 3 Mancos Black-on-white; 5 Mesa Verde Corrugated--Mancos Variety; and 5 other corrugated) all suggest a Pueblo II dating if the ceramic association is valid. This particular shrine lies on the ridge that terminates in the point of Soda Canyon just north of Balcony House (Site 615).

Site 270. On a small ridge spur a short distance south of Balcony House is a smaller U-shaped shrine with its open end facing southwest. It measures about 4½ by 3 feet with rough dry masonry walls up to 20 inches high. There is no associated habitation site or refuse.

Site 879. The third U-shaped shrine stands on the crest of the ridge spur that runs along the west rim of Navaho Hill overlooking Navaho Canyon. Its dry masonry walls stand only about 12 inches high and outline an area about 4 by 6 feet with an opening on its north end. The closest house site lies over 350 yards away.

Site 295. This shrine, located near the end of the ridge north of Balcony House and southeast of Site 291, consists of a number of rough, flat stones piled up on a projecting point of rimrock in a roughly oval shape about 2 feet high. There is no open space in the center of the heap, as characterizes other shrines. Two plain jar sherds probably drifted in from nearby Site 294. It would be logical to expect to find more shrines built on this pattern, but to date only this one rock pile is so clearly unnatural as to warrant assignment to a prehistoric human origin.

Site 266. A low circular wall, about 6 feet in diameter, built of thin slabs and spalls of sandstone, stands on a slight promontory at the end of a low ridge crest overlooking Cliff Canyon to the southwest. There is so little rubble lying about that the structure's original height probably did not exceed 12 inches.

At this point, let me insert a comment about several of the sites to be discussed in the following section. Five of them (Sites 272, 273, 274, 276, 278), all located on the same secondary tongue of Chapin Mesa as Site 266, resemble that shrine in specific situation, general construction, and lack of occupational refuse. They tend to be somewhat larger, and vary considerably in shape. I suspect they were shrines, but I have grouped them with a more general category, because their larger size could indicate uses more characteristic of a structure like Cedar Tree Tower (Site 383).

Site 786. Completely excavated in 1958, this small shrine stood on top of the stabilized ruins of an earlier Pueblo I house. Small unshaped stones were "piled" up in mud mortar on top of a base course of larger horizontal building stones, to form an arc of masonry around a space 5½ feet across its open end and 2½ feet deep (fig. 42). The present wall height of 12 inches could easily be tripled by the addition of available fallen stones, which means the original height probably exceeded 3 feet. Both ends of the arc were finished as corners, precluding any possibilities that the structure may once have been a complete oval or circle. Most of the potsherds found in the fill surrounding this structure can be classified as Pueblo II (Mancos Black-on-white and corrugated), and they contrast sharply with the purely Pueblo I sherds associated with the underlying house.

Figure 42. Remains of masonry shrine at Site 786.

It is very difficult to ignore the thought that the Pueblo II builders of this shrine knew they were working on top of ruins of an earlier house. Did they also realize or believe that these earlier inhabitants were their own ancestors? Did their traditions recognize this specific site as the home of long departed family or lineage members? In one other case, a shrine-like structure was recorded during the survey atop the ruins of a late Pueblo II chipped-edge stone masonry house at Site 296.

When these 14 shrines are compared with historic Pueblo structures of known usage (Mindeleff 1891, Fewkes 1898,

Stevenson 1904), several additional intriguing questions arise.
Many of the modern shrines are capped with stone slabs or
boards. Were more of the prehistoric structures similarly
equipped than Site 11 and presumably Site 1911? Many more
modern shrines have no artificial construction, but consist of
some unmodified or slightly altered natural phenomenon, such as
a spring, cave, or unusual rock formation. Even though such
features would be as noticeable today as they were in prehistoric times, how can we determine if any such places received
special attention from the ancients? Finally, Stevenson (1904:
233 and pl. 48) refers to a sacred place covered with
pictographs, permitting an easy analogy for several similar
spots surveyed on Chapin Mesa (See Petrographs).

Mesa Top Structures of Possible "Ceremonial" Use

One of the most nebulous groupings, yet one of the
most interesting, is formed by the sites discussed under this
heading. Most of the similar characteristics are negative, but
the primary negative inference is all important: none of these
sites were inhabited as dwellings. Customary house forms,
sizes, construction, locations, refuse, are all absent.
Positive similarities are limited to site situations. Here
again each individual site deserves separate treatment.

Site 352 (Sun Temple). J. W. Fewkes, who excavated
Sun Temple in 1915 (Fewkes 1916b), presents a strong case in
support of the idea that inhabitants of nearby cliff houses
constructed this edifice for religious rather than for secular
purposes. Whether or not the building was ever completed, its
unity of construction in plan of the letter D, the great effort
expended in dressing almost every stone by pecking and
grinding, its commanding situation, the three kiva-like
circular rooms, and the small shrine at the southwest corner
all duplicate features that are assignable to religious
activities elsewhere on Chapin Mesa.

Even though the overall theological character of Sun
Temple can be adequately supported, several specific aspects
deserve additional comment. The massive rubble-filled masonry
walls, averaging around 4 feet thick, do not typify domestic
architecture on the Mesa Verde, but seem to be more consistently associated with probable religious construction. Similar
but slightly less massive walls are found at Far View House,
(Site 808; Fewkes 1917), Site 16 (Lancaster and Pinkley 1954),
Site 52 (Luebben, Herold, and Rohn 1960), Site 1 (O'Bryan
1950), Site 388 (Rohn 1963b), and in defensive walls at Alcove

House (Site 529) and Casa Colorado (Site 669). The so-called towers occasionally exhibit rubble-filled masonry: e.g., Site 16, Sun Point Pueblo (Site 7 Lancaster and Van Cleave 1954), and Site 499 (Lister 1964), in addition to the isolated circular structure at Sun Temple. I suspect all of these except the defensive walls and the walls at Far View House represent religious architecture.

All three round rooms resembling kivas in Sun Temple were equipped with sub-floor ventilators, quite like those so commonly found in kivas of the Chaco Canyon, New Mexico ruins. This trait has so far been found on Chapin Mesa only in four of the five kivas at Far View House and in the lone kiva at Pipe Shrine House (Site 809), and all but one of these five kivas had been remodeled to include above-floor vents. The sub-floor ventilator, not requiring a separate deflector, is a complex architecural trait not likely to be duplicated by sheer chance or in parallel development. This would indicate that Sun Temple and the ruins of the Far View Group are linked in some manner, a point to which I shall return when discussing population groupings. It would also suggest some tie between the Mesa Verde and Chaco Canyon, a line of research that lies beyond the scope of this study.

Sun Temple is doubly important, not only because it represents a special building dedicated to religious ideology, but also because it helps to establish criteria by which other sites, whose purposes are less clear, may be judged.

Site 397 (Cedar Tree Tower). In 1920, Fewkes excavated another ruin whose religious implications are quite clear (Fewkes 1921). What originally appeared to be an isolated ovoid tower was shown to be a tower and kiva connected by a tunnel, plus a small rectangular subterranean room joined to one side of the tunnel. The kiva contained all of the customary features (excellent pecked-face masonry, recess, banquette, six pilasters, ventilator, deflector, hearth, and wall niches) found in cliff house kivas. Only the sipapu was lacking. The tower, on the other hand, was expertly formed of double-coursed masonry walls in which virtually every stone was dressed by pecking to fit the curvature of the walls, and its floor contained a sipapu excavated out of the bedrock sandstone. A low retaining wall supported a level plaza-like space over the kiva roof.

The absence of refuse indicates no one inhabited Cedar Tree Tower. Such an elaborate building, however, must have been the scene of rituals performed most likely by occupants of the cliff houses, and probably some paraphernalia was stored in the subterranean room. Once again this site is situated on a secondary ridge crest where the slight, even slope of the mesa top breaks to a steeper talus-covered slope beginning the descent into Soda Canyon. This spot possesses a spectacular view southeastward into the canyon.

Site 810 (Far View Tower). Another complex, closely similar to Cedar Tree Tower, was excavated by Fewkes in 1922 in the Far View group (Fewkes 1922, 1923). Here a circular tower had been constructed on top of the ruins of a late Pueblo II house (see chipped-edge stone masonry pueblos) and used in conjunction with one, or possibly two kivas. One of the kivas may have been built contemporaneously with the tower, while the other seems to have been remodeled from an already existing structure. The extensive necropolis mentioned by Fewkes may have housed the deceased from the earlier pueblo, or from several of the surrounding pueblos, or it may indeed have been a specialized burial place associated with the kiva-tower complex. Unfortunately, there is no published description of burials from here, and vandals had destroyed a large portion even before Fewkes excavated it.

Far View Tower is situated on the open mesa top at no distinctive topographic feature. Only the ruined Pueblo II house differentiates this spot from its surroundings. Features of the various buildings have not been described in print, but characteristics of the preserved tower and kivas suggest contemporaneity with the later occupations at Far View House (Site 808) and Pipe Shrine House (Site 809) in Pueblo III.

Site 383. This isolated unexcavated tower with about a 15-foot inside diameter, is situated on the end of a low ridge near the rim of Soda Canyon. Its double-coursed walls with pecked-face building stones resemble those of Cedar Tree Tower, but there is only enough rubble to permit a maximum height of around 4 feet. Thus, either the structure was robbed for building materials or it was never intended to stand higher. There is no trace of refuse or a kiva depression. Sixteen potsherds gathered from the surrounding surface verify an early Pueblo III building date. This building is situated in an exceptionally poor location to serve as a lookout.

Site 1. When considered in the light of the preceding three sites, Site 1 pueblo, excavated by O'Bryan (1950) in 1942, is more easily explained as a kiva-tower unit than as a dwelling. Three-foot thick rubble-filled and masonry-faced walls form a D-shaped room that O'Bryan thought did not exceed one story in height. Immediately to the south lies a six-pilaster masonry-lined kiva yielding tree-ring dates up to A.D. 1024. Attached to one corner of the D-shaped room is a small single-coursed masonry room. These three structures seem to be

analogous to Cedar Tree Tower, its kiva, and the subterranean
room, respectively. A sub-floor passageway opening toward the
kiva from the D-shaped room suggests the presence of a tunnel,
but the near side of the kiva was not entirely dug out to test
this possibility.

The presence of a refuse mound, which cannot be dis-
counted as belonging entirely to the underlying Pueblo I site,
presents an anomaly, however. Two burials and about 2,600
potsherds (two-thirds of which must be classified as Pueblo II)
were recovered from about nine-tenths of the mound. Aside from
this, none of the artifacts or features found on the floors of
any of the buildings argues against a possible ceremonial
connotation. Is it possible that some religious functionary
actually did dwell here between periods of ritual use, and that
he acted as a sort of custodian? Without completely abandoning
the idea that someone simply built a "futuristic" house in
which to live, I would strongly suggest that Site 1 pueblo more
properly belongs to the class of sites including Cedar Tree
Tower, Far View Tower, and Sun Temple. It certainly predates
all of these, probably by one to two centuries.

Site 233. One circular tower and two rectangular
rooms have been arranged in a row forming a building about 8 by
5 yards in size. Rough building stones were used rather than
shaped or dressed blocks. There is no evidence of a kiva
depression or of refuse, although 33 sherds were collected.
Most of these represent a single vessel that had been nearly
reduced to cinders by extreme reheating. Once again, this site
is situated toward the end of a ridge crest between tributaries
to Cliff Canyon.

Similar situations characterize eight other sites
that are all located on the tongue of mesa extending between
Cliff Canyon and Soda Canyon:

Site 253.   8 x 3 yard mound, walls of rough
             masonry blocks.

Site 272.   5 x 5 yard mound, walls of rough
             unshaped stone slabs.

Site 273.   6 foot-square masonry room of rough
             unshaped stones.

Site 274.   5 yard masonry arc with nearby
             hearth.

Site 276.   5 x 7 feet rectangular masonry room
of   rough unshaped sandstone blocks.
There seems to be a small habitation
site (Site 276A) close by.

Site 278.   2-yard diameter, roughly circular
structure of crude stone blocks with
hearth nearby.

Site 1033.   2-yard diameter, roughly circular
structure   of   crude   masonry   with
hearth nearby.

Site 1037.   5 x 3 yard mound, with walls of
large   unshaped   masonry   blocks
showing.

None of these eight sites has kiva depressions or
accumulations of refuse, but all were built directly on
outcropping bedrock ledges. I believe that all eight were
shrines, but I have included them among this more generalized
group of sites because their poor state of preservation
prohibits a more positive designation until they are excavated.
Actually there are striking resemblances between these eight
sites and several of the sites already identified as   shrines,
in apparent construction, situation, occasional presence of
hearths, and the negative presence of habitation features and
refuse.   Their size fills the gap between the smaller shrines
and the larger ceremonial structures such as Cedar Tree Tower.

Site   198.   This   peculiar rough stone masonry
structure, with several large upright stones, measures 3 yards
square.   It is situated on a low ridge with a possible hearth
10 yards away.   One Mesa Verde Black-on-white sherd could not
have drifted from the earlier house sites located uphill, and
no other sign of refuse is present. This site differs from the
preceding eight only in the use of large upright stones and the
failure to build on an outcropping sandstone ledge.

Site 1910.   Traces of a curved stone masonry wall
bound one side of a faint hollow, clear of stones on its
surface, and situated on top of a rocky ridge that slopes into
Soda Canyon. There is an insufficient number of stones visible
to indicate a structure any higher than the visible 1-foot-high
wall, and not enough soil depth to permit the existence of a
subterranean kiva. Part of the wall shows reddening from fire,
but no trash is visible around this roughly circular area,

which measures about 6 yards in diameter.

Site 52. A desire to evaluate several pueblo-like sites, situated in atypical spots and possessing no occupational debris, motivated the excavation of this ruin in 1955 (Luebben, Herold, and Rohn 1960). The excavators suggest this may have been a low platform--implied by two stepped abutments, and several other features--of ceremonial significance. Certainly the various unusual architectural characteristics, including rubble-core walls, find closer parallels among those sites already identified as ceremonial in nature than among dwelling sites. While discussing the probability that the long Far View Ditch (Site 1059) supplied water to the occupants of Cliff and Fewkes Canyons, I have already noted the seeming coincidence of Site 52's position at the point where need for an artificial canal would cease in favor of the natural draw leading to the reservoir (Site 26) at the head of Fewkes Canyon (Rohn 1963b). Thus, in the total context of prehistoric Chapin Mesa, Site 52 does indeed seem to bear religious connotations.

Closely related to Site 52 in pre-excavation surface appearance are four other ruins with large rectangular thick-walled enclosures that seem to have stood less than one full story in height. Site 38 consists of two 21-foot-square rooms located on a slope near the rim of Navaho Canyon. Site 55 is a large 9 by 6 yard rectangle of double-coursed masonry located on the main ridge of Chapin Mesa. Site 121 is a 15 by 18 yard mound concealing perhaps three masonry rooms formed by large stones both on edge and horizontal. It is situated on a slope close to the rim of Cliff Canyon. Site 193 contains two rectangular rooms, built of rough multiple-coursed stone masonry on different levels situated on the west slope of the main ridge not far from the rim of Navaho Canyon. Both rooms cover an area about 9 by 6 yards. Potsherds from Sites 38 and 193 indicate contemporaneity with Site 52, but only masonry details at the other two suggest a Pueblo III date. At present, any claim for the religious significance of these sites rests on the interpretation of Site 52.

Site 388. This low rectangular building with rubble-core walls (Rohn 1963b, and section on Reservoirs and Ditches in this volume) is situated on top of the east bank of the Far View Ditch near the lower end of its traceable segment. While there are no habitation site ruins near enough to have been served by this as a small water storage tank, neither can it be satisfactorily identified with ritual practice. Water could have been stored here to irrigate adjacent field areas. Its general appearance, however (large, low-walled space, rubble-core walls, lack of kiva and refuse), does fall within the pattern established at other so-called ceremonial sites.

There are two additional sites that seem out of place among the ordinary habitations because of their plans and construction. One of these is the Unit Pueblo No. II at Site 16 (Lancaster and Pinkley 1954) with its crudely rectangular main building, three "towers," and eight-pilaster kiva. All of the above-ground structures exhibit massive rubble-filled walls of low height, although some building materials could have been robbed by later builders. The peculiar combination of attributes found in this structure, while requiring profuse explanations as a house, agrees rather closely with attributes at other ceremonial sites: large rectanguloid, low-walled enclosure; massive rubble-filled walls; towers and kiva associated with towers. Furthermore, the exceptionally large kiva is matched in size by only one other yet known, at Far View House (Site 808), also with eight pilasters and oblong floor vaults. The situation of this component at Site 16 on top of the ruins of older houses is also compatible with this interpretation.

Site 297. The plan of this site virtually disqualifies it as a habitation, but is reminiscent of the plans of Sites 16 and 52. A circular wall may represent a kiva, and a high mound of stone could conceal some structure taller than the main building.

Thanks to the characteristics of Sun Temple, Cedar Tree Tower, Site 52, and the 14 shrines described above, it is possible to speculate that all the sites treated in this category once possessed some religious significance. It may be possible to consider all of these sites as "shrines" of various sorts, with Sun Temple by far the largest. Sun Temple's builders may have intended that ceremonies held there would be attended by persons coming from many communities, and indeed this site may have provided a sort of ceremonial center for them. Fewkes points out that the building of this imposing structure could hardly be accomplished by a small group of people, but must have required the cooperative efforts of several groups, united possibly by theological direction.

Petrographs

There is hardly room within the confines of this

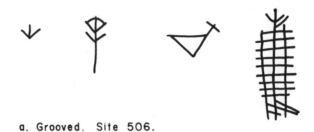

a. Grooved. Site 506.

b. Pecked. Site 588.

c. Pecked. Site 583.

d. Pecked. Site 544.

e. Pecked. Site 577.

f. Pecked.
Site 594.

Figure 43. Chapin Mesa petrographs.

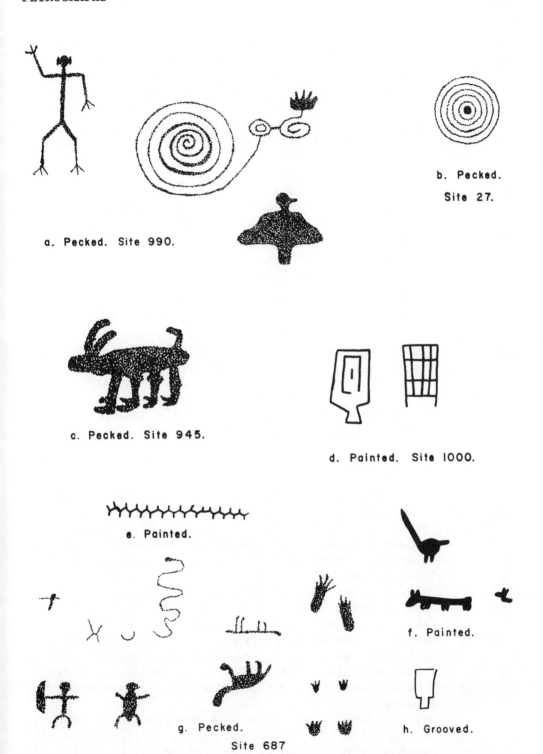

a. Pecked. Site 990.

b. Pecked.
Site 27.

c. Pecked. Site 945.

d. Painted. Site 1000.

e. Painted.

f. Painted.

g. Pecked.
Site 687

h. Grooved.

Figure 44. Chapin Mesa petrographs.

study to include an analysis of the art forms expressed in pictographs and petroglyphs found on Chapin Mesa. Nevertheless, the basic information should be made available to other students who might wish comparative data for their own studies. Thus, a fairly complete range of illustrations is presented with discussion focused primarily on their patterns of occurrence. For convenience in the following discussion the term "petrograph" (Turner 1963) will apply to any naturalistic or geometric figure inscribed on rock surfaces whether by painting, pecking, or incising.

Most often, petrographs are found on cliff or cave walls directly associated with cliff dwellings (14 such sites are recorded in table 10). These have the distinct advantage of being at least roughly datable. At five other sites, though, petrographs are completely isolated from other cultural manifestations.

Some of the representative petrographs found at cliff house sites are shown in figures 43 and 44e-h. Most of them occur singly or in small groups, and they may represent simple adornment of the habitation site, magical charms, the inclination to express some scene or event artistically, or mere doodling. The peculiar groove figures from Site 506 (fig. 43a) seem to best fit this last explanation, partly because they are located on a sloping surface within the site's limits, where it would be only natural to sit and while away idle moments. Groups of hand prints are found at Sites 581, 572, and 700, and a single pecked hand figure at Site 617, but most figures appear to represent some human or animal beings.

Five sets of petrographs are not found in direct association with any habitation sites, and therefore cannot be explained simply as embellishments or idle compositions. The makers of these designs were away from home at the time of their formulation. Four of them consist of from one to three figures and could have been executed on a single visit, but the fifth, Pictograph Point (Site 1001), must have been visited and revisited many times. The many figures pecked into the cliff face here (fig. 45), apart from any house sites yet within easy walking distance of several, present an analogous situation to a decorated cliff near Zuni, revered as a shrine by these people (Stevenson 1904: 233). Both of these rock surfaces exhibit a wide range of anthropomorphic, zoomorphic, and geometric figures.

Unfortunately, no kind of precise date can be assigned to the work at Pictograph Point. Artistically, the figures resemble those found in association with Pueblo III cliff houses, and there is no evidence suggesting any later

origin for them.   Of course, preceding Puebloan peoples could
have produced some or all of them too.

The small series of concentric circles (Site 27: fig.
44b) pecked into the bare rock area at the head of Fewkes
Canyon was noted by Charles Mason and Richard Wetherill in 1888
(Mason 1918) and related to the spring beneath the adjacent
pour-off.   About 30 yards upstream is the reservoir dam (Site
26), that helped provide valuable water to the large community
nearby.   It requires some imagination to view this site as
having a supernatural association, but any other possible
explanation falls even shorter.   The isolated figures at Sites
990 (fig. 44a), 945 (fig. 44c), and 100 (fig. 44d) may fit a
similar interpretation.

All "petrographs" were produced by one of three
techniques: pecking, grooving, or painting.   The first two are
more durable, possibly explaining in part the predominance of
pecking.   However, even though all three techniques were
employed at one sheltered spot near Site 687 (fig. 44e-h),
pecked figures outnumber those made by the other two techniques
combined.   The technique employed on each figure illustrated is
listed in the legend for that figure.

Occupied Caves

Five caves contained signs of former human occupation
but lacked any visible structural remains.   Their ceilings were
blackened by smoke and some trash lay on their floors.   All
pottery found in these caves indicates contemporaneity with the
cliff dwellings.

Two of the caves, Sites 611 and 1038, lie only 40
yards apart along the cliff between Balcony House (Site 615)
and Site 515.   Numerous axe-sharpening grooves and several
"doodlings" in Site 611, and clusters of fire-reddened stones
in both, demonstrate limited use, almost certainly by persons
living in the Balcony House ruin group.

The three other caves are located within the Cliff-
Fewkes Canyon group and are situated near cliff dwellings.   The
soot-covered roofs of both Sites 513 and 525 have peeled off,
but this appears to have happened after their use periods. Site
503 contained a considerable quantity of perishable refuse
material and produced remnants of a mummy, apparently placed
there by neighboring Cliff Dwellers and later damaged by a
nineteenth-century campfire.

Figure 45. Pictograph Point, Site 1001.

Historic Navaho Sites

        Four sites (916, 943, 1042, 1043) could positively be
identified as sweat houses built and used by Navahos employed
by the National Park Service during construction of an
automobile road into the Park and for various maintenance work
up to the present time. Even though these sites are historic
and do not pertain to the prehistoric occupation of Chapin
Mesa, they have been recorded by the survey and are mentioned
here because of their implications for interpretation of
surface remains.
        Everywhere, especially on Chapin Mesa, are the signs
of twentieth-century conservation work, road building,
quarrying for raw building material or ballast, clearing dead-
falls from the forest, old camps of horseback-traveling
visitors, corrals for horses and cattle, and so forth. Many of
these activities disturbed prehistoric sites (e.g., Site 369 or
the Far View Ditch). The Navaho sites represent historic
disturbance by persons whose traces are more easily confused
with prehistoric remains. For example, the cave roof at Site
661 is completely blackened by smoke, although no architecture
is visible. Superficially, this cave resembles the other
occupied caves, and the tantalizing prospect that Basket Makers

once dwelled there stimulated the digging of five unproductive
test holes in 1954. Five unusual biomorphic pictographs and the
proximity to two of the sweat lodges introduce the possibility
that much of the occupational evidence or all of it could be
due to use by Navahos in recent years.

       A further potential source of confusion may be
visualized in the huge heap of fire-cracked and reddened stones
associated with three of the sweat houses. Within a few short
decades this stone heap will be the sole survivor of the site,
and how would an archaeologist interpret such a massive pile of
fire-altered stones?

IV

CERAMICS

As each site was recorded during the survey, the usual array of potsherds and occasional artifacts of stone, bone, and perishable materials was collected from the surface. In addition, collections in the Mesa Verde Museum contain numerous specimens recovered through stabilization work or found by visitors at some of these same sites. Test excavations have also added to the already large total collection.

However, only selected items will be treated here-- those that promise to add some information to the story of Chapin Mesa. Pottery, of course, will receive the most atten- tion. Sherds were gathered from most of the sites in sufficient quantities to serve as one of the major criteria for the temporal placement of each site. These, together with a number of whole vessels in the Museum's collections and the pottery from the many small and partial excavations, form the basis for the suggested classification of Mesa Verde pottery that follows.

The pottery collected during the course of the Archaeological Site Survey was first combined into one large pile, and then sorted into various classificatory groups. This permitted a practical test for the most recent and compre- hensive pottery classification for the Mesa Verde region (Abel 1955). The results suggested that a revised taxonomy might even better express Mesa Verde's ceramic history (many of these concepts have been included in Breternitz, Rohn, and Morris 1974), although Abel's contribution in ordering Mesa Verde pottery types for the first time cannot be minimized. Before launching into type descriptions, however, it will be useful to review both the ends to be furthered by pottery classification and the approach to be utilized in formulating it.

The Approach and Assumptions

Ceramic classification produces a set of abstract categories for the purpose of ordering a great mass of raw data in the form of individual potsherds and vessels. Its aim is to utilize these arbitrary categories as part of an expression of cultural units and cultural processes (e.g., culture change), without having to return constantly to lengthy descriptions of the raw data themselves. Thus it is important to approach as nearly as possible the never really attainable goal of reproducing in classification what was in the minds of the potters and pottery users.

This requires a careful weighing of the various criteria available for classification, together with recognition that no distinct or sharp lines can be drawn between any two contiguous categories of data. Hence a suitable classification of pottery would be based primarily on those factors reflecting most strongly individual choices that are regulated by the enclosing culture. It should not expect to classify satisfactorily all sherds and even vessels, especially those that represent the dividing lines between categories. In other words, a varying percentage of unclassifiable pieces must be expected in any classification that attempts to parallel actual cultural variation.

This disadvantage does not plague classifications that are based on purely objective criteria, such as certain physical or measurable properties, because there are objective means of placing a single specimen on one or the other side of a dividing line. The more objective the criteria used for classification, the sharper the dividing lines may be, and the farther from actual cultural parallels the system becomes. True, objective classifications may avail themselves of quantitative methods of analysis and comparison, but what can quantitative methods produce out of raw data that by their very means of coming into being are non-quantitative? Any such quantitatively-produced results must be expected to lack significant cultural implications.

From the standpoint of cultural implication, the many criteria will bear unequal weight, according to the factors that set limits on their occurrence and the narrowness of those limits. Raw materials are limited by the physical environment, although occasionally augmented by trade carried on with peoples in other physical environments. Even though many different materials have proved satisfactory for making pottery in various parts of the world, any one potter rarely has a wide choice. For example, on most of Chapin Mesa potters could choose their temper from the native sandstone, the fine sand into which the sandstone breaks down, or potsherds, unless they were willing to travel to the south end of the mesa to procure igneous rocks from ancient gravels deposited there by the Mancos River. Actually, all four of these materials were used.

However, there was a distinct preference for the materials that had to be crushed, such as potsherds and the igneous rocks.

Techniques of manufacture for pottery are limited primarily by the number of possible ways in which a specific operation can be accomplished. The atmosphere in which a vessel is fired provides a suitable example. Oxygen may be withheld from the fire, or its presence may be permitted. Although this is a purely cultural choice, its significance is almost totally negated by the availability of only two possibilities, and therefore but one choice between them. The technologist will rightly protest this commentary as an oversimplification, since there are many different degrees of oxidation in the firing of pottery. However, the primitive methods practiced by prehistoric Southwesterners usually resulted in a considerable range of oxidation on a single pot, including an occasional fire cloud produced by reduction where a piece of fuel fell against the vessel. Some features of decoration and design also suffer from a limited number of possibilities: particularly primary design layout and simple individual design elements.

Then, features such as design motifs, specific combinations of elements, secondary design layout, plus some aspects of choice in field of decoration, vessel shape, and surface finish, essentially reflect only limitations imposed by the cultural community in which the individual potter operates. Because of this cultural control, these traits take on a growth pattern similar to that of fads in our own society. Following its inception, a new trait will increase in popularity and spread through geographic space until it reaches its peak (this may be a widely pervasive peak or one that hardly makes a splash compared to its contemporaries), after which it will decline in popularity and become discontinuous in space until it finally disappears altogether, or is rejuvenated in a new form. Wherever the decline of a trait has been prolonged or reversed by rejuvenation, there has been a significant qualitative reformulation of the original trait.

In contrast, those traits that reflect other than local cultural controls generally lack the pattern described above. They frequently show an alternating pattern of peaks and troughs in popularity (or occurrence) instead. An example is the course followed by the black dot on Chapin Mesa pottery. As a single element of design, there are only so many other possible substitutes should the dot temporarily go out of favor, and so it continually regains usage from time to time, sometimes in new contexts and sometimes in almost exactly the same format as in an earlier period of popularity. It is therefore suggested that one means of weighing the effectiveness of a particular ceramic trait as a reflection of local cultural limitation or control--and thereby its usefulness as a classificatory tool--is by examination of its pattern of growth and decline in popularity.

For most of the Southwest, I would rate aspects of design as least likely to be influenced or affected by factors other than cultural limitations, thus as most useful in classification. Second would be means of treating vessel surfaces and the shapes of vessels, frequently represented by rim shapes. Of least value are such traits as type of paste and temper because of their great dependence on the physical environment, and paint types, firing atmosphere, and vessel wall construction because of the limited number of possibilities. Another important consideration in this ranking is the practicability of determining certain differences. For example, although detailed laboratory analysis can recognize a wide variety of pastes and paints, how many archaeologists can subject all of their potsherds to such an analysis?

Design could serve as the only basis for classification if it were not for a number of limitations inherent in the nature of the material to be classified. A large proportion of Southwestern pottery bears no decoration at all, and many individual potsherds are either too small, too badly eroded, or bear such a small portion of the full design as to be totally unclassifiable from the standpoint of design alone. Where present, however, design should be considered as first in importance. Particularly specific motifs--such as the interlocking scroll with barbs or ticks along the convex edges of the curved lines seen on many sherds and vessels of Cortez Black-on-white--and details of secondary design layout--such as the custom of building designs on Mesa Verde Black-on-white pottery by a process of constantly subdividing the design area into smaller and smaller units before finally filling in certain portions solid or with hatching to bring out the overall design--are most useful and most closely related to the culture whose patterns are under scrutiny.

A number of relatively subjective aspects of design also belong in this top priority group of criteria: especially symmetry and balance. It may be argued that such subjective criteria have no place in classification, or that at best they should only be accorded a low priority status. However, in the case of these two qualities, at least, partial objectivity can be retained if the concept of balance is qualified in its use by specific application to the relationship between decorated and undecorated areas, light and dark, between solid and hatched design elements, in the placement of unconnected

clusters of design, and so forth. Symmetry has been treated in
an organized manner by Shepard (1948; 1957) in such a way as to
make the analysis of symmetry applicable to a wide range of
geometric styles on a comparable level.

Surface treatment is faced with a somewhat limited
number of possibilities, but not so limited as to hamper
seriously its use for classificatory purposes. In fact, the way
in which the surface has been treated is the primary means for
classifying undecorated pottery. In the Southwest, kinds of
surface treatment include the obliteration or lack of obliteration of coils, various forms of smoothing including polishing
(and of course the lack of any smoothing after scraping), the
addition of a slip, or coating a surface with pigment after
firing, smudging, the elaboration of unobliterated coils, and a
limited variety of texturing such as scoring, grooving,
incision, and punctation. Surface texturing, coil elaboration,
and slipping can contribute to decoration or even occasionally
carry very simple designs, thereby blurring the line of
distinction between decorated and undecorated pottery.

Vessel shape is, of course, dependent on the function
for which the vessel was made--primarily as a container,
frequently for liquids. However, even within this limitation,
shape can vary in many ways so long as a given amount of space
is enclosed within the vessel walls and access to this space is
kept within the range of practicability for the substances that
are to be contained. Hence shape can vary a great deal
according to cultural fads or dictates, and has even been
satisfactorily used as the primary criterion for pottery
classification in the post-Neolithic phases of Europe and the
Near East.

The remaining characteristics of pottery can still be
useful in combination even if they have only limited value
individually. Paint pigments that can be satisfactorily
distinguished on large groups of potsherds with the naked eye,
or at most with the aid of a 10-power hand lens, are essentially limited to two: mineral versus organic pigment. To be
sure minute laboratory analysis by chemical, thermal, or micro-
scopic means could distinguish a rather large variety of
specific pigments, but this type of analysis can be performed
effectively on only a very small proportion of all the
potsherds that are collected. Secondly, mineral pigments were
probably applied while suspended in a solution of some plant
extract dissolved in water (Colton 1953), thus complicating the
distinction in any single case. Thus, the usefulness of paint
pigments for classification is virtually limited to cases of
clear identification. The mineral paint of Mancos-Black-on-

white and the organic paint of Mesa Verde Black-on-white and
its varieties are relatively easily distinguished from one
another.   But even in this case paint can only serve as one of
several criteria for the assignment of individual sherds to one
type of the other, since there are numerous exceptions to the
general pattern (witness the organic paint deviation of Mancos
Black-on-white and the "organic look" to many sherds because of
the organic medium, and the mineral paint deviation of Mesa
Verde Black-on-white).

         Major categories of temper can also be recognized
without detailed laboratory analysis, although precise mineral
identifications cannot be made.   In this way temper classes can
also be useful for classification.   Vessels assignable to a
single pottery type on the basis of all other criteria often
contain different classes of temper. For example, Shepard found
crushed potsherds and crushed rock temper in several samples of
Mesa Verde Black-on-white pottery (Shepard 1939; and Shepard in
O'Bryan 1950), and I have observed both these categories of
material in sherds of the same type from sites on Chapin Mesa,
as well as several clear cases of sand temper.

         The cultural values concerning the choice of
tempering materials vary from one pottery-making group to
another. One group will be satisfied with any material that the
environment may provide and will use materials from different
sources indiscriminantly.   Another group will find a given
material acceptable only if it came from one of a few specified
sources, regardless of the existence of nearer or better
sources of the same material.

         Other features by which pottery specimens may differ
from each other have been referred to above as subject to a
small number of possibilities, especially in the Southwest.
None of these should be entirely neglected on these grounds,
however, but rather they should be used in conjunction with all
other discernible features, although they would carry the least
significance in the process of classification.

Classification

         The system employed in the following classification
of Mesa Verde pottery centers around the type-variety concept
expressed by Wheat, Gifford and Wasley (1958), Phillips (1958),
Smith, Willey and Gifford (1960), and Gifford (1960).   My
application of this concept recognizes an abstract description
of an "ideal" type, which is also characterized by a range of
variation from that "ideal." This range of variation may be

subdivided into two degrees of significance: 1) variation that bears either spatial or temporal significance is termed a "Variety" and assigned a formal name; 2) variation that bears neither spatial nor temporal significance and that may be attributed to "the vagaries of individual potters" (Colton 1946: 315), is termed a "deviation" and referred to by a purely descriptive term, such as "unslipped deviation."

Although the Type remains the smallest classificatory unit, the Variety becomes the primary sorting unit. The chief value of a deviation is to aid in reconstructing past events, in recognizing a difference that might ultimately become significant and therefore graduate to the status of a Variety or even a Type, and to reduce the tendency for taxonomists to create hosts of new Types and Varieties on the basis of minor variations. It also permits expression of many exceptions that might otherwise be ignored or that might tend to weaken the distinctiveness of Type and Variety descriptions. Where a Type comprises a single Variety, the Type name applies to that Variety; when a second Variety is recognized, it is contrasted with the established or the first described Variety which then takes on the Type name (e.g., Chapin Gray--Chapin Variety).

The concept of ware as a group of pottery types embodying identical characters of manufacture such as paste and surface properties (Colton 1953: 51) is severely limited by the requirement for absolute identity of attributes and by the view that it is a taxonomic unit on a level above that of types. The association of ware with the physical properties of pottery relating to manufacture can be very useful, however, if it is thought of as a different kind of classificatory device, in the same manner in which design styles are handled. A ware might best be considered a technological tradition of pottery making closely tied to the features of the physical environment. It would thus embrace both cultural and geographic factors. Within a given territory, two wares might be distinguished by differences in technique, while between two separate territories, two wares might be distinguished primarily by the raw materials used.

The actual description of ceramic wares in the Southwest has come quite close to this view in spite of the too rigid definition. Therefore, I have retained most of the existing ware descriptions for Mesa Verde pottery (Abel 1955). Mesa Verde Gray Ware and San Juan Red Ware seem to be consistent with both concepts stated in the preceding paragraph. The two white wares, though, satisfy neither. To carry the requirement for identical physical properties to its logical extreme, two separate white wares are not sufficient. Abel's present line of separation falls between Mancos and McElmo Black-on-whites, and places greater emphasis on the character of the paint, implying that Mesa Verde Black-on-white decorated in mineral paint really belongs to San Juan White Ware (Abel 1955: 4 and Ware 12A). This would suggest that Chapin Black-on-white with organic paint should belong to Mesa Verde White Ware.

Another worker might wish to emphasize temper in separating wares, draw his line of distinction between Cortez and Mancos Black-on-whites, and admit to each ware sherds of non-member pottery types that contain the proper temper. Presence or absence of a slip provides yet another useful criterion. If we carried such a concept of ware to its logical conclusion, we would establish eight separate wares, accounting for each actual combination, with future provision to accomodate any other variables deemed important, including single vessels with two or more kinds of temper, and so forth. Lest we soon be disappointed that our exercise in systematics is not absurd enough, we can then proceed to describe separate pottery types for each design style in each of our wares.

In the Mesa Verde region, there was a definite tradition of manufacturing gray-white pottery decorated in a blackish paint. Individual attributes of this pottery varied from time to time, from place to place, and from potter to potter as new ideas were tried and either discarded or accepted. I do not think it is necessary to recognize each of these experiments taxonomically as separate pottery types and wares. In the Mesa Verde, painted gray-white pottery began with crushed rock temper and no slip and ended with a predominance of crushed potsherd temper and slipped surfaces. There is no indication that the paste changed or that methods of construction and firing varied from start to finish. Both mineral and organic paints were used for decoration throughout the tradition, although in varying proportions. I have retained the name Mesa Verde White Ware for this technological tradition.

The following classification of Mesa Verde pottery is based on the detailed study of approximately 21,000 potsherds from Chapin Mesa, plus a survey of pertinent literature and of several collections of sherds and whole vessels from the Mesa Verde and its surroundings. Unfortunately, data on Hovenweep Gray and Hovenweep Corrugated are insufficient for proper evaluation at present. Actually, there does not seem to be a large enough sample of these proposed types to warrant separate descriptions. The research and basic descriptions were completed in 1959.

MESA VERDE WHITE WARE

DESCRIPTION: (Originally described by Colton and Hargrave 1937:
            229; revised by Abel 1955: Ware 10B)
    Construction: Coiling and scraping.
    Firing: Without free access of oxygen.
    Paste: (a) Color - Medium to light gray.
            (b) Temper - Crushed rock in earlier types and
        crushed potsherds in later types with some examples
        of all types containing crushed rock. Some sand and
        crushed sandstone in most types.
            (c) Carbon streak - Not common, but more common in
        latest types.
    Surface Finish: Rough and unslipped in earliest types with
        an increase in polishing and in the proportion of
        slipped vessels toward the later types. Latest
        types have thick, white, crazed slip.
    Surface Color: Light gray to white; fire clouds common.
    Recorded Wall Thickness: 2.5 to 9 mm., average increasing
        from about 4.5 to 6 mm. from early to late types.
        Complete range exists in earliest type, only
        minimum and average increase.
    Vessel Shapes: Bowls predominate in all types; number of
        shapes increases from early to late and includes
        dippers, pitchers, mugs, seed jars, kiva jars,
        water jars or ollas, and canteens.
    Paint: Black or brownish black. Varying proportions of
        mineral and organic pigments with the former
        predominant in the early types and the latter pre-
        dominant in Mesa Verde Black-on-white--both vari-
        eties. Some glaze paint in Chapin Black-on-white.
        Some vessels bear no painted decoration.
NAMED FOR: The Mesa Verde in southwestern Colorado.
NAMED BY: Colton and Hargrave 1937: 229.
POTTERY TYPES IN THIS WARE: 1. Chapin Black-on-white
                            2. Piedra Black-on-white
                            3. Cortez Black-on-white
                            4. Mancos Black-on-white
                            5. Mesa Verde Black-on-white--two
                               varieties
CULTURAL ASSOCIATION: The sub-culture normally found in the

Mesa Verde region on the northern tributaries of the San Juan River in Utah, Colorado, and New Mexico, from Basket Maker III through Pueblo III.

TIME: <u>Ca</u>. A.D. 600 to 1300.

RANGE: Northern tributaries of the San Juan River in Utah, Colorado, and New Mexico with late extensions southward into the region around Chaco Canyon, New Mexico, and Canyon de Chelly, Arizona.

REMARKS: Abel has included Galisteo Black-on-white in this ware on the oft-stated assumption that it is virtually indistinguishable from Mesa Verde Black-on-white. There is a marked difference, however, probably stemming a great deal from the different raw materials available in the two different regions where these types are found. It would seem more logical to place Galisteo Black-on-white in the same ware with Santa Fe Black-on-white and observe that many features of both these types, especially their style of design, may have originated with Mesa Verde Black-on-white.

Figure 46. Chapin Black-on-white sherds from Chapin Mesa.

CHAPIN BLACK-ON-WHITE

DESCRIPTION: (Originally described by Abel 1955: Ware 12A –
          Type 1)
     Paste: (a) <u>Color</u> – Light to dark gray.
          (b) <u>Temper</u> – Predominantly crushed rock, usually
          igneous rocks such as andesite or diorite (Shepard
          1939; and in O'Bryan 1950). Sand has been noted
          very rarely from the La Plata District and in
          sizable proportions from the area of Durango,
          Colorado (<u>Ibid</u>).
          (c) <u>Carbon streak</u> – uncommon; often weak when
          present.
          (d) <u>Texture</u> – Coarse to medium.
     Surface Finish: Scraped, then rubbed, but not polished to
          the same degree as found in later decorated pottery
          types. The "highly polished" surface described by
          O'Bryan for Twin Trees Black-on-white (1950: 91)
          occurs rarely and grades imperceptibly into the more
          common smoothed surfaces.
     Surface Color: Medium to very light gray; fire clouds
          common.
     Recorded Wall Thickness: Ranging from 2.5 to 9 mm.,
          average ca. 4.5 mm.
     Vessel Shapes: Hemispherical bowls predominate; squash
          pots (seed jars), ladles, pitchers, and one
          submarine-shaped canteen (Morris 1939) appear to be
          late, possibly Pueblo I.
     Rims: Distinctly tapered, giving a pinched appearance, and
          rounded on the lip. Occasionally painted solid, but
          usually undecorated.
     Paint: Mineral paint predominates, but organic paint can
          be recognized on from 5-67% of specimens from a
          single site, and numerous individual sherds appear to
          exhibit both. This probably results from experimen-
          tation with the beginnings of applying mineral
          pigments in an organic medium leading to the
          consequent imperfections that may be noted on
          individual sherds. Glaze paints occur on a very small
          proportion of the total specimens and seem to con-
          centrate in the Durango area where lead ores that

could produce a glaze effect are available. Specific references for paints may be found in Shepard 1939; Shepard in O'Bryan 1950: 90-91; Brew 1946; and Reed 1958. The pottery from Chapin Mesa exhibited a ratio of two mineral to one organic with something less than 10% showing clear signs of both.

Field of Decoration: Bowl interiors; ladle interiors and handles; exteriors of squash pots and pitchers above widest diameter.

Decoration: Designs usually consist of elaborations built up from single or double lines radiating outward on the field of decoration (mostly bowl interiors) in straight, arced, or zigzag paths. A small circle frequently marks the center of the decorative field and two, three, or four units may be constructed. Elaborating elements that may occur include various forms of triangles, short dashes or ticks, dots, hooks, and combinations of these. Repeated small elements were frequently used as fillers between parallel lines or in open clusters-- ● ↳ ↲ ✝ ╱ -- and occasionally to outline other segments of design. Occasionally, isolated units occur in opposition to one another, usually having been built up in the same way. Rarely did designs take on a concentric layout, and those that have been illustrated seem to be varying in the direction of later types. The construction of designs is very suggestive of that found on basketry where design must necessarily be built up from the bottom of the container toward the top. In fact, one particular motif--that of an outlined area filled with repeated "z's"--has been compared to basketry stitching. The individual components and elements of the design were almost always drawn very minutely in relation to the size of the field of decoration and were most likely done with very short strokes. Some specific motifs are: "Basket stitch"-

DEVIATIONS:

(a) Fugitive red deviation - exteriors of bowls coated with red paint, presumably after firing since it easily washes off.

COMPARISONS: Lino Black-on-gray, La Plata Black-on-white, and Piedra Black-on-white are most likely to be confused with Chapin Black-on-white. The distinctions between Chapin and Piedra are emphasized in the following description. La Plata and Lino both contain predominantly sand temper

according to the published descriptions (Roberts 1929;
Hawley 1936; Colton 1955), although Shepard (in O'Bryan
1950: 90) lists one sherd each with organic paint and
crushed rock temper from Shabik'eschee Village. The paint
of Chapin Black-on-white is also somewhat distinctive in
that either mineral or organic pigments or both may be
present and glaze paint occurs part of the time. Such
distinctions hardly seem sufficient to set off Chapin
Black-on-white as a separate type, but the separation of
La Plata Black-on-white from Lino Black-on-gray solely on
the basis of paint pigments is no better. A thorough
restudy of all these pottery types is badly needed.
(Wasley found a small proportion of crushed rock temper,
smoothed and polished surfaces, and very little organic
paint in his Cerro Colorado Variety of La Plata Black-on-
white.)

NAMED FOR: Chapin Mesa, in Mesa Verde National Park, Colorado,
   where the type sites listed below are located.

NAMED BY: Abel 1955.

SYNONYMS: La Plata Black-on-white (in part); Lino Black-on-gray
   (in part); Twin Trees Black-on-white.

ADDITIONAL REFERENCES AND ILLUSTRATIONS: Morris 1939: pls. 196,
   197, 199-207. Shepard 1939. O'Bryan 1950: 89-92; pl. 39.
   Reed 1958: 75-78. Abel 1955: Ware 12A – Type 1.
   Lancaster and Watson 1954: pl. 17. Brew 1946: figs. 103,
   106, 107. Hayes 1964: 53-56 (As La Plata Black-on-white).
   Breternitz, Rohn, and Morris 1974: 25-27.

EXAMPLES: (Figs. 46 and 61) In Museum, Mesa Verde National
   Park, Colorado.

TYPE SITES: Site 101 (Deep Pithouse), Mesa Verde National Park
                (Lancaster and Watson 1954).
            Site 117 (Pithouse B), Mesa Verde National Park
                (Lancaster and Watson 1942).
            Site 283 (Pithouse C), Mesa Verde National Park
                (Lancaster and Watson 1942).
            Site 145, Mesa Verde National Park (O'Bryan 1950).
            Site 118 (Pithouse A – Linton's Earth Lodge A),
                Mesa Verde National Park.
            Basket Maker III sites from the La Plata District
                (Morris 1939), Alkali Ridge (Brew 1946),
                and Mancos Canyon (Reed 1958).

STAGE: Basket Maker III and Pueblo I.

TIME: Ca. A.D. 575 to 900. Direct evidence is currently lacking
   for the existence of any Basket Maker III pithouse with
   decorated pottery in the range of Chapin Black-on-white
   earlier than A.D. 575. The pithouse from which O'Bryan

recovered a 477 date (O'Bryan 1950) also produced dates ranging from 430 to 587+ (complete file of tree-ring dates from the Mesa Verde by Gila Pueblo). In other words, there are no grounds for dating that pithouse any earlier than its latest date, or, until shown otherwise, 587+.

RANGE: The literature suggests that the geographic range includes the area from around Durango, Colorado, to that around the Abajo Mountains, Utah, north of approximately the Colorado-New Mexico state line and the San Juan River in Utah. There is as yet no reported occurrence north of the Dolores River in Colorado.

REMARKS: Since the relationships among the various Basket Maker III decorated pottery types are inadequately known, especially for La Plata and Rosa Black-on-whites, it is probably better to retain the more thoroughly studied and described groups such as Lino Black-on-gray and Chapin Black-on-white as distinct types. When the data become comparable, several of these types could easily be accorded variety status rather than separate type status. Twin Trees Black-on-white is discarded as a separate pottery type, or even a variety.

Figure 47. Piedra Black-on-white sherds from Chapin Mesa.

PIEDRA BLACK-ON-WHITE

DESCRIPTION: (First described by Reed 1958: 78-81)
    Paste: (a) <u>Color</u> - Light gray.
         (b) <u>Temper</u> - Crushed igneous rock.
         (c) <u>Carbon Streak</u> - Occasional.
         (d) <u>Texture</u> - Medium.
    <u>Surface Finish</u>: Smoothed, fairly well polished; mostly
        unslipped--a thin, even slip on 27-47% of the speci-
        mens in La Plata collections, 46% of these from the
        Piedra, much less on the specimens from the lower
        Mancos River and from Chapin Mesa.
    <u>Surface Color</u>: Generally pale gray, sometimes white; fire
        clouds uncommon.
    <u>Recorded Wall Thickness</u>: Ranging from 2.5 to 8 mm.,
        average <u>ca</u>. 4.5 mm.
    <u>Vessel Shapes</u>: Hemispherical bowls, scoop ladles, jars,
        pitchers, seed jars, effigies, and some unusual forms
        (see Roberts 1930: fig. 19).
    <u>Rims</u>: Distinctly tapered, and rounded on the lip; slightly
        beveled from the outside; rarely tapered and squared.
        Usually painted solid, but rarely undecorated.
    <u>Paint</u>: Mineral pigment applied in an organic medium,
        better controlled than in Chapin Black-on-white so
        that sherds appearing to show evidences of both
        mineral and organic paint are now rare. Organic paint
        may appear on up to 5% of specimens, and glaze paints
        are not uncommon, especially in the Durango area
        where lead ore is available. Color ranges from a
        reddish-brown to black with a much greater occurrence
        of black than in Chapin Black-on-white.
    <u>Field of Decoration</u>: Bowl interiors; ladle interiors and
        handles; exteriors of pitchers, jars, seed jars, and
        effigy forms above widest diameter. Very rarely on
        bowl exteriors.
    <u>Decoration</u>: Many earlier designs were employed, but
        executed with larger strokes and in a bold manner as
        if they were drawn or composed almost as a unit
        rather than being built up carefully from the vessel
        bottom. Designs are more appropriate in size to the
        field of decoration. Unattached designs are common,

but are placed in symmetrically defined areas. Rather common elements and combinations of elements include barbed lines ┼┼┼ , lines and solids ticked with dots or dashes ●●●● ⊤⊤⊤⊤ ⊤⊤⊤⊤ , two or more parallel lines ⌐─┐ ≡ , wavy lines ∼∼ , wavy lines laid over straight lines ∿∿ , bounded areas filled with dots ⣿ , small plain or hooked triangles attached to a line ⌐⌐ . Checkerboard is rare as are zigzag lines and solid triangles. Some specific motifs are:

Occasionally wavy lines and barbed lines appear as space fillers, but the resemblance to straight and squiggle hatchure is superficial. Band layout is rare.

DEVIATIONS:
    (a) Unobliterated coil deviation.
    (b) Tooled-coil deviation.

COMPARISONS: Chapin Black-on-white and La Plata Black-on-white are most likely to be confused with Piedra Black-on-white, but designs on the former tend to resemble basketry designs and were executed with smaller strokes than those of Piedra. Smoother surfaces, some slipped, and a higher proportion of mineral paint also help to distinguish Piedra specimens. Cortez Black-on-white differs primarily in design and in the predominance of white-slipped surfaces.

NAMED FOR: Piedra River and district where first described pottery of this type (Roberts 1930) was found.

NAMED BY: Mera 1935: 3.

SYNONYMS: Pueblo I Black-on-white (Roberts 1930; Morris 1939); Mancos Black-on-white (in part) (Martin 1939: 463).

ADDITIONAL REFERENCES AND ILLUSTRATIONS: Roberts 1930: 80ff; pls. 25-31. Morris 1939: 160-179; pls. 226, 237-240, 246-254, 263-268. Shepard 1939: 269. Reed 1958: 78-81, fig. 36. Martin 1936: pl. CIX. Martin 1938: pls. CXLIX, CL. Hayes 1964: 55-56, 58. Lister and Lister 1969: figs. 12-13, 16-17. Breternitz, Rohn, and Morris 1974: 29-31.

EXAMPLES: (figs. 47, 62, and 63) In Museum, Mesa Verde National Park, Colorado.

TYPE SITES: Site 103, Mesa Verde National Park (O'Bryan 1950: Site 102 - village).
           Site 786, Mesa Verde National Park.
           Site 33, La Plata District (Morris 1939).
           Site 11, Mancos Canyon (Reed 1958).

STAGE: Pueblo I.

TIME: <u>Ca</u>. A.D. 750 to perhaps 900 (Reed 1958).

RANGE: Piedra Black-on-white has so far been reported only from the drainages of the Piedra, Pine, Animas, La Plata, and Mancos Rivers, and from the Yellow Jacket-Hovenweep drainage. Reed (1958: 80) mentions its presence in Chaco Canyon. Missing from Pueblo I sites in the Montezuma Creek drainage of southeastern Utah.

REMARKS: While Piedra Black-on-white pottery was thoroughly described by Roberts (1930), and it has been frequently treated as a type orally in the Southwest, Reed (1958) is to be thanked for describing it as a type and recognizing its distribution outside the Piedra district. In fact, I would go one step further and suggest that Piedra Black-on-white appears to have developed directly out of the local Basket Maker III decorated pottery, while to the south and southwest, in New Mexico and Arizona, the typical Pueblo I decorated pottery types (Kiatuthlanna Black-on-white, Red Mesa Black-on-white, Kana'a Black-on-white, etc.) show a marked discontinuity, especially in design, with Lino and La Plata; this is strongly suggestive of outside influences (a similar conclusion has been reached by Bullard 1962: 55).

Figure 48. Cortez Black-on-white sherds from Chapin Mesa.

CORTEZ BLACK-ON-WHITE

DESCRIPTION: (Originally described by Abel 1955: Ware 12A-
          Type 3)
     Paste: (a) Color - Light gray to white.
            (b) Temper - Crushed rock in the distinct majority;
            crushed potsherds in a sizable minority.
            (c) Carbon Streak - Rare.
            (d) Texture - Medium.
     Surface Finish: Scraped and polished, except for jar
          interiors which were neither polished nor slipped;
          usually covered with a smooth white slip, although
          not necessarily so. Bowl interiors may not always be
          slipped.
     Surface Color: Grayish-white to chalky white; fire clouds
          occasional.
     Recorded Wall Thickness: Ranging from 3 to 8.5 mm.,
          average ca. 4.5 mm.
     Vessel Shapes: Hemispherical bowls, narrow-necked ollas,
          pitchers, ladles with scoop or flat or tube handles,
          occasional bird-shaped vessels,   submarine-shaped
          vessels and other eccentric forms.
     Rims: Distinctily tapered, and rounded on the lip. Usually
          painted solid, but occasionally undecorated. Rarely
          untapered and   partly squared.   Occasionally only
          slightly tapered and rounded.
     Paint: Mineral pigment applied in   a   well-controlled
          organic medium, but occasional sherds show traces of
          the organic medium where mineral pigment was not
          thoroughly bound. Very few specimens of organic
          paint; no glaze paint. Color ranges from reddish-
          brown to black, the latter regularly achieved.
     Field of Decoration: Bowl interiors, ladle interiors and
          handles; exteriors of jars, pitchers, ollas, and
          effigies above greatest diameter. Rarely on bowl
          exteriors.
     Decoration: Many elements, combinations of elements, and
          motifs that do not appear on the earlier types.
          Lines, dots, and triangles dominate the scene, but
          scrolls, squiggle hatching, straight-line hatching
          are new.   Band layouts show a marked burst of

popularity, although they do not constitute a majority; interlocking scrolls are consistently found employed in bands or panels. Line decorations such as 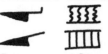 are still common, and narrow, parallel lines often make up much of the total design. Common elements or combinations of elements include:  (frequently opposed),

Some specific motifs are:

DEVIATIONS:
   (a) Unslipped deviation - background surface to which decoration is applied lacks a white slip.
   (b) Exterior corrugated deviation - corrugation on the exterior of Cortez Black-on-white bowls.
COMPARISONS: Cortez Black-on-white incorporates many of the designs found in Kiatuthlanna and Red Mesa Black-on-whites along with carry-overs from Piedra Black-on-white. While the most conspicuous differences from Kiatuthlanna and Red Mesa are in paste and temper, close scrutiny can find several design differences also; e.g., squiggle hatching occurs very sparsely in Cortez, and classic features of both Kiatuthlanna and Red Mesa occur together on occasion. It is impossible to differentiate many individual sherds from Mancos Black-on-white as a result of the gradual change from one to the other.
NAMED FOR: Town of Cortez, Colorado, located just northwest of the Mesa Verde.
NAMED BY: Abel 1955.
SYNONYMS: Mancos Black-on-white (in part) (Martin 1936; Lancaster and Pinkley 1954); Pueblo II Black-on-white (in part) (Morris 1939).
ADDITIONAL REFERENCES AND ILLUSTRATIONS: Morris 1939: pls. 262-268. Abel 1955: Ware 12A - Type 3. Hayes 1964: 57-59. Lister 1965: pls. 30-31. Lister and Lister 1969: fig. 20. Swannack 1969: 74-78. Breternitz, Rohn, and Morris 1974: 33-35.
EXAMPLES: (figs. 48 and 64) In Museum, Mesa Verde National Park, Colorado.
TYPE SITES: Site 16, Mesa Verde National Park, Colorado (Lancaster and Pinkley 1954).
STAGE: Early Pueblo II.

TIME: <u>Ca</u>. A.D. 900-1000 (Abel 1955).

RANGE: Evidence indicates distribution from the Durango, Colorado, area to the area around the Abajo Mountains, in Utah, and north of the San Juan River in both New Mexico and Utah; probably not north of the Dolores River, in Colorado.

REMARKS: Many features of design and surface slip effect a rough discontinuity from Piedra Black-on-white, although several Piedra features carry through. The great similarity to pottery types in the Puerco Valley and around Gallup, New Mexico, during Pueblo I strongly suggests the derivation of much of the Cortez design from that area with appropriate time lag, thereby superseding the local development of pottery decoration seen in Piedra Black-on-white. Some sherds labeled as Morfield Black-on-gray by Abel (1955), which do not differ from Cortez except in the absence of a slip, can be designated Cortez Black-on-white--unslipped deviation.

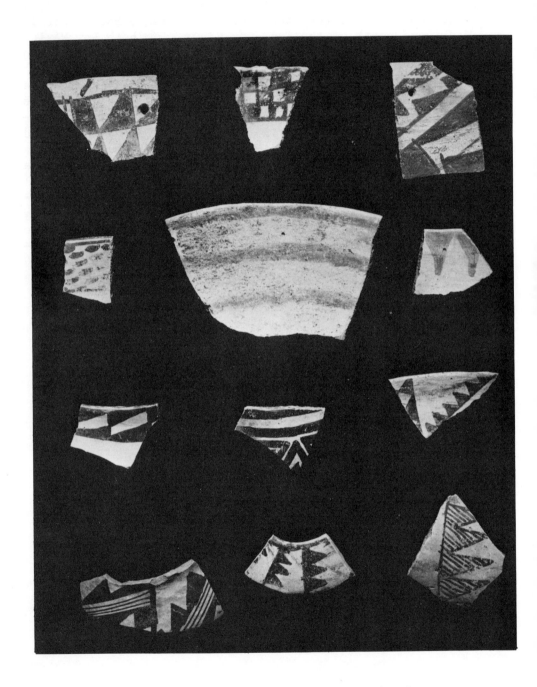

Figure 49. Mancos Black-on-white sherds
with solid and triangular designs from Chapin Mesa.

MANCOS BLACK-ON-WHITE

DESCRIPTION: (First described by Martin 1936: 80-94: revised by
    Colton and Hargrave 1937: 230-231; and by Abel 1955: Ware
    12A - Type 5)
    Paste: (a) Color - Gray to blue-gray.
            (b) Temper - Crushed   potsherds   predominate,
        although crushed rock temper is found in up to 1/3
        of specimens. Where sherd temper occurs, particles
        of rock appear also, probably derived from the
        sherds crushed for use.
            (c) Carbon Streak - Common.
            (d) Texture - Medium to fine.
    Surface Finish: Usually well polished with the   following
        exceptions: jar interiors are not polished; bowl
        exteriors are frequently poorly polished. Most
        surfaces are slipped with a smooth, white slip except
        jar interiors and frequently bowl exteriors. Some
        poorly polished and unslipped specimens would be
        classified by Abel (1955) as Morfield Black-on-gray
        but are here undifferentiated. Corrugated bowl
        exteriors and olla necks occur occasionally. Crazing
        of the surface is common. Slip is often so thin that
        the gray surface shows through.
    Surface Color: Chalky white to slate gray.
    Recorded Wall Thickness: Ranging from 2.5 to 7 mm.,
        average ca. 5 mm.
    Vessel Shapes: Hemispherical bowls, narrow-necked ollas,
        ladles with scoop or tubular handles, duck pots,
        pitchers, squash pots (seed jars), miniature vessels
        (rare), and possibly mugs.
    Rims: Distinctly   tapered, and rounded on the lip in most
        cases; occasionally only slightly tapered and rounded
        on the lip; and rarely untapered and either rounded
        or partially flattened. Rims are often undecorated,
        but often painted solid. Ticked painted decoration
        does occur on some rims and possibly should be
        distinguished as a ticked-rim deviation.
    Paint: Mineral pigment applied in an organic medium, well
        controlled so as to only occasionally show evidence
        of the underlying organic medium; organic paint does

Figure 50. Mancos Black-on-white sherds
with hatched designs from Chapin Mesa.

occur on a very small number of sherds and may be expressed as an organic paint deviation. Color ranges from an orange-red (in cases of extreme overfiring) through reddish-brown to black. No glaze paint.

<u>Field of Decoration</u>: Bowl interiors; ladle interiors and handles; exteriors of jars, pitchers, ollas, and effigies above greatest diameter. Rarely on bowl exteriors.

<u>Decoration</u>: Designs are organized into allover patterns, segmented layouts such as quartered, and in broad bands, the latter of which appears on less than half the specimens. The bands are rarely segmented, but treated as a panel of allover design. Elements and figures are large and have been boldly executed. Triangles are arranged in an infinite variety of ways, either filled in solid or hatched (rarely filled with dots), and make up the predominantly used figures or element. Triangles may be used in opposition to one another, attached to a line and sometimes repeated in echelons, set pendant from the rim, used in combination to produce negative rhomboids (parallelograms) and diamonds, and arranged in checkerboard fashion. Hatching occurs on up to 40% of specimens and is usually used as a filler between two parallel lines. Bands are never framed with lines. Design is often built-up from two or more parallel lines that do not parallel the vessel rim, and thus produce numerous panels. Designs are usually carried right to the rim or onto it. Symmetry within bands is confined to simple translation or a combination of translation with longitudinal reflections (Shepard 1948; 1957). Commonly found elements and figures include:

Some specific motifs are:

DEVIATIONS:
(a) Unslipped deviation - background surfaces to which decoration is applied lack a white slip.
(b) Exterior-corrugated deviation - corrugation on the exterior of Mancos Black-on-white bowls.
(c) Ticked-rim deviation - rim is decorated with dots or ticks.
(d) Organic paint deviation - an organic paint pigment was

Figure 51. Mancos Black-on-white sherds from Chapin Mesa:
top row - corrugated exterior; second row - unslipped;
bottom two rows - organic paint.

used in decoration, rather than a mineral pigment.

COMPARISONS: Gallup, Escavada, Puerco, Chaco, and Cortez Black-on-whites are most likely to be confused with Mancos Black-on-white. Cortez Black-on-white differs most in features of design, while the first four differ primarily in technological details. However, the frequency with which solids and hatching are found on the same specimens (almost in the budding Tularosa Style) and the preoccupation with the triangle in design, both tend to set Mancos apart.

NAMED FOR: Probably the Mancos River valley and town of Mancos, Colorado.

NAMED BY: Gladwin and Gladwin 1934: 28.

SYNONYMS: Chaco Pueblo III Black-on-white (Morris 1939).

ADDITIONAL REFERENCES AND ILLUSTRATIONS: Morris 1939: pls. 285, 287, 290, 291, 293-298. Shepard 1939: 274. Lancaster and Pinkley 1954: pls. 47-51 (some sherds shown are Cortez Black-on-white). Reed 1958: 81-95. Abel 1955: Ware 12A - Type 5. Martin and Willis 1940: pls. 58-59. Brew 1946: 275-280; figs. 111-142. Martin 1936: 80-94; figs. 26-36, 38-39. Hayes 1964: 59-63. Lister 1965: 82-86. Lister 1966: 38-40. Lister and Lister 1969: figs. 5, 9, 16, 19-20, 22, 26, 31, 37. Swannack 1969: 78-94. Breternitz, Rohn, and Morris 1974: 37-40.

EXAMPLES: (figs. 49, 50, 51, 65, and 66) In Museum, Mesa Verde National Park, Colorado.

TYPE SITES: Lowry Ruin, 9 miles west of Pleasant View, Colorado (Martin 1936). Site 16, (Lancaster and Pinkley 1954), Site 866 (Lister 1966), Site 875 (Lister 1965), Big Juniper House (Swannack 1969) in Mesa Verde National Park, Colorado.

STAGE: Pueblo II.

TIME: Ca. A.D. 950-1150 (Abel 1955).

RANGE: An area bounded by the region of Durango, Colorado, the San Juan River, the region around the Abajo Mountains in Utah, and the Dolores River in Colorado. Mancos Black-on-white is also found on the west to the Colorado River and in the region around Chaco Canyon.

REMARKS: It would seem unwise to break Mancos Black-on-white into separate types based on the use of hatching or on the use of solids (as in Sosi and Dogozshi Black-on-whites), since the two features are so consistently associated both on the same sherds and in the same site assemblages. Furthermore, the "style" of Mancos is unified by such crosscutting features as the multiple uses of the triangle, panel arrangement, large sloppy designs, and, of

course, many technological features. The numerous devia-
tions help to show how some attributes that characterize
Mesa Verde Black-on-white had their beginnings in Mancos
Black-on-white.

MESA VERDE BLACK-ON-WHITE

DESCRIPTION: (Originally described by Nordenskiöld 1893: 82-
     84.)
     Paste: (a) Color - Dark gray to white.
          (b) Temper - About 3/4 of specimens from Chapin
          Mesa have crushed potsherd temper and ¼ have
          crushed igneous rock. Shepard (1939) found crushed
          rock in the majority on many La Plata District
          sites. At least a few sherds from the Mesa Verde
          contain sand temper, and sand predominates in the
          lower San Juan Valley. Temper is a very poor
          criterion for Mesa Verde Black-on-white.
          (c) Carbon Streak - Visible in slightly less than
          half the specimens.
          (d) Texture - Very fine to fine.
     Surface Finish: Usually, but not always, slipped on bowl
          interiors and exteriors and on jar exteriors with a
          thick, creamy-white slip that is often crackled or
          crazed and well polished. Exceptions are seen in the
          unslipped deviation where either bowl exteriors or
          all surfaces are unslipped.
     Surface Color: Ranges from a grayish white to a creamy
          white, but most specimens show a good white.
     Recorded Wall Thickness: Ranges from 4.8 to 9 mm., average
          ca. 6 mm.
     Vessel Shapes: Hemispherical bowls, narrow-necked ollas,
          kiva jars, mugs, dippers with tubular handles,
          canteens, seed jars, pitchers, submarine-shaped
          vessels (canteens).
     Paint: Organic. Mineral paint rarely appears and may be
          designated as a mineral paint deviation, or, if in
          conjunction with organic paint, as a mineral and
          organic paint "polychrome" deviation.
     Field of Decoration: Bowl interiors; frequently on bowl
          exteriors; jar exteriors above the maximum diameter;
          olla necks; pitcher and mug exteriors and handles;
          ladle interiors and handle rims; frequently jar
          handles.
COMPARISONS: Only in the case of specimens marginal to this
     type is there liable to be confusion with other types.

McElmo Variety can often be distinguished from Mancos Black-on-white and from Sosi and Dogozshi Black-on-whites only by assessing clusters of attributes including characters of slip and polish, rim form and decoration, and design layout and construction. Some design features are also found on Tusayan Black-on-white and Tularosa Black-on-white.

NAMED FOR: The Mesa Verde, of which Mesa Verde National Park, Colorado, is a part.

NAMED BY: Kidder 1924: 63-66.

SYNONYMS: Decorated Smooth Ware (Morris 1919b: 174).

ADDITIONAL REFERENCES AND ILLUSTRATIONS: Fewkes 1909: 1911; Morris 1939: pls. 302-320. Shepard 1939; 1948. Brew 1946: figs. 166-169. O'Bryan 1950: pls. 47-49. Abel 1955: Ware 10B - Types 1, 2, and 3. Nordenskiöld 1893: pls. 25-29. Rohn 1971: 145-185.

EXAMPLES: (figs. 52, 68, and 69 Mesa Verde Variety; figs. 53 and 67 McElmo Variety) In Museum, Mesa Verde National Park, Colorado.

TYPE SITES: Spruce Tree House (Site 640), (Fewkes 1909), Cliff Palace (Site 625), (Fewkes 1911), Mug House (Rohn 1971) in Mesa Verde National Park, Colorado. Aztec Ruin, New Mexico, (Morris 1919a).

STAGE: Pueblo III.

TIME: Ca. A.D. 1050 or 1100 to 1300.

RANGE: The region bounded by the vicinity of Durango, Colorado, the San Juan River, the Colorado River in Utah, and the Dolores River in Colorado. Also found at Chaco Canyon in New Mexico and at Canyon de Chelly and along the Chinle Wash in Arizona, and on Cummings and Paiute Mesas south of the San Juan and Colorado Rivers in Utah and Arizona.

REMARKS: The marked differences between Mesa Verde Black-on-white--Mesa Verde Variety and Mancos Black-on-white, its temporal antecedent, has led several observers to postulate an influx of people, or at least new traits, into the Mesa Verde region in early Pueblo III coming from the north or west. The McElmo Variety and its minor deviations, however, provide a rather complete transition from Mancos Black-on-white instead of confirming the view of a discontinuity. Most of the earlier McElmo specimens bear Mancos-like designs treated much as on Mesa Verde vessels or in a Mesa Verde manner. Many also bear designs closely related to those of the Mesa Verde Variety (in fact, the gradation between these two varieties has prompted their inclusion in one type). Paint, rim forms and decoration, and some designs that are all typical of

Mancos Black-on-white are found with consistency on McElmo
specimens, while paint, rare rim forms, rim ticking, and
degree of polish that characterize McElmo are also found
on specimens of Mancos Black-on-white and its deviations.
The general replacement of mineral paint by organic paint
assumes less importance when we realize that mineral
pigments were applied in organic vehicles in the Mesa
Verde region, and when we recognize organic-painted Mancos
Black-on-white and mineral-painted Mesa Verde Black-on-
white. Finally, specimens of the Mesa Verde Variety
display a strong tendency toward standardization of
pottery manufacture and decoration, while McElmo Variety
specimens exhibit a wide range of variation and seeming
experimentation.

Figure 52. Mesa Verde Black-on-white--Mesa Verde Variety
sherds from Chapin Mesa.

MESA VERDE BLACK-ON-WHITE--MESA VERDE VARIETY

DESCRIPTION: Conforms to the type descriptions for Mesa Verde
     Black-on-white with the additions stated below.
     Surface Finish: Highly polished so as to produce a luster,
          and often compacting the surface so as to reduce the
          loss of moisture through porous vessel side walls.
     Surface Color: Larger proportion of whites than average
          for the whole type.
     Vessel Shapes: Mugs and kiva jars are represented in
          higher proportions than in the McElmo Variety and
          dippers, water jars, seed jars, and pitchers in
          smaller proportions.
     Rims: Non-tapering and flat; rarely slightly tapering and
          rounded. Almost always decorated with various
          combinations of dots and short dashes (called
          ticking).
     Field of Decoration: Bowl exteriors are more often
          decorated than on McElmo Variety specimens.
     Decoration: Designs were built up by a process of
          constantly dividing and subdividing the decorative
          field into smaller and smaller units and then filling
          in certain of the spaces to bring out the total
          pattern. As a result, designs are well organized and
          integrated. Almost all elements, figures, motifs,
          and even segments of the pattern are placed in
          symmetrical relationship with other units of
          equivalent status. Symmetry is usually maintained too
          within segments of the design. Layout is generally
          symmetrical or balanced. There is balance between
          light and dark, painted and unpainted zones within
          the design, and often in solids versus hatching.
          Bands are the most commonly used layouts and are
          frequently bounded or framed by broad and narrow
          lines, either singly or in groups, on each side.
          Designs are remarkably independent of vessel shapes.
          Most designs are abstract and geometric, except for
          some stylized biomorphic figures that may appear on
          bowl exteriors and in some bowl centers. Bowl
          interior decoration may consist simply of a series of
          concentric lines (usually narrow), frequently

embellished with dots or some filled-in solid areas. Designs are rarely carried up to the rim and never onto the rim. Hatching occurs always as a background filler between solid figures (thus in irregular shapes rather than between parallel lines) and never alone in a design (actually the peculiarities of breakage produce quite a few sherds that show only hatching from the hatched portions of designs). The dot element is used extensively (generally very round) in rim ticking, embellishing lines and triangles, between parallel lines, and in the center of negative figures. Some specific motifs and figures include opposed stepped triangles, opposed ticked triangles, opposed plain triangles, diagonal checker-board, interlocking scrolls, triangular and rhom-boidal scrolls, zigzag lines and frets, and numerous combinations of parallel lines.

DEVIATIONS:
    (a) Mineral paint deviation.
    (b) Mineral and organic paint "polychrome" deviation.
    (c) Unslipped deviation.

COMPARISONS: See separate descriptive headings above.

SYNONYMS: Mesa Verde Polychrome (Abel 1955).

ADDITIONAL REFERENCES AND ILLUSTRATIONS: Abel 1955: Ware 10B – Types 2 and 3. Lister and Lister 1969: figs. 12, 16, 25-26, 29-36. Breternitz, Rohn, and Morris 1974: 45-47.

TIME: Ca. A.D. 1150 to 1300.

REMARKS: This variety apparently represents the culmination of Mesa Verde Black-on-white pottery that began to develop in very late Pueblo II. It stands as the established variety only because it was recognized and distinguished first.

Figure 53. Mesa Verde Black-on-white--McElmo Variety
sherds from Chapin Mesa.

MESA VERDE BLACK-ON-WHITE--McELMO VARIETY

DESCRIPTION: (Originally described by Kidder 1924: 67) Conforms
    to the type description for Mesa Verde Black-on-white with
    the additions stated below.
    Surface Finish: Generally less highly polished than Mesa
        Verde Variety, but often as well polished. There is a
        slightly higher proportion of unslipped examples.
    Surface Color: There are more gray or light gray surfaces
        and fewer white ones than on Mesa Verde Variety.
    Vessel Shapes: Dippers, ollas, seed jars, and pitchers
        occur in higher proportions than in the Mesa Verde
        Variety, while mugs and kiva jars are less common.
    Rims: May be non-tapering and flat but are more frequently
        slightly tapered and at least partially rounded on
        the lip. Some tapered rims have been segregated in a
        tapered rim deviation. Rims are commonly undecorated
        or ticked with series of dots or groups of dots. A
        few are painted solid.
    Field of Decoration: Rims and bowl exteriors are less
        frequently decorated than in Mesa Verde Variety.
    Decoration: Many designs are decidedly transitional
        between Mancos Black-on-white and the Mesa Verde
        Variety of Mesa Verde Black-on-white; some are almost
        purely Mancos while others even recall earlier
        motifs. Many other designs are simply crudely
        executed Mesa Verde Variety patterns as might be done
        by novices or physically ailing potters. There are
        frequently well-executed combinations or recombina-
        tions of typical Mancos figures. Preoccupation with
        the triangle, which is so marked in Mancos Black-on-
        white, is lacking. Figures made up of heavy solid
        lines are common and may be reminiscent of Sosi
        Black-on-white, but they were painted in a less bold
        manner and are more often closer together to produce
        a cumulative effect in a more complex figure; in
        addition, series of triangles along a broad, solid
        line, common on Sosi Black-on-white, do not occur in
        McElmo. In general, the range of variation in McElmo
        Variety may be seen as distributed along a continuum
        between Mancos Black-on-white and Mesa Verde Variety

of Mesa Verde Black-on-white.

DEVIATIONS:

(a) Mineral paint deviation – design applied in mineral rather than organic paint.

(b) Unslipped deviation – decorated surfaces or just bowl exteriors lack a slip.

(c) Tapered rim deviation – bowls have tapered and rounded rims.

(d) Exterior-corrugated deviation – bowl exteriors are corrugated.

COMPARISONS: Most likely to be confused with Mesa Verde Variety, with Sosi and Dogozshi Black-on-whites, and even on occasion with Mancos Black-on-white.

SYNONYMS: McElmo Black-on-white (Gladwin and Gladwin 1934: Abel 1955); Proto-Mesa Verde Black-on-white (Kidder 1924: Morris 1939).

ADDITIONAL REFERENCES AND ILLUSTRATIONS: Abel 1955: Ware 10B – Type 1. Hawley 1936: 31–32. Reed 1958: 102–110. Brew 1946: 285–288. Kidder 1924: pl. 27a. Hayes 1964: 65–69. Lister and Lister 1969: figs. 2, 5, 12, 16, 19, 27, 29–31, 37. Breternitz, Rohn, and Morris 1974: 41–44.

TIME: Ca. A.D. 1050 or 1100 to 1300.

REMARKS: McElmo pottery may ultimately be distinguished as a type, but at this time it seems more feasible to consider it as a variety of Mesa Verde Black-on-white, because attempts to separate collections of local Pueblo III black-on-white pottery into these two categories always results in a large pile of indistinguishable sherds. Furthermore many McElmo specimens are obviously just sloppily or poorly executed specimens of Mesa Verde Black-on-white, such as might be produced by a young girl experimenting with her first pottery making, by a potter with little or no aptitude for potting, or by an aged potter who could no longer see well enough or hold her hand steady enough for the fine line execution so often found on the classic pottery.

McElmo Variety is thus viewed both as a transition from Mancos Black-on-white to Mesa Verde Black-on-white-- Mesa Verde Variety and as the product of inferior or careless potters who worked contemporaneously with the makers of the finest Mesa Verde Black-on-white. The occurrence of specimens in the latest dated ruins on the Mesa Verde in direct association with Mesa Verde Variety and at Aztec Ruin during the Mesa Verde occupation supports this view.

MESA VERDE GRAY WARE

DESCRIPTION: (Originally described by Abel 1955: Ware 10A)
    Construction: Coiled concentrically   and   spirally,   and
        scraped.
    Firing: Without free access of oxygen.
    Paste: (a) Color - Light to dark gray with   some   tan
        patches.
            (b) Temper - Crushed rock in the vast majority of
        cases--usually a dark-colored igneous rock   such as
        andesite or diorite, but frequently some   crushed
        sandstone was included, rarely sand.
            (c) Carbon Streak - Occasional.
            (d) Texture - Medium to coarse.
    Surface   Finish: Scraped,   sometimes   smoothed,   even
        polished; unslipped; coils may be obliterated or not.
    Surface Color: Light to dark gray with some tan patches.
    Recorded Wall Thickness: Ranging from 2.5 to 9 mm.;
        average about 4.5 mm.
    Vessel Shapes: Jars of many shapes--seed jars, wide-
        mouthed jars, ollas, pitchers; bowls;   platters;
        dippers; some eccentric forms.
    Rims: Tapering and rounded.
    Decoration: Some fugitive red paint on   exteriors of
        earliest vessels; simple patterning of surface areas
        by alternating treatments of coil obliteration, non-
        obliteration, or elaboration such as tooling; simple
        figures rarely painted just   inside   mouth of
        corrugated jars; applique scrolls or strips on later
        vessels.
COMPARISONS: Differs from Tusayan Gray Ware and the gray
    pottery from the region of the Chaco Canyon by having
    crushed rock temper rather than sand temper and by a
    tendency toward smoother, often crackled surfaces. It
    exhibits far less incising and punctation than the Chaco
    ware. There also seem to be some shape differences,
    especially in details, but these have not yet been   thor-
    oughly studied.
NAMED FOR: The Mesa Verde, in southwestern Colorado.
NAMED BY: Abel 1955.
STAGE: Basket Maker III through Pueblo III.

TIME: <u>Ca</u>. A.D. 600 to 1300.

RANGE: The northern drainages of the San Juan River from the Piedra River Valley to the Colorado River.

REMARKS: Unlike decorated wares, Mesa Verde Gray Ware displays a remarkable uniformity in manufacture throughout its life history. Most of this results simply from the practice of using the same materials throughout. Vessel shapes and techniques of treating the surfaces show many changes, most of them for non-functional reasons. Thus the types in this ware are separated from one another primarily by these culturally-influenced criteria.

TYPES IN THIS WARE: Chapin Gray--Chapin Variety
                                        Moccasin Variety
                                        Mummy Lake Variety
                    Mancos Gray
                    Mesa Verde Corrugated--Mesa Verde Variety
                                        Mancos Variety

CHAPIN GRAY

DESCRIPTION: (Originally described by Abel 1955)
    Construction: Coiled concentrically and spirally, and
        scraped.
    Firing: Without free access of oxygen.
    Paste: (a) Color - Light to dark gray with some tan
        patches.
        (b) Temper - Crushed rock in the vast majority of
        cases--usually a dark-colored igneous rock such as
        andesite or diorite, but frequently some crushed
        sandstone is included, rarely sand.
        (c) Carbon Streak - Occasional.
        (d) Texture - Medium to coarse.
    Surface Finish: Scraped and usually smoothed, occasionally
        even polished. Finish ranges from rough to smooth
        with particles of temper often protruding. Surface
        frequently shows where particles have been dragged
        during scraping.
    Surface Color: Light to dark gray. Fire clouds show up
        frequently on lighter-colored surfaces.
    Recorded Wall Thickness: Ranging from 2.5 to 9 mm.;
        average ca. 4.5 mm.
    Vessel Shapes: Globular jars without necks (seed jars);
        wide-mouthed jars with short necks; ollas; pitchers;
        bowls; platters; dippers; some eccentric forms.
    Rims: Tapering and rounded.
NAMED FOR: Chapin Mesa, in Mesa Verde National Park, Colorado.
NAMED BY: Abel 1955.
STAGE: Basket Maker III through early Pueblo III.
TIME: Ca. A.D. 600 to 1150.
RANGE: The northern drainages of the San Juan River from the
    Piedra River Valley to the Abajo Mountains in Utah.
REMARKS: Since it is impossible to separate body sherds of the
    three varieties of this type from one another, sorting
    practicability argues for the inclusion of all of these
    into a single type. Any ceramic researcher working with
    pottery from the northern San Juan drainages is forced to
    recognize that he can distinguish Chapin, Moccasin, and
    Mummy Lake gray varieties only on whole vessels or on rim
    and neck sherds. Designation of this whole group as one

type, with the three varieties recognizable in distinctive
specimans, permits taxonomic comparison with similar types
from other regions. The term "plain gray" will always
require further description in any such comparisons.

Figure 54. Chapin Gray--Chapin Variety sherds from Chapin Mesa.

CHAPIN GRAY--CHAPIN VARIETY

DESCRIPTION: (Originally described by Abel 1955: Ware 10A –
     Type 1)
     Construction: Concentric coiling and scraping.
     Paste: (a) Color – Light to dark gray with some tan
          patches.
          (b) Temper – Crushed rock in the vast majority of
          cases--usually a dark-colored igneous rock such as
          andesite or diorite, but frequently some crushed
          sandstone is included, rarely sand.
          (c) Carbon Streak – Occasional.
          (d) Texture – Medium to coarse.
     Surface Finish: All coils obliterated. Scraped and
          usually smoothed, occasionally even polished. Finish
          ranges from rough to smooth with particles of temper
          often protruding. Surface frequently shows where
          particles have been dragged during scraping.
     Recorded Wall Thickness: Ranging from 2.5 to 9mm.;
          average ca. 4.5 mm.
     Vessel Shapes: Globular jars without necks (seed jars or
          squash pots); short-necked jars; large ollas with
          long slender necks and horizontal lugs or handles;
          pitchers; bowls; platters; half-gourd dippers; and
          eccentric forms such as bird-shaped vessels and
          miniatures.
     Rims: Tapering and rounded.
     Decoration: Fugitive red pigment was sometimes applied to
          the exteriors of some vessels during Basket Maker
          III.
DEVIATIONS:
     (a) Fugitive red deviation – exteriors of bowls and jars
     coated with red paint, presumably after firing as it
     easily washes off.
COMPARISONS: Differs from Lino Gray in having crushed rock
     rather than sand temper and in surface finish. Chapin Gray
     surfaces tend to be smoother with less protruding temper
     particles. Lacks the sand temper and polished surfaces of
     Obelisk Gray, except for some polished specimens. Lacks
     the sand temper and frequent basket impressions of Rosa
     Gray. Body sherds are indistinguishable from body sherds

of Moccasin and Mummy Lake Varieties.

NAMED FOR: Chapin Mesa, in Mesa Verde National Park, Colorado.

NAMED BY: Abel 1955.

SYNONYMS: Lino Gray (in part); Twin Trees Plain (O'Bryan 1950; Abel 1955).

ADDITIONAL REFERENCES AND ILLUSTRATIONS: Abel 1955: Ware 10A - Types 1 and 2. O'Bryan 1950: 91; pl. 39, f, g; pl. 40, h; pl. 41, a-d, f. Lancaster and Watson 1954: 15-19; pls. 14, 16. Morris 1939: 144-145 and 157-160; pls. 180-182, 185-193, 211-214, 241-242. Reed 1958: 111-112. Shepard 1931: 277-278. Brew 1946: fig. 99, a-h, j-o, t, w, kk; fig. 100. Hayes 1964: 42-44. Lister and Lister 1969: figs. 5-6, 10, 15. Breternitz, Rohn, and Morris 1974: 1-3.

EXAMPLES: (figs. 54, 70a and b, and 71a and b) In Museum, Mesa Verde National Park, Colorado.

TYPE SITES: Site 117 (Pithouse B), Mesa Verde (Lancaster and Watson 1942).

Site 101 (Deep Pithouse), Mesa Verde (Lancaster and Watson 1954).

Site 145, Mesa Verde (O'Bryan 1950).

Site 1285 (Step House), Mesa Verde.

Site 19, La Plata District (Morris 1939).

STAGE: Basket Maker III; Pueblo I.

TIME: Ca. A.D. 575 to 900.

RANGE: The northern drainages of the San Juan River from the Piedra River Valley to the Abajo Mountains in Utah.

REMARKS: Pottery described as Twin Trees Plain by both Abel (1955: Ware 10A - Type 2) and O'Bryan (1950: 91) has been included here because any given series of plain gray pottery from early sites in the Mesa Verde may show a complete range in degree of smoothing from a very roughly-scraped surface to a surface that is definitely polished, with no easy separation within the series. In fact, smoothing of some kind or other occurs on a majority of excavated specimens. Thus, only a purely arbitrary dividing line can be drawn between "unpolished" and "polished" surfaces. Should such an arbitrary division be set, so-called "Twin Trees" could at best only be assigned the status of a "polished" deviation of Chapin Gray, since no spatial or temporal significance has yet been noted. O'Bryan's notation of sand temper and Abel's revision of this both tend to obscure the fact that both crushed rock and sand temper are found throughout the whole range of rough, smoothed, and polished surfaces.

Figure 55. Chapin Gray--Moccasin Variety
sherds from Chapin Mesa.

CHAPIN GRAY--MOCCASIN VARIETY

DESCRIPTION: (Originally described by Abel 1955: Ware 10A –
    Type 3)
    Construction: Concentric coiling and scraping.
    Surface Finish: Scraped particles of temper protruding
        through surface with occasional streaks where temper
        particles were dragged during scraping; rarely if
        ever smoothed. Concentric bands, half an inch or
        more wide, left unobliterated around the neck
        exterior. Rare use of tooling between coils after
        partial obliteration.
    Vessel Shapes: Short-necked wide-mouth jars, narrow-necked
        ollas, pitchers.
    Rims: Tapering and rounded.
DEVIATIONS:
    (a) Finger-grooved deviation – the slight troughs formed
    where two bands or fillets are joined have been smoothed
    and slightly deepened by dragging a finger along these
    joints before firing the vessel.
COMPARISONS: Differs from Chapin Gray--Chapin Variety in the
    presence of unobliterated neck bands and the absence of
    smoothed and fugitive red surfaces. Differs from Kana'a
    Gray in temper. Differs from Mancos Gray in band width,
    the use of concentric bands versus spiral coils, and the
    absence of grooving frequently seen on Mancos Gray.
NAMED FOR: Moccasin Mesa, in Mesa Verde National Park,
    Colorado.
NAMED BY: Abel 1955.
SYNONYMS: Kana'a Gray (in part); Kana'a Neck-banded (in part);
    Moccasin Gray.
ADDITIONAL REFERENCES AND ILLUSTRATIONS: Abel 1955: Ware 10A –
    Type 3. O'Bryan 1950; pl. 41, e. Brew 1946: fig. 99,
    p-s; fig. 110, d-f, h-k. Morris 1939: 158-160 and pls.
    183, 215-220. Hayes 1964: 44-46. Breternitz, Rohn, and
    Morris 1974: 5-8.
EXAMPLES: (figs. 55 and 71c) In Museum, Mesa Verde National
    Park, Colorado.
TYPE SITES: Site 103, Mesa Verde (O'Bryan 1950) Site 102
    Village).
        Site 786, Mesa Verde National Park.

           Site 111, Mesa Verde National Park.
           Site 33, La Plata District (Morris 1939).
           Site 13, Alkali Ridge (Brew 1946).
STAGE: Pueblo I.
TIME: Ca. A.D. 800 to 900.
REMARKS: This variety may serve as an index for Pueblo I,
    although its duration in time is probably much less than
    the Pueblo I stage. It has been made a Variety of Chapin
    Gray because only rim and neck sherds can be distinguished
    from the Chapin Variety. Whether or not temper provides
    an adequate distinction between this variety and Kana'a
    Gray must await further study. Such a study should also
    explore the feasibility of considering Kana'a Gray as a
    variety of Lino Gray.

Figure 56. Chapin Gray--Mummy Lake Variety
sherds from Chapin Mesa.

CHAPIN GRAY--MUMMY LAKE VARIETY

DESCRIPTION: (Described by Rohn and Swannack 1965)
   Construction: Spiral coiling followed by scraping.
   Paste: (a) Temper - Crushed igneous rock in the great
         majority of cases; some sherds have rock and sherd
         temper; a few contain sand or crushed sandstone.
   Surface Finish: Exteriors are scraped, usually leaving a
         rough and grainy surface with temper particles
         protruding. Some surfaces are quite smooth. Ver-
         ticle striations often appear on the neck. Interior
         surfaces are usually smoother than exteriors. Coils
         have not always been completely obliterated,
         indicating that some, but not all, vessels were
         originally constructed as corrugated jars.
   Recorded Wall Thickness: Ranging from 3 to 9 mm.; average
         ca. 4 to 5 mm.
   Vessel Shapes: Small to medium-sized wide-mouth jars and
         pitchers. Jar shapes generally parallel those of
         Mancos Variety of Mesa Verde Corrugated with hemi-
         spherical base and bell-shaped mouth whose diameter
         is only slightly less than the vessel's maximum
         diameter; pitchers are roughly jar-shaped with a
         vertical strap handle; occasionally pitchers have a
         cylindrical neck rising from a globular body. Bottoms
         are either rounded or flat.
   Vessel Sizes: Small in comparison to contemporary
         corrugated vessels. The mean capacity of ten vessels
         measures approximately 2.3 liters; five hold less
         than 1.0 liter, two between 1.0 and 1.6 liters, and
         three from 4.8 to 6.4 liters. Twelve vessels range
         from 11 to 25 cm. in total height with five at 13 to
         14 cm. high. Maximum diameters range between 11 and
         26 cm. with five between 11.5 and 12.5 cm. (These
         figures are not meant to be restrictive, only
         indicative.)
   Rims: Formed by the addition of a fillet of clay after
         obliteration of the body coils. Occasionally the rim
         fillet is partially obliterated. Rims are tapered
         with rounded lip. Rim profiles vary from a slight
         flare to sharp eversion.

Decoration: Appliqued conical nodes or small spirals
    just below the rim fillet. Occasional simple figures
    painted inside the rim. (All these features are
    found also on Mesa Verde Corrugated.)

COMPARISONS: Differs from Chapin and Moccasin Varieties in
    having corrugated vessel shapes and in the flaring or
    everted filleted rim. Kiet Siel Gray has generally larger
    vessels with thicker walls and sand temper, and lacks the
    filleted rim. Hovenweep Gray seems to be a crushed
    sandstone-tempered variety of Kiet Siel Gray. Body sherds
    of Chapin, Moccasin, and Mummy Lake Varieties of Chapin
    Gray cannot be separated.

NAMED FOR: Mummy Lake, a prehistoric reservoir in the Far View
    ruin group on the north end of Chapin Mesa.

SYNONYMS: Mummy Lake Gray (Rohn and Swannack 1965).

ADDITIONAL REFERENCES AND ILLUSTRATIONS: Morris 1939: 193–194
    and pls. 220j; 270c, e, g–k. Lister 1965: pl. 29b.
    Swannack 1969: 66–67. Breternitz, Rohn, and Morris
    1974: 13–15.

EXAMPLES: (figs. 56 and 70e) In Museum, Mesa Verde National
    Park, Colorado.

TYPE SITES: Site 875, Mesa Verde (Lister 1965).
        Site 1595 (Big Juniper House), Mesa Verde (Swannack
    1969).
        Site 1645 (Two Raven House), Mesa Verde (Swannack
    Ms).
        Site 1452 (Badger House), Mesa Verde (Hayes and
    Lancaster Ms).
        Site 41, La Plata District (Morris 1939).

STAGE: Pueblo II and early Pueblo III.

TIME: Total span - ca. A.D. 950 to 1200.
    Period of abundance - ca. A.D. 1000 to 1150.
    The early date depends on the association of a pitcher
    with a Cortez Black-on-white bowl in a Badger House grave.
    The terminal date is derived from the presence of Mummy
    Lake Variety sherds in the late Pueblo II and early Pueblo
    III components of Mug House on Wetherill Mesa and its
    absence from the late Pueblo III component (Rohn 1971).

RANGE: Vessels and sherds are known from the La Plata District,
    the Mesa Verde, the McElmo Valley northeast of Cortez, and
    from the Goodman Point and Yellowjacket Districts, all in
    southwestern Colorado. A vessel probably belonging to this
    group has been found near Waterflow, New Mexico, on the
    north side of the San Juan River.

DISCUSSION: Rough-surfaced plain gray pottery occurs in Mesa
    Verde ceramic assemblages from Basket Maker III through

early Pueblo III, although its proportion relative to
other types steadily decreases through time. Body sherds
of any of these vessels are indistinguishable from one
another and from portions of narrow neck-banded and some
corrugated jars where the construction coils have been
obliterated. Plain gray body sherds can then represent
vessels made throughout most of the Mesa Verde sequence.
Their total disappearance from the ceramic record,
however, may provide one of the sharpest distinctions
between early and late phases of Pueblo III. Almost all
known associations are with Mancos and Mesa Verde Black-
on-whites and with Mesa Verde Corrugated.

Figure 57. Mancos Gray sherds from Chapin Mesa.

MANCOS GRAY

DESCRIPTION: (Originally described by Abel 1955: Ware 10A – Type 4)

Construction: Spiral coiling and scraping.

Firing: Without free access of oxygen.

Paste: (a) Color – Light to dark gray; rarely a brownish-gray.
      (b) Temper – Crushed igneous rock.
      (c) Carbon Streak – Occasional.
      (d) Texture – Medium.

Surface Finish: Coils on lower portions of vessel exteriors obliterated by scraping, and sometimes by smoothing; coils on upper portions vessel exteriors left unobliterated, often down almost to the shoulder. Unobliterated coils usually overlap slightly giving a sort of "clapboard" appearance. Coils are frequently smoothed. Three or more coils per inch.

Surface Color: Medium to dark gray; frequently almost black with adhering soot.

Recorded Wall Thickness: Ranging from 2.9 to 8.2 mm.; average 4.8 mm.

Vessel Shapes: Necked jars, pitchers, bell-shaped jars with mouth diameter almost equal to maximum diameter.

Rims: Markedly tapered and rounded on the lip. Usually formed by the addition of a fillet of clay from 1 to 3 times the height of the average coil in the vessel neck. This fillet was added after the neck coiling had been terminated.

DEVIATIONS:

(a) Grooved deviation – the troughs between coils have been deepened by the use of a pointed instrument, forming grooves.

COMPARISONS: Differs from Chapin Gray--Moccasin Variety in the narrower coils, greater overlap of coils, spiral construction, and frequent grooving of the troughs between coils with a pointed instrument. Medicine Gray and Coconino Gray (Colton and Hargrave 1937: 199-202) contain quartz sand temper and have a rougher and coarser surface finish. Body sherds from below the unobliterated coils are almost impossible to distinguish from body sherds of Chapin Gray, while very small sherds could also just as easily come from an unindented band of a Mesa Verde Corrugated vessel.

NAMED FOR: The Mancos River, which drains the Mesa Verde, and the town of Mancos, in southwestern Colorado.

NAMED BY: Abel 1955.

SYNONYMS: Clapboard Corrugated (Kidder 1936: 304); Plain Corrugated (Martin 1938: 268, 270).

ADDITIONAL REFERENCES AND ILLUSTRATIONS: Abel 1955: Ware 10A – Type 4. Martin 1938: pl. CLXXVI, upper rows. Morris 1939: pl. 259, c-i, x-b'. Brew 1946: fig. 150. Hayes 1964: 45-46, 48. Swannack 1969: 65. Breternitz, Rohn, and Morris 1974: 9-11.

EXAMPLES: (fig. 57) In Museum, Mesa Verde National Park, Colorado.

TYPE SITES: Site 16, Mesa Verde National Park (Lancaster and Pinkley 1954).
             Sites 1-4, Ackmen-Lowry Area, Colorado (Martin 1938).

STAGE: Early Pueblo II.

TIME: Ca. A.D. 875-950 (Abel 1955).

RANGE: Northern drainages of the San Juan River between the Animas River and the Abajo Mountains in Utah.

DISCUSSION: As Morris pointed out (1939: 185), Mancos Gray seems to represent a short-lived stage of development through which culinary pottery passed on the way from the neck-banding of Pueblo I to the indented corrugation of Pueblo II. As such, its duration in time is quite limited. It is customarily associated in the Mesa Verde with Cortez Black-on-white and also probably with jacal pueblos and the earliest forms of the "true" kiva.

MESA VERDE CORRUGATED

DESCRIPTION:
    Construction: Spiral coiling and some scraping.
    Paste: (a) Color - Light to dark gray.
            (b) Temper - Crushed igneous rock; rarely sand or
            crushed sherds.
            (c) Carbon Streak - Occasional.
            (d) Texture - Medium to coarse.
    Surface Finish: Interiors were scraped and sometimes
            smoothed; exteriors show the unobliterated coils
            embellished by pinching or crimping in a regular
            pattern from the bottom of the jar to the rim.
    Surface Color: Light to dark gray; frequently almost black
            with adhering soot.
COMPARISONS: The primary difference from corrugated wares to
    the south and west (Exuberant and Tusayan Corrugated)
    comes from the use of crushed rock rather than sand
    temper. Interior surfaces tend to be smoother, often
    crackled, and temper particles are less conspicuous on the
    surfaces than for Tusayan Corrugated.
NAMED FOR: The Mesa Verde, in southwestern Colorado.
NAMED BY: Abel 1955.
SYNONYMS: Corrugated Ware (in part) (Cushing 1886: 490); Coiled
    Ware (in part)(Holmes 1886: 273); Gray Corrugated (in
    part) (Colton 1932: 10).
STAGE: Pueblo II; Pueblo III.
TIME: Ca. A.D. 900 to 1300.
RANGE: The northern drainages of the San Juan River between the
    Animas River and the Colorado River.
DISCUSSION: In spite of the presence of several distinguishing
    features of vessel shapes and surface treatment between
    the Mancos and Mesa Verde Varieties of Mesa Verde
    Corrugated, the two are lumped into a single type for the
    purely practical reason that a majority of individual
    sherds cannot honestly be distinguished. If two separate
    types are retained, all these specimens are left unclassi-
    fied; using the present outline permits their assignment
    to a type description, albeit broad, without destroying
    the utility of the temporal distinction between varieties.
    Hovenweep Corrugated (Abel 1955: Ware 10A - Type 8) may

become most useful as a regional variety of Mesa Verde Corrugated distinguished by squarish indentations, coarse protruding crushed rock temper, and a trace of smoothing over the indentations.

Figure 58. Mesa Verde Corrugated--Mesa Verde Variety
sherds from Chapin Mesa.

MESA VERDE CORRUGATED--MESA VERDE VARIETY

DESCRIPTION: (Originally described by Abel 1955: Ware 10A -
     Type 6)
     Surface Finish: Interiors are scraped and sometimes
          smoothed; exteriors show the unobliterated coils
          embellished by pinching or crimping in a regular
          pattern from the bottom of the jar to the rim.
     Recorded Wall Thickness: Ranging from 3 to 6.5 mm.;
          average ca. 4.5 mm.
     Vessel Shapes: Generally egg-shaped jars with the greatest
          diameter near the base and an inward-sloping neck
          that leads to a sharply everted rim. Both large and
          small jars occur.
     Decoration: Occasional use of appliqued fillets in   the
          form of a single or double spiral made from a small
          rope of clay, or sometimes in   the   form of small
          cones or nodes made by pressing small lumps of clay
          onto the jar. These features usually occur   a
          short distance below the rim. Most common patterning
          consists of alternating horizontal bands of indented
          or unindented coils. Occasionally, very simple
          figures were painted on the interior of rims.
DEVIATIONS:
     (a) Patterned deviation - narrow horizontal bands of
     unindented coils contrast with the otherwise overall
     indentation.
     (b) Rim-corrugated deviation - in place of a high rim
     fillet, the spiral coils are continued above the point of
     eversion of the rim to the vessel lip.
COMPARISONS: Mancos Variety differs primarily in shape: bell-
     mouthed jars versus the egg-shaped jars of Mesa Verde
     Variety; the former also exhibits a wider range of
     patterning in coil treatment, incision, and diagonal
     ridging, (see Brew 1946: 281-283). Although Brew also
     observed a slight difference in coil size, this feature
     does not readily aid classification, since both the widest
     and narrowest coils may appear on both Varieties. Mesa
     Verde Variety everted rims form an angle to the side
     walls; Mancos rims continue the side wall profile.
NAMED FOR: The Mesa Verde, in southwestern Colorado.

NAMED BY: Abel 1955.

SYNONYMS: Standardized Corrugated (Reed 1958: 121-122).

ADDITIONAL REFERENCES AND ILLUSTRATIONS: Abel 1955: Ware 10A –
    Type 6. Brew 1946: 288; fig. 153, i; fig. 156. Morris
    1939: 196-200; pls. 273-282. Reed 1958: 121-122 and fig.
    50. Hayes 1964: 49-53. Lister and Lister 1969: fig. 28.
    Rohn 1971: 130-145. Breternitz, Rohn, and Morris 1974:
    21-23.

EXAMPLES: (figs. 58 and 72B) In Museum, Mesa Verde National
    Park, Colorado.

TYPE SITES: Spruce Tree House (Site 640), Mesa Verde (Fewkes
    1909).
                Cliff Palace (Site 625), Mesa Verde (Fewkes 1911).
                Mug House (Site 1229), Mesa Verde (Rohn 1971).
                Site 39, La Plata District (Morris 1939).
                Site 41, La Plata District (Morris 1939).

STAGE: Pueblo III.

TIME: Ca. A.D. 1100 to 1300.

RANGE: The northern drainages of the San Juan River between the
    Animas and Colorado Rivers.

Figure 59. Mesa Verde Corrugated--Mancos Variety
sherds from Chapin Mesa.

MESA VERDE CORRUGATED--MANCOS VARIETY

DESCRIPTION: (Originally described by Abel 1955: Ware 10A –
    Type 5)
    Surface Finish: Interiors were scraped and sometimes
        smoothed; exteriors show the unobliterated coils
        embellished by pinching or crimping, usually from the
        bottom of the jar to the rim. Frequently the lower
        exterior portions are scraped or smoothed often up as
        far as the shoulder.
    Recorded Wall Thickness: Ranging from 2.8 to 8 mm.;
        average ca. 5 mm.
    Vessel Shapes: Bell-mouthed jars where the mouth diameter
        is nearly as great as the greatest diameter of the
        body, round-bottomed, roughly cylindrical sides;
        small, short-necked jars; pitchers.
    Rims: Slightly tapered and rounded on the lip; formed by a
        fillet of clay from two to four times the height of
        the average coil, added after the spiral coiling had
        been terminated; this fillet continues the general
        outward arc of the neck and does not form an angle
        with it.
    Decoration: A wide range of variation in patterning of
        various surface treatments are listed as deviations.
        Occasionally one or two cone-shaped lumps of clay are
        attached to the neck over the corrugations. Rarely
        spiral ropes of clay are similarly applied.
        Occasionally, very simple figures are painted on the
        interior of rims.
DEVIATIONS:
    (a) Patterned deviation – the techniques of unindented
    coils, indented coils, smoothed areas employed in various
    combinations to produce generally horizontal or diagonal
    patterns.
    Illustrations: Brew 1946: figs. 152e, n, p; 157; 159h.
                   Morris 1939: pl. 260 b-e.
    (b) Impressed deviation – simple geometric designs formed
    by incising, engraving, punctation, dragging of fingers or
    other blunt tools over the finished corrugation.
    Illustrations: Brew 1946: figs. 152g, c; 158-161.
                   Morris 1939: pl. 272d.

Figure 60. Mesa Verde Corrugated--Mancos Variety sherds
with diagonal finger-ridging from Chapin Mesa.

(c) Diagonal-ridged   deviation – the   crests   of   the
individual crimps are diagonally aligned and so pronounced
as to catch the eye more rapidly than the horizontal coil
lines.
Illustrations: Morris 1939: pl. 271.
(d) Diagonal-finger-ridged   deviation – the   crests   of
individual crimps are diagonally aligned and a finger has
been dragged   down   the   diagonally running   troughs,
deepening them and emphasizing the ridges, and usually
obliterating the signs of the individual coils.
Illustrations: fig. 70; Lancaster and Pinkley 1954:   pl.
                  54, row 4, nos. 3–4.
COMPARISONS: See comparisons under Mesa Verde Corrugated--Mesa
     Verde Variety.
NAMED FOR: The Mancos River, which drains the Mesa Verde, and
     the town of Mancos, in southwestern Colorado.
NAMED BY:Abel 1955.
SYNONYMS: Mancos Corrugated (Abel 1955); Pueblo II Corrugated
     (in part)(Roberts 1935: 13); Variable Corrugated (Reed
     1958: 118-121).
ADDITIONAL REFERENCES AND ILLUSTRATIONS: Abel 1955: Ware 10A –
     Type 5. Brew 1946: 281-283; figs. 152, 157-163. Morris
     1939: 185-187, 194-196; pls. 260, 261d-e, 271-272. Reed
     1958: 118-121. Martin 1938: pls. CLXXVII, CLXXVIII 1-5,
     7-9. O'Bryan 1950: pl. XLIII f. Lancaster and Pinkley
     1954: pls. 54-55. Hayes 1964: 48-50. Lister 1965: pl.
     29c-f. Swannack 1969: 67-73.   Breternitz, Rohn,   and
     Morris 1974: 17-19.
EXAMPLES: (figs. 59, 60, and 72a) In Museum, Mesa Verde
     National Park, Colorado.
TYPE SITES: Site 16, Mesa Verde (Lancaster and Pinkley 1954).
          Big Juniper House, Mesa Verde (Swannack 1969).
STAGE: Pueblo II; Morris (1939: 194-196) suggests also   early
     Pueblo III.
TIME: Ca. A.D. 900 to 1100.
RANGE: Northern drainages of the San Juan River between the
     Animas and Colorado Rivers.
DISCUSSION: The diagonal finger-ridged deviation may or may not
     have any temporal significance, and therefore could rate
     designation as a Variety. It seems to occur early in
     Pueblo II and could conceivably be linked with the
     development of indented corrugation in the San Juan area.
     Specific evidence, however, is direly needed.

RED WARES

Type descriptions are not repeated here for the various redware types because nothing can be added to those already presented by Abel (1955). Application of type-variety taxonomy, however, allows for some reorganization of the different categories that have been described.

For Alkali Ridge, Brew describes three separate red pottery types: Abajo Red-on-orange, Abajo Black-on-gray, and Abajo Polychrome (1946: 254-255). Following a full description of the first, he states only how the next two differ in some few details from the red-on-orange type. Brew's handling of the Alkali Ridge pottery and occurrences of similar red pottery on the Mesa Verde strongly suggest that we are dealing with a single pottery type--Abajo Red-on-orange--within which extreme variations in surface and paint color can be distinguished as black-on-gray and polychrome deviations. Indeed, a third, or black-on-red deviation, might even be suggested to account for the darker color of paint and darker background surface exhibited by most specimens from the Mesa Verde.

In like manner, the relationship between Bluff and La Plata Black-on-reds as described by Abel (1955) rests primarily on the presence of a slip on the latter and its absence on the former. The unslipped pottery apparently equates with La Plata Black-on-orange (Martin 1939). The situation is perhaps best stated by Brew: "Hargrave's Bluff Black-on-red seems to be identical with the pottery known taxonomically in the Mesa Verde area as La Plata Black-on-red, described and illustrated by Morris, Shepard, and Martin, which is the immediate successor in the Mesa Verde red series to Abajo Red-on-orange in later Pueblo I times" (Brew 1946: 296). Reed, too, recognizes a basic unity, although he separates an early, unslipped La Plata Black-on-orange from a later, slipped Bluff Black-on-red that bears a close resemblance to Deadmans Black-on-red from the region around Flagstaff, Arizona (Reed 1958: 128-131). I would go one step farther than Reed and consider all this red pottery as a single type containing two subdivisions based on the presence or absence of a slip. Since unslipped specimens consistently appear with Pueblo I assemblages and slipped examples show up on later Pueblo I and early Pueblo II sites (Chapin Mesa; Shepard 1939; Reed 1958), these subdivisions should be recognized as varieties. Bluff Black-on-red has prioritiy for the type name (Hargrave 1936), and La Plata remains to be assigned to the slipped variety. Breternitz,

Rohn, and Morris (1974) include the La Plata Variety in Deadmans Black-on-red.

Red pottery from the Mesa Verde region, then, should fall into one of the following taxonomic groupings:

Abajo Red-on-orange
polychrome deviation
black-on-gray deviation
Bluff Black-on-red--Bluff Variety (unslipped)
Bluff Black-on-red--La Plata Variety (slipped)

Martin presents an excellent comparison of design between the two types (Martin 1939).

Discussion

Several of the type names utilized by Abel (1955) are missing from the foregoing classification. McElmo Black-on-white, Mancos Corrugated, Moccasin Gray, and La Plata Black-on-red have here been described as Varieties of other Types; Mesa Verde Polychrome, Morfield Black-on-gray, Abajo Black-on-gray, and Abajo Polychrome have all been described as deviations of other Varieties and Types. Twin Trees Black-on-white has been discarded since the first description was based on only 10 sherds from Site 145 and an unknown number from Step House Cave (O'Bryan 1950: 91). According to the sherd tables for Site 145 (ibid.: 120-121), a larger number of corrugated and Mancos Black-on-white sherds were found in the same levels as Twin Trees Black-on-white. Since smoothing and even polishing are clearly part of the cluster of traits associated with Chapin Black-on-white, a separate designation seems unnecessary. Twin Trees Plain poses a related problem: where should the line be drawn between a smoothed and a polished surface? I personally would not draw such a line, because both smoothed and polished surfaces can appear on different portions of the same vessel. Hovenweep Gray and Hovenweep Corrugated seem to be very rare, even in collections from Hovenweep itself. If Abel's diagnosis of Hovenweep Gray is accurate, this might best be described as a Variety of Kiet Siel Gray. Hovenweep Corrugated may ultimately end up as a Variety of Mesa Verde Corrugated. Galisteo Black-on-white appears to be clearly distinguishable from Mesa Verde Black-on-white.

Chapin Mesa Pottery

Sherds from the Chapin Mesa survey appear in the

preceding illustrations (figs. 46 to 60) as examples of the various pottery types. A few additional observations on the relative proportions of certain features on the Chapin Mesa sherds are in order here. Those features not mentioned agree closely with the type descriptions.

Chapin Black-on-white. Survey workers collected 294 sherds of this type from 173 unexcavated sites, few of which appeared to have been occupied during Basket Maker III. Only three sherds represented jars, the rest bowls. Crushed rock was normally used for temper (88%), but sand appeared as temper alone or in combination with rock in 12% of the sherds. The 35 sand tempered pieces came from 28 widely scattered sites. Most of the surfaces (56%) were at least slightly polished; 27% were smoothed; and 17% were still rough, having been only scraped. Mineral paint appeared on 67% of these sherds and a glaze paint on 3% (8 sherds). On many of these, the organic vehicle that carried the mineral pigments showed. The remaining 30% were decorated in an organic, or carbon paint. Of the 67 rim sherds, 24 (36%) were painted solid and 43 (64%) were left undecorated.

a

b

Figure 61. Chapin Black-on-white bowls from a grave at Site 364.

All sites on which Chapin Black-on-white was found also yielded Chapin Gray pottery. Seventeen sites, most of them Pueblo I, contained both Chapin and Piedra Black-on-whites. Another 41 sites had Pueblo I red sherds, and 54 of the 173 had a Pueblo II or later component.

Excavations and tests in Basket Maker III sites produced three whole Chapin Black-on-white bowls. One from Site 111 has crushed rock temper and mineral paint. The two bowls from Site 364 have

crushed rock temper, one with mineral paint (fig. 61a) and the
other with organic paint and a fugitive red exterior wash (fig.
61b).

 Piedra Black-on-white. Only 143 sherds of Piedra
Black-on-white--14% of them from jars--were gathered from 69
unexcavated sites. These sherds evidence much more uniformity
than do those of Chapin Black-on-white; only two have sand
temper, both from Site 368, and only five sherds were decorated
in organic paint. Thirty-five of forty-six bowl rims (77%)
were painted solid. Thin slips on 15% of the sherds herald the
inception of slipping as a form of surface treatment, and
painted decorations appear on three bowl exteriors.

 Chapin Gray was found on all but one of the 69 sites
with Piedra Black-on-white, but the Moccasin Variety was
collected from only 31 sites and red sherds from 37. All these
categories of pottery appear together consistently in assemblages from excavated and tested sites on Chapin Mesa. Thus,
the inconsistency of association in surface collections from
unexcavated sites must reflect the shortcomings of most of
these usually small surface samplings as indicators of the
contents of the sites themselves. Pueblo II or later components
are present at 34 sites.

 Test excavations in Site 111 produced one dipper, a
large bowl sherd, and 16 other sherds of Piedra Black-on-white.

Figure 62. Piedra Black-on-white sherds
from fill of pithouse at Site 786.

Figure 63. Piedra Black-on-white sherds from fill of pithouse
at Site 768. Lower left is probably Cortez Black-on-white.

With few exceptions, these specimens are unslipped, mineral
painted, and tempered with crushed rock. Four sherds, including
the only two from jars, are decorated with organic paint. These
same two jar sherds contain sand temper. Three of four bowl
rims were painted solid.

Similar testing in Site 786 yielded no whole vessels
but 122 sherds of Piedra Black-on-white (figs. 62 and 63). None
were slipped. Mineral paint and crushed rock temper typified
most, but 16 (13%) had organic paint, 3 were sand tempered, and
14 others contained both sand and crushed rock. Twenty-three
sherds belonged to jars; 37 of 42 bowl rims (88%) were painted
solid; one bowl sherd exhibited decoration on its exterior.

Cortez Black-on-white. There are 491 sherds of this
type from 138 unexcavated sites. Two-thirds (66%) of these
came from bowls. Crushed potsherd temper makes its first
appearance here, usually in combination with crushed rock, in
30% of the sherds. Five sherds (1%) contain sand. All but 14
sherds (3%) were slipped, and all were decorated in mineral
paint. No organic pigment was observed on the specimens,
although two sherds with two tones of mineral paint, probably
from a single vessel, were collected from Sites 287 and 296
near Balcony House. A solid black stripe decorated 128 out of
143 bowl rims (90%); the rest had no decoration. Corrugation
appears on five bowl exteriors, painted decoration on five

others.

Although Mancos Gray and Cortez Black-on-white are contemporaries, they were found together on only 55 sites. Cortez Black-on-white was associated with corrugated on 123 sites, with Chapin Gray on 118 sites, and with Mancos Black-on-white on 105 sites. All these types may be expected to occur together.

Other types occasionally collected from sites with Cortez Black-on-white include: Piedra Black-on-white from 19 sites, Mesa Verde Black-on-white from 45 sites, and Mesa Verde Variety of Mesa Verde Corrugated from 18 sites. Most, if not all, of these occurrences are from sites with several occupational components.

One Cortez Black-on-white dipper bowl with crushed rock temper (fig. 64a) was found at Site 642. The organic vehicle that carried its mineral paint pigment is clearly visible. Another dipper with open trough handle (fig. 64c) came from Site 528. A small jar (fig. 64b) was picked up from Site 16 in 1942, before that site was excavated.

Mancos Black-on-white. A total of 310 unexcavated sites yielded 2,468 sherds of this pottery type. Forty-four per cent belonged to jars. Ten per cent lacked slips, most of these from jars. Sixteen bowl rims were decorated with painted dots or ticking, painted designs decorated 18 bowl exteriors, and 73 (5%) other bowl exteriors were corrugated. Sixty sherds (about 2½%) were decorated in organic paint; the rest had mineral paint, apparently applied in an organic vehicle. Crushed potsherd temper clearly predominated.

Many other types occur in association with Mancos Black-on-white: Chapin Gray at 255 sites, Mancos Gray at 68 sites, Mesa Verde Corrugated--Mancos Variety at 184 sites, indeterminate corrugated where no varieties were recognized at 70 sites, Mesa Verde Corrugated--Mesa Verde Variety at 51 sites, Cortez Black-on-white at 105 sites, and Mesa Verde Black-on-white

Figure 64. Cortez Black-on-white vessels from Site 642 (a), Site 16 (b), and Site 528 (c).

at 118 sites.

Eleven Mancos Black-on-white vessels have been collected from salvage or test excavations on Chapin Mesa over the years. Two bowls (fig. 65a and b), one dipper bowl, and two unslipped small pitchers (fig. 66b) came from sites in the Mummy Lake group, although they were collected before the sites were numbered. Two bird effigy pots (figs. 66c and 77a) came from Site 542 and from a grave at Site 200. Another grave at Site 828 gave up a pitcher decorated in organic paint (fig. 66d) and a bowl with corrugated exterior (fig. 65c). Both have crushed sherd temper. Still another bowl with corrugated exterior (fig. 65d) came from Site 41, and a small unslipped dipper bowl (fig. 66a) accompanied a burial at Site 299. Evidence of an organic vehicle can be seen on several of these mineral-painted vessels.

Mesa Verde Black-on-white--McElmo Variety. The survey collected 678 sherds of this variety from 138 unexcavated sites. Eighty per cent belonged to bowls; 82% were slipped. Organic paint decorated 98%, mineral paint only 2%. Side walls tapering to the rim were recorded on 35 bowl sherds. Only six bowl sherds had corrugated exteriors. Two tones of organic paint produced a "polychrome" effect on three sherds. One sherd contained sand temper.

McElmo Variety of

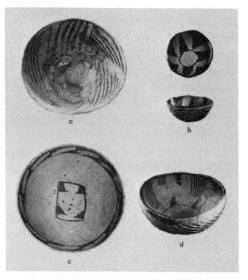

Figure 65. Mancos Black-on-white bowls from sites in Mummy Lake Group (a & b), Site 828 (c), and Site 41 (d).

Figure 66. Mancos Black-on-white vessels from Site 299 (a), the Mummy Lake ruin group (b), Site 542 (c), and Site 828 (d).

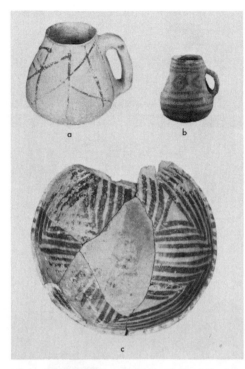

Figure 67. Mesa Verde Black-on-white--McElmo Variety vessels from Site 835 (a), Site 201 (b), and Site 529 (c).

Mesa Verde Black-on-white was found in the following combinations: 1) with Mancos Black-on-white and earlier decorateds at 40 sites; 2) with Mesa Verde Variety of Mesa Verde Black-on-white at 25 sites; 3) with both Mancos Black-on-white and Mesa Verde Variety at 53 sites; 4) with no other decorated pottery at 20 sites; 5) with Mesa Verde Corrugated--Mancos Variety at 34 sites; 6) with Mesa Verde Corrugated--Mesa Verde Variety at 34 sites; and 7) with both varieties of Mesa Verde Corrugated at 31 sites. It clearly occupies a position intermediate between Mancos Black-on-white and Mesa Verde Variety, rarely occurring by itself, but largely overlapping both.

A whole mug (fig. 67a) was found on the trash dump of Site 835 during survey, and a restorable bowl (fig. 67c) was excavated with a burial from a rock crevice near Site 529. Both vessels were unslipped and decorated in organic paint. The bowl was associated with a Mesa Verde Variety mug. A small pitcher (fig. 67b) accompanied one of the burials from Site 201.

Mesa Verde Black-on-white--Mesa Verde Variety. The 875 sherds of this variety came from 121 unexcavated sites. Bowl sherds outnumber jar sherds 83% to 17%. Both kiva jars and mugs are also represented. Four per cent of the specimens lack the characteristic white slip; eleven sherds were decorated in mineral paint; two have sand temper; one bowl exterior was grooved; and two bowl rims are slightly everted.

The Mesa Verde Variety of Mesa Verde Black-on-white is customarily associated with McElmo Variety (78 sites) and with Mesa Verde Corrugated--Mesa Verde Variety (63 sites). There is also a considerable overlap with Mancos Black-on-white, at least in the surface collections.

Twelve whole vessels of this Variety from Chapin Mesa sites in the Mesa Verde Museum collections have not yet been

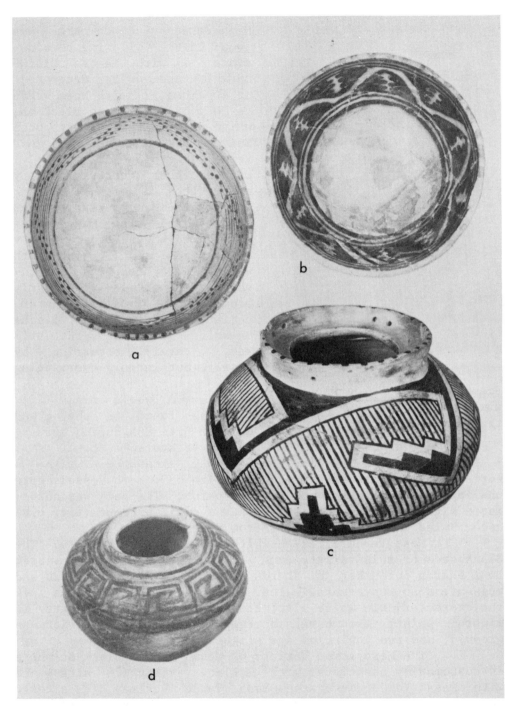

Figure 68. Mesa Verde Black-on-white--Mesa Verde Variety
vessels from Site 542.

reported in print. Half of
them--two bowls, two kiva jars
(fig. 68), and two ollas--were
found together in Site 542.
Another bowl and another jar
(fig. 69b) came from Site 626.
The other vessels include a
canteen from Site 524, a dipper
from Site 808, an olla (fig.
69a) from Site 201, and the mug
associated with the McElmo
Variety bowl in a grave near
Site 529.

Mesa Verde Black-on-
white--indeterminate. Sherds
that could not be differentiated into McElmo or Mesa Verde
Varieties numbered 349 from 120
unexcavated sites. Seventy per
cent came from bowls, a smaller
proportion than in either Variety. This discrepancy reflects
the greater ease of distinguishing between the two varieties on bowls, probably
because the ancient potters
expressed their cultural con-
ventions more consistently on
the bowl form. Individual
specimens revealed such unusual
features as a corrugated jar
neck, basket impression on a

Figure 69. Mesa Verde Black-on-
white--Mesa Verde Variety
ollas from Site 201 (a) and
Site 626 (b).

bowl exterior, and the combination of both organic and mineral
paint producing a sort of "polychrome" effect.

Chapin Gray. The survey yielded 8,393 sherds of
Chapin Gray from over 600 unexcavated sites. Most of these
(7,228) were plain body sherds that could have belonged to any
of the three Varieties. Of the remaining 1,165 sherds, 15
could be assigned to the Mummy Lake Variety, 174 (15%) to the
Moccasin Variety, and 976 (84%) to the Chapin Variety. Jars
accounted for all sherds of the two less common Varieties.
Three major shapes are represented in the Chapin Variety: bowls
(215 sherds--22% of the distinguishable sherds), seed jars or
squash pots (111 sherds--11%), and necked jars including ollas
(640 sherds--66%). Ten sherds of Chapin Variety retain traces
of fugitive red paint.

Test excavations on Chapin Mesa also produced many Chapin Gray sherds, which are listed under the respective sites, as well as 11 complete or restorable vessels. Two Chapin Variety seed jars came from Site 106, the larger one from the pithouse floor. The smaller jar, restored from sherds in the fill of the same pithouse, was only weakly fired and had been tempered with fine sand or crushed sandstone. Numerous bits of vegetal material also left their impressions. Although the jar measures only 3 inches high, its walls range from 7 to 11 mm. thick. One small necked jar of Chapin Variety (fig. 70a) was found with an infant burial at Site 341; another (fig. 70b) came from the talus slope in front of Site 640 (Spruce Tree House). This last provides a further suggestion of Basket Maker III use of Spruce Tree House cave. Both contained crushed rock temper. Morris and Nusbaum found a small U-shaped vessel (fig. 70c) while testpitting Site 115. Two wide-mouthed jars (fig. 71a and b) and a shallow bowl of Chapin Variety and two neck-banded jars of Moccasin Variety (fig. 71c) were unearthed together in the test at Site 111. All five contained crushed rock temper and had rough surfaces. A grave at Site 201 yielded a small jar of Mummy Lake Variety with a vertical handle (fig. 70e). A small dipper with a trough handle (fig. 70d), from Site 828, fits none of the Variety descriptions, but equates in age with Mummy Lake Variety.

Mancos Gray. Only 346 sherds of this type were gathered from about 120 unexcavated sites. Of these, 76 sherds or 22%, had shallow tooled grooves between the coils, two specimens had been incised over the coils, and the coils on eight had been partly smoothed with something like a finger. Some of these sherds could conceivably belong to unindented portions of Mesa Verde Corrugated jars on which patterns had been formed by alternating indented and unindented areas. Some of the plain gray body sherds classified under Chapin Gray could also have come from the plain bottoms of Mancos Gray jars. Chapin Mesa produced no whole jars, but the sherds indicate that many of the jars had unobliterated coils only on their necks or upper bodies.

Mesa Verde Corrugated. A total of 3,843 sherds of this type were gathered during survey from over 460 unexcavated sites. The greatest number of these (2,783) could not be differentiated into one of the Varieties. The Mancos Variety accounts for 808 sherds, or 76% of these specimens that could be assigned to a variety. Most of these are rim and neck sherds. Relatively great variation in surface treatment is reflected in the numbers of the four deviations of this Variety: 1) diagonal-ridged deviation--220 sherds (27% of

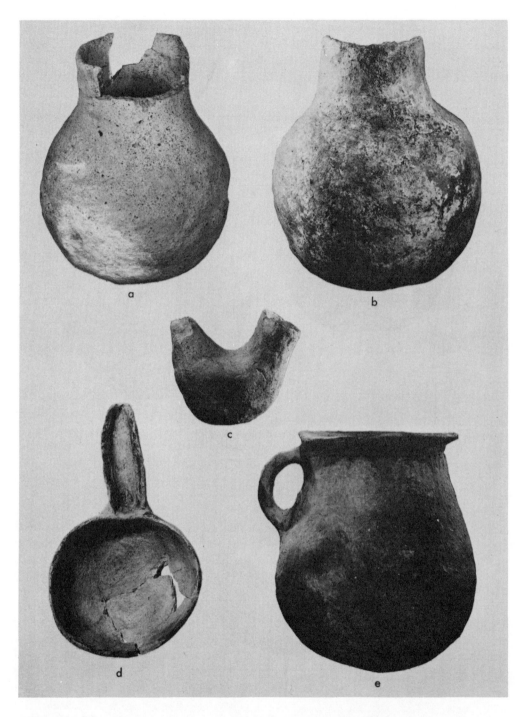

Figure 70. Chapin Gray vessels from Chapin Mesa sites: (a-c) Chapin Variety, (d) indeterminate, and (e) Mummy Lake Variety.

Figure 71. Chapin Gray vessels from Site 111, room 2:
(a-b) Chapin Variety, (c) Moccasin Variety.

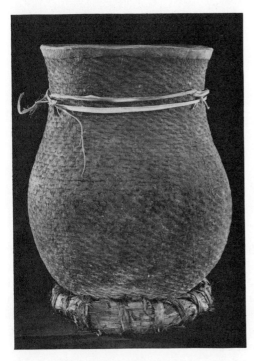

Figure 72. Mesa Verde Corrugated jars: (above) Mancos Variety from Site 519; (below) Mesa Verde Variety from Site 640.

these classed as Mancos Variety); 2) diagonal-finger-ridged deviation--84 sherds (10%); 3) patterned deviation--95 sherds (12%); and 4) impressed deviation--15 sherds (2%). Two of the rim sherds have simple painted figures just inside the rim. Recognizable Mancos Variety sherds came from close to 200 unexcavated sites. Site 519 yielded one complete Mancos Variety jar (fig. 72a) with yucca strips tied around the neck.

There are 252 sherds of Mesa Verde Variety making up 24% of the differentiable specimens. Seven per cent of these (17 sherds) have patterned surfaces. Five rim sherds have figures painted in organic paint on or just inside the rim.

Four whole vessels of Mesa Verde Variety were recovered from various tests and salvage work on Chapin Mesa. The one large jar (fig. 72b) came from Spruce Tree House (Site 640). Sites 534 and 626 each contained a small form of the same kind of vessel. A third small jar was one of the two pots accompanying the burial at Site 200 with which the unusual cache of stone objects was placed (fig. 77b).

Red Wares. Although 530 red sherds, apparently of local origin, were collected from unexcavated Chapin Mesa sites, most of them lacked characters definitive for classification. Of these unclassified sherds, 232 were plain and 58 painted.

One hundred sixteen sherds were classified as Abajo Red-on-orange, although the paint tends toward a dark brown and the background tends more toward a red than on specimens of this type from Alkali Ridge (Brew 1946). Ten of these would fit the black-on-gray deviation. There were 95 bowl sherds and 21 jar sherds. Abajo Red-on-orange was collected from 51 mesa-top sites.

Figure 73. Unpainted white olla from Cliff Palace (Site 625).

Bluff Black-on-red is represented by 89 sherds (15 of them from jars) of Bluff Variety from 30 sites and by 35 sherds (3 from jars) of La Plata Variety from 25 sites. The two Varieties appeared together on only six sites. Bluff Variety was associated with Abajo Red-on-orange at 14 sites, La Plata Variety with this same type at six sites. Only twice did all three categories of decorated red pottery occur together.

Although red sherds were collected from more than 140 sites, they were found in quantity on very few. The following sites produced more than ten sherds: 112 from Site 370; 28 from Site 793; 21 from Site 373; 16 each from Sites 58, 376, and 386; 15 from Site 851; and 11 each from Sites 747 and 824.

A restorable Abajo Red-on-orange bowl was excavated from Site 111, and a restorable Bluff Black-on-red--Bluff Variety seed jar from Site 58.

Unclassified. A great many kinds of specimens are grouped among the 3,047 unclassified sherds from unexcavated sites. There are 1,551 sherds with slipped and polished surfaces that probably represent unpainted portions of black-on-white vessels. Bowls accounted for 463 sherds and jars 1,088.

However, 32 slipped and polished rim sherds could not have come from painted pots. These specimens represent portions of bowls--in only one case a jar--that always bear parts of any decoration that is present. Consequently, the vessels themselves must have lacked painted decoration (Rohn 1971: 185-186). A complete jar without paint, but with all other attributes common to typical Mesa Verde Black-on-white vessels, including a polished white slip (fig. 73), has come from Cliff Palace (Site 625). Site 620 has produced half a small white bowl with the same characteristics.

Unclassified black-on-white sherds numbered 826, with 459 from bowls and 367 from jars. Two black-on-white jars from the Mummy Lake group of sites could not be classified. Another 638 sherds include indeterminate plains, corrugateds, handle fragments, and just plain unknown specimens. An unclassified plain miniature bowl, only an inch and a quarter in diameter, was found on the surface of Site 267.

A unique dipper deserves special mention. Its decoration was drawn in a thick white paint applied over a thin black wash that covered the dipper's interior. Total length is 6 1/8 inches. Salvage excavation of a burial from the trash heap of Site 80 unearthed the dipper on the floor in the southeast corner of a bathtub-shaped pit. The pit's sides had been heavily burned, before it was filled with Pueblo II refuse (Lancaster 1968b).

CHAPTER V

OTHER REMAINS

In most stone and bone artifact classes, too few
items were collected to be useful in this study. In most cases,
the recovered specimens merely duplicated already published
materials (e.g., in O'Bryan 1950 and Lancaster et al. 1954).
The hammerstones, scrapers, choppers, and utilized flakes
yielded no new information. A good series of projectile points
is described here as well as an unusual cache of objects found
in a grave. Perishable items are generally rare enough to
justify the description of several uncommon objects as
additions to Mesa Verde material culture.

Projectile Points

Most of these are sufficiently lightweight to have
tipped arrowshafts, but some may have been dart or spear
points. Only the obvious knife blades are excluded from this
category. It is possible to segregate several styles of
projectile points, using form primarily and weight secondarily,
and to observe what appears to be a sequential development.
Small triangular points with opposed lateral notches
and straight or nearly straight bases (fig. 74, top two rows)
consistently turn up in sites of late Pueblo II and Pueblo III
vintage. They commonly weigh less than one gram, but may reach
1.7 grams. The two sides vary from slightly concave to slightly
convex, and, like the base, seem intended to be straight.
Materials include quartzite, chalcedonies, and cherts. Most of
those found during the survey came from cliff dwellings and
from the large early Pueblo III mesa-top pueblos. Several small
aberrant points with markedly convex bases came from Oak Tree
House (Site 523). A couple of points with oblique side notches
may be transitional between the typical late side-notched
arrow point and its predecessor.
The Archaeological Site Survey and the Mesa Verde
Museum collections produced 18 side-notched points from the
following sites: cliff dwelling 523, mesa-top pueblos 808,

217

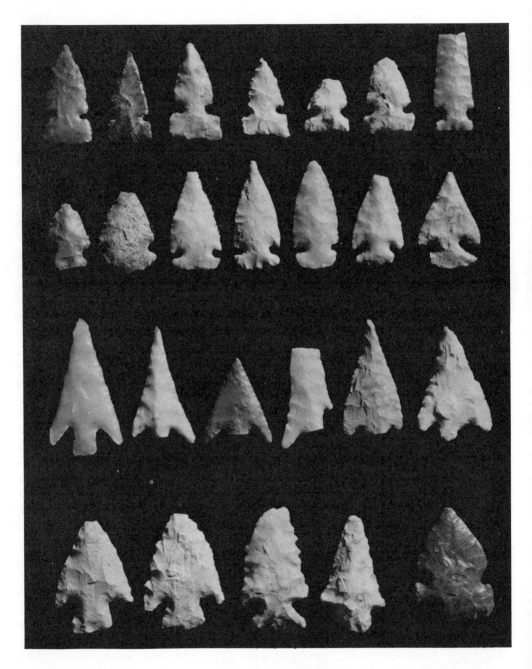

Figure 74. Projectile points from Chapin Mesa: bottom row –
Basket Maker III; second row – Pueblo I; top two rows –
Pueblo II and III.

809, 303, 829, 866, 867, 201, 786, 981, 484, 465, and 359.

Another group of small triangular points is characterized by narrow stems, either expanding or contracting toward
a convex base, long pointed barbs, and straight or concave
sides (fig. 74, third row). In weight they cluster around one
gram with a maximum of 1.8 grams recorded. Quartzites,
chalcedonies, and cherts again are the usual materials. There
are eight specimens in the museum collections and from the
survey; two from the refuse heap at Site 370, one from the
backdirt at Site 1, one from the Pueblo I site 793, one from
either Site 137, 154, or 159, all Pueblo I sites, and three
from the early Pueblo II Sites 809, 831, and either 281 or 282.
O'Bryan (1950: pl. 27) illustrates two more from Site 103
(Site 102 Village) and one from Site 102 Pueblo. Thus, the
temporal distribution of this kind of point includes both
Pueblo I and early Pueblo II associations. Points in the latter
provenience tend to have shorter barbs and slightly convex
sides.

A third group of larger points has a broad stem
expanding toward the base with short blunt barbs and convex
sides (fig. 74, bottom row 1-4). Their weights vary between
2.5 and 3 grams. Quartzite and cherts predominate as materials.
One has serrated sides, and the base of another's stem was
ground smooth. Of the six known specimens, one came from Site
145 (O'Bryan 1950: pl. 27), two from Site 101 (Lancaster and
Watson 1954: pl. 13) and one from its backdirt, one from Site
405, and one with no site association. All of these sites are
Basket Maker III.

A chalcedony point of the same size and weight as
this last group, but with a different shape, was found on the
Basket Maker III Site 847. It seemingly has no stem, but two
lateral notches instead (fig. 74, bottom row right). This point
is obviously eccentric, but should perhaps be considered with
the above group. Still another of chert from Site 792 (Basket
Maker III) differs in weight--1.7 gm.--and slightly in shape--
with concave sides--and may be a late transitional piece.

Large triangular points with side notches present a
curious dilemma. In form they resemble closely the small
triangular side-notched points already described, but they are
much larger, exceeding 3 and 4 grams in weight (fig. 76, lower
row left). Quartzites and chalcedony predominate. A wide
variety of proveniences is represented: Masket Maker III Site
35, Site 710 belonging to late Pueblo II, and the non-ceramic
Site 801. O'Bryan (1950: pl. 27) illustrates one from Site
103 (Pueblo I) and another from Site 34 (Pueblo III, although
not within the Chapin Mesa Study area). These artifacts should

perhaps be classed as knife blades designed for hafting.

There are five points in the collections from Chapin
Mesa typologically similar to points that belong to preceramic
assemblages in surrounding areas. Three of these, all of
quartzite, have broad stems or tangs, concave on both sides and
on the base so as to produce ear-like projections at both
corners (fig. 75, top row 1-3). They all possess markedly
convex blade sides and two are deeply serrated. The sides of
the stem on one specimen are ground. Very similar points are
described and illustrated by Mohr and Sample (1959: fig. 2a-c)
from the Aneth assemblage in southeastern Utah, by Wendorf and
Thomas (1951: fig. 49b-e) from the Concho Complex in Arizona,
and by Bryan and Toulouse (1943: pl. 19w-e) from the San Jose
Complex near Grants, New Mexico. All these complexes have been
assigned a pre-Basket Maker date. If the three points from
Chapin Mesa belong in this broad group, and I see no reason why

Figure 75. Projectile points from Chapin Mesa: bottom row –
probable Basket Maker II styles; top row – preceramic styles.

Figure 76. Miscellaneous projectile points from Chapin Mesa.

they would not, it would certainly suggest that pre-Basket Maker peoples were at least hunting over Chapin Mesa even if they did not live here. All three were found on the mesa top, not clearly associated with any known sites; one near Site 1909, one east of the head of Spruce Canyon alongside the Far View Ditch, and the other in the vicinity of Site 650 (Square Tower House).

A fourth point (fig. 75, top row fourth from left) recovered from Site 650 (Square Tower House) nearly duplicates two shown by Wendorf and Thomas (1951: fig. 49n-o) as part of the Concho Complex, but listed as "rare" and "not reported from all sites of the complex." This point certainly does not match the typical side-notched points found in cliff dwellings in either form or size (weight exceeds 1.6 gm.). It can either be ascribed to eccentricity of manufacture or to the finding and collection of an older point by a Square Tower House inhabitant.

The fifth point is an obvious case of re-use by its Spruce Tree House (Site 640) owner. It has a broad stem with deeply indented base and pronounced but low shoulders (fig. 75, top row right). Both sides are ground from the base to slightly above the shoulder. One shoulder and part of the blade have been broken away and that side resharpened for subsequent use, probably as a knife blade. Because we cannot tell exactly how the thirteenth-century cliff dweller acquired his antique knife blade, it would be foolish to try to claim it was originally lost on Chapin Mesa. He could have acquired it through trade from a relatively great distance. It does bear a striking resemblance to Duncan Points from the northern Great Plains (Wheeler 1954).

Under the circumstances just described, one would expect also to find some Basket Maker II points in the Chapin Mesa collections. In fact two points were found apart from sites during survey that bear a gross resemblance in form and size to those figured by Morris and Burgh (1954: figs. 81 and 82) from the Basket Maker II sites near Durango, Colorado. They have broad stems, expanding toward the convex base, short but sharp barbs, and long convex blade sides (fig. 75, bottom row). These sides on one specimen were ground smooth. Both exceed 4.5 gm. in weight; one is quartzite, the other chert. One was found on the mesa top about half a mile south of the Mummy Lake ruin group and the other came from the northern part of Little Soda Canyon. Two other similar points were picked up near Sites 1097 and 923, but are not necessarily associated with them. We should not overlook the crude similarity of these two points to some knife blades in use during the later phases.

The remaining 14 points are quite variable and not so easy to characterize as those already described. Their range of variation in form can best be seen in figure 76, so I shall refrain from further description here.

Site 200 Burial Cache. One particular grave in the refuse heap of Site 200 contained an adult male in a flexed position and on his right side (fig. 17). With him in death his mourners placed a Mancos Black-on-white bird effigy jar (fig. 77a), a small Mesa Verde Corrugated--Mesa Verde Variety jar (fig. 77b), and a coiled basket. The basket contained the following 90 objects (fig. 78).

4 bone awls
2 small sandstone abraders
7 chipped knife blades, four of them broken
1 chipped double pointed drill or eccentric
1 broken turquoise pendant
4 turquoise inlay pieces

29 stone flakes and cores, many of them with utilized edges
28 pieces of red hematite, mostly soft
1 large lump of yellow ochre
1 small lump of tan ochre
1 large discoidal lump of white kaolin with a hole through it
3 polished concretions of hard hematite
3 small lumps of azurite
3 small lumps of malachite
1 large gizzard stone
1 squash seed

Several kinds of cherts, chalcedony, and quartzite are represented among the flakes and cores (bottom three rows of fig. 78). The sharp edges on some were used for cutting or scraping, while other pieces were probably stock to be made into tools. One of the two sandstone abraders, resembling a miniature mano, appears in the top row center of the flakes and cores. Immediately above are

Figure 77. Pottery vessels Site 200 burial.

Figure 78.   Cache of stone objects from Site 200 burial.

the many pieces of red hematite. In the upper left corner is
the lump of yellow ochre; the kaolin is in the upper right.

    All four bone awls were manufactured from split
portions of large mammal long bones, three from shaft splinters
and one with most of the articular head worked off. The three
complete awls range in length from 2 3/4 to 4 7/8 inches.

    The chipped knife blades all have a generalized leaf-
shaped outline, although only three are complete and measure
from 3 1/8 to 3 1/2 inches long. If the blades had broken after
being buried, the missing pieces would have been found by the
excavators. We must assume, therefore, that the man in the
grave had owned them as fragments and not as whole objects.

    A similar conclusion must be reached concerning the
five pieces of turquoise. The four inlay pieces are rectangular
with sharp corners and neatly beveled edges. This man probably
salvaged them when the object to which they originally belonged
became damaged or partially destroyed.

    The many pieces of minerals, the wide variety of
paint pigments, the gizzard stone, and the squash seed all
recall the variety of items often considered sacrosanct by the

historic Pueblo Indians
(Parsons 1939). One wonders if
the basket once contained also
several kinds of feathers,
various soft parts of plants
and animals, string, some
carved sticks, pollen, and
meal. The presence of several
tools and probably some "stock"
for future manufactures suggests that most of this man's
personal possessions were
buried with him. Further interpretation of this burial must
await complete excavation of
Site 200.

Perishables

<u>Bark Bucket</u>. What may
be a unique object for the Mesa
Verde is this bucket found in
the late Pueblo III two-room
cliff site 643. It was made
from a long strip of cottonwood
bark folded in the middle and
spirally whipped along its
sides with split strips of

Figure 79. Bark bucket from
Site 643.

yucca leaves (fig. 79). The completed object stands 14 inches
high with a maximum opening of 9½ inches by 7 inches. There is
a separate row of split yucca strip stiching through the sides
2¼ inches below the rim, which may have been an attachment for
a carrying strap. This bucket certainly held no liquids as no
signs of pitch are visible along the seams.

<u>Bark Cradle</u>. A second unusual specimen made from
cottonwood bark is shown in figure 80. A rectangular piece of
bark measuring 23 by 16 inches was formed into an apparent
cradle by curling the two long sides over about 2 inches on the
smooth inner side of the bark. The two ends were then tipped
upward slightly and an arc of oak attached to one end with
split yucca leaf strips. The finished product had an overall
length of 22 inches, was 9 inches wide and 3 deep. In size it
is a near duplicate of other wooden cliff dweller cradles. As
the bark dried out and suffered the hardships of use, it began
splitting lengthwise. Repair was effected by stitching across

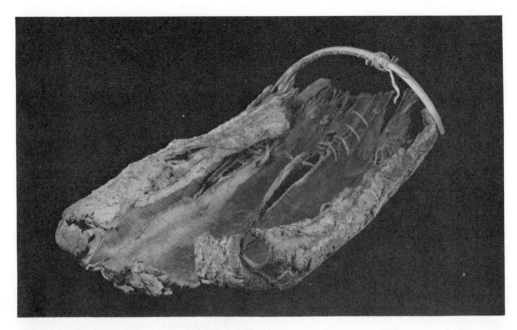

Figure 80. Bark cradle from Site 528.

two main cracks with split yucca leaf strips.

The cradle, along with several other pieces of
unworked cottonwood bark, was found in Site 528, a five-room
cliff house not far from Spruce Tree House. At the present
time, cottonwoods are quite rare in the Mesa Verde although one
now stands above the head of Spruce Tree Canyon. The recovery
of two artifacts (including the bark bucket) and a bundle of
cottonwood bark from sites in this canyon suggests that several
such trees may have grown there in the past.

Coiled Basket. While the Mesa Verde Museum collections include several fragments of basketry from Chapin Mesa
cave sites, there is only one reasonably complete specimen
(fig. 81). This is a bottomless coiled basket with straight
sloping sides 4 3/4 inches high. It has a diameter at the mouth
of 11 3/4 inches and at its base of 7 3/4 inches. A thick pad
of grass now forms a sort of false bottom. Stitching was done
with strips of willow; each foundation coil consists of 2 reds
and a splint bundle. There is no evidence of decoration. This
basket was collected from Site 519.

Sandals. The Mesa Verde Museum collections contain
26 whole and fragmentary sandals from Chapin Mesa sites, 17 of
them from Spruce Tree House and 5 from Cliff Palace. Twenty of
these sandals were made by plaiting yucca leaves, or strips

split from yucca leaves, in a diagonal twill. Six were twined
with yucca cordage. Rather than pursue the subject of sandals
at length, I will describe one example of each kind, from small
cave sites that are not likely to be reported in the near
future.

Site 528 produced a fine twilled yucca strip sandal
for the right foot (fig. 82). Sets of loops along the sides
permitted criss-cross lacing. The total length is 9 3/4
inches, the width 4 inches. This style of twill sandal, with
round heel and toe and a small jog at the outside of the toe,
characterizes late Pueblo III on Chapin Mesa.

A decorated twined sandal was found at Site 519 in
Fewkes Canyon. Its outline is essentially rectangular, 10
inches long by 3¼ inches wide, with a concave, or "scallop",
toe and the heel drawn up at the corners (fig. 83). There are
ties at the heel and at the toe. A large hole has been worn
through the heel. The foundation consists of 28 warps,

Figure 81. Coiled basket from Site 519.

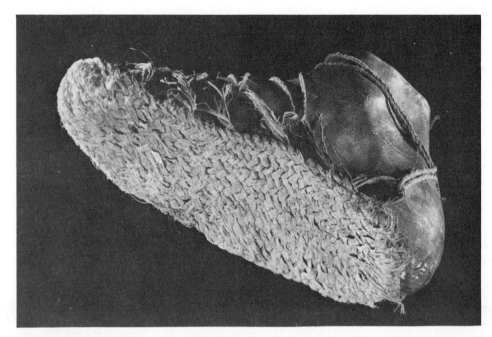

Figure 82. Twilled yucca sandal from Site 528 shown on
model foot.

each one   a   2-ply S-twist medium   degree   cord   about 2 mm. in
diameter, made with smooth, well-separated yucca fibers, and
running the length of the sandal. Weft   cords were twisted
in   the   same manner, but   harder, to about half the diameter
of   the   warps. From   the toe to the patterned section, the
wefts   were   twill-twined   around   pairs   of   warps   completely
covering them; elsewhere, the warps were used singly.   Two
colors of wefts, rust and gray-brown, formed a patterned
band under the arch of the foot.

A heavy   cord was drawn through the warp loops   at
the heel and tied. For the heel tie, two loops were formed
by a 6 to 7 mm. multi-twist cord passing through an overhand
knot of this loomstring and tied to both raised sides of
the heel.   This rope is 3-ply Z-twist, made up of 3-ply S-twist
elements, which are in turn composed of 2-ply S-twist twine.
Each single ply is Z-twist bringing the complete formula
to Z-S-S-Z and 1-2-3-3. At the toe, two overlapping loops were
made with 2-ply S-twist cord 6 mm. in diameter.

Twined cord sandals with concave toes are a Basket
Maker III style and are thought to indicate Basket Maker III
use of the sites where they are found. Similar sandals have
been found in Site 503, a burial cave, and from beneath the
north end of Cliff Palace. Several fragments of twined sandals

have also come from Spruce
Tree House.

Hafted Axe

Axes with their
wooden handles preserved are
scarce enough to warrant
description whenever they are
encountered. This particular
specimen came from a cave (Site
519) opposite Fire Temple in
Fewkes Canyon, and was probably
associated with the late Pueblo
III occupation. The stone axe
head is typically single-
bitted and full-grooved, 6
inches long by 2 3/4 inches
wide and 2 inches thick (fig.
84). An unpeeled stick ½ inch
in diameter, was wrapped completely around the groove twice
so that both ends extended side
by side for 13½ inches from one
side of the stone head, where
they were bound together with
2-ply Z-twist yucca cordage.

Figure 83. Twined cord sandal
from Site 519.

Figure 84. Hafted stone axe from Site 519.

VI

CULTURAL SEQUENCE

With as wide a variety of sites as has been recorded
on Chapin Mesa, it is essential to arrange them into some kind
of chronological system before one can study the nature of
culture at any one time or enumerate the way in which certain
aspects of culture changed or developed through time. It would
be ideal to be able to assign precise calendar year dates to
the construction and length of occupation for each site.
However, even if our dating techniques were absolutely accurate
and could be applied to all sites, the shuffling of remains due
to human occupation and its duration dull the precision of any
dates. As it is, where we have to rely on the changing fashions
expressed in cultural phenomena to place most sites, especially
unexcavated ones, in relative sequence, we are forced into the
use of time periods or of cultural units that exist within time
periods.

There is a certain degree of circular reasoning in
the use of cultural phenomena to define units by which those
phenomena are then studied. An artificiality creeps in that
cannot be ignored. If several traits are employed as hallmarks
of one unit, the occurrence of those traits is usually assigned
to that unit to the exclusion of others. Shifts within units
and transitions between them are usually obscured by the inclu-
siveness of unit definitions. In other words, the constancy of
modification or change is distorted by efforts to recognize
successive stations along the continuum as aids in dating. For
several reasons, I shall outline in this study a cultural
sequence developed especially for Chapin Mesa and based on
local data. First, in a region where there are still hosts of
undug sites, the greatest possibilities for the discovery of
anthropologically useful data can be realized through the
establishment of local sequences. The extensive work done
recently on Wetherill Mesa should provide an excellent body of
comparable data from another similar locality. Peculiarities of
geography would suggest that several interesting differences
may be expected between local sequences on the Mesa Verde and
in the Montezuma Valley to the northwest. Fortunately, too,
there is sufficient information available to permit not only a

reasonable description of local phases, but to establish the
chronological relationships.

        In terms of geographical space over which there are
certain cultural uniformities, within the Northern San Juan
Region (Bullard 1962: 53), the Mesa Verde proper north of the
Mancos River may be considered a district (Herold 1961: 47),
and Chapin Mesa might qualify as a locality (Willey and
Phillips 1958: 18) if that concept is broadened somewhat.
Locality is better defined as a convenient unit of space with
physiographic bounds small enough to permit extensive but not
necessarily exhaustive investigation within the space of a few
years. It contains many sites, usually representing more than
one village-size community, dependent of course on the density
of settlement. Identification with a local group--a body of
people held together and recognized primarily through their
sharing of a given geographical space for living and
subsistence--is not clear since any unit from a household to a
tribe may qualify as such a local group. Using this expanded
view, Chapin Mesa is considered a locality, and its local
sequence will be outlined.

        With this modification of the concept locality, the
stages within our local sequence will resemble what Willey and
Phillips would call phases. But phases are supposed to represent units within a regional sequence. However, rather than
introduce a new term, it would be better to use this term with
the understanding that it synthesizes components within a
locality and that any "phase" on Chapin Mesa probably belongs
to a larger phase characteristic of much of the Northern San
Juan Region. Of course, it is tempting to describe a phase
sequence for the whole region. But with extensive work
conducted in recent years and still going on, I believe it will
promote clarity and utility to describe a local sequence that
can be compared to others and used in the formulation of a true
regional sequence. The modern tendency for each worker to
redefine the sequence in his region every time he publishes
only leads to ultimate confusion over a muddle of competing
names and assignments.

        Chapin Mesa may have had some preceramic occupation,
although no definite sites have been found. Several early
projectile points, resembling points from sites of the San Jose
or Concho Complexes, suggest that pre-agricultural people may
have wandered across Chapin Mesa, even if they did not live
there. Surface finds also yielded a number of projectile points
like those found in Basket Maker II sites near Durango (Morris
and Burgh 1954). With so little evidence, however, it is impossible to postulate phases or even complexes for

these manifestations.

Meat of the Chapin Mesa sequence consists of six units. Each includes several excavated sites on the basis of which the unexcavated ones were both interpreted and assigned. The designations for these units are best left noncommittal, and I shall use the terminology of the Pecos Classification (Kidder 1927) since the units fit the stage descriptions so well. For those who insist on specific names, I shall suggest some local names by which they could also be called, and indicate the regional phases proposed by O'Bryan (1950: 103-111) to which they probably belong.

Basket Maker III (Twin Trees)

Regional phase: Four Corners.
Time placement: A.D. 590-750.
Sites and/or components: Site 145 (O'Bryan 1950); Site 118 (Earth Lodge A); Sites 117 (Pithouse B) and 283 (Pithouse C) (Lancaster and Watson 1942); Site 405 (Pipe Line Pithouse) (Smiley 1949); Site 101 (Deep Pithouses) (Lancaster and Watson 1954); Site 1060 (Hayes and Lancaster 1968); Site 354 (Lancaster 1968a); and Site 1061. A total of 11 pithouses have been excavated at these sites. Eighteen others have been partially excavated or tested, and 26 mesa-top sites probably include at least 36 unexcavated pithouses (this includes all the sites listed in table 1). In addition Basket Maker III remains were found by Nusbaum in several cave sites. He found no structures, only pottery and perishable artifacts in Sites 510, 519, and 640 (Spruce Tree House).

Site situations: All known house sites are located along the low ridges of the mesa top. However, the finds of Nusbaum suggest at least some limited use of rock shelters.

Architecture: No complete village or cluster of pithouses has been excavated on Chapin Mesa, although two have been investigated by testing. These indicate a definite conglomeration of as many as seven or eight separate structures in close proximity to one another, and it may be assumed that similar groupings exist wherever pithouses are found. House floors are all roughly circular to squarish in plan and excavated from 2 to 4 feet below the ground surface. An antechamber, connected to the main room by a raised passageway, a crude banquette, central clay-lined circular hearth, storage bins and pits, irregular wing walls, and four-post roof support are common to all. Upright stone slab deflectors and clay-plastered sipapus are also typical, but not always present.

Where determinable, groups of four posts also held up the antechamber roof. The later houses tend to be squarer and deeper with smaller antechambers and more extensive wing walls. The second pithouse at Site 101 displays the earliest known ventilator tunnel in place of the antechamber. Upright sandstone slabs frequently appear as partial lining for the dirt bank, for wing walls, bin sides, and deflectors. Site 283 had a partially slabbed floor. All pithouses are oriented with their antechambers toward the south. Trash seems to have been scattered in sheets around the houses.

Pottery: Chapin Gray predominates in relatively small vessel forms including seed jars, short-necked jars, and probably bowls. Some bowls are painted with small open designs--Chapin Black-on-white. Fugitive red washes occur on some vessel exteriors. Unfired mud platters and miniatures in unusual shapes have also been found.

Objects of clay: Simple human figurines, nipple-shaped objects, miniature cradle, tubular pipe, "plugs."

Stone: Trough metates made on irregular blocks of sandstone; unificial manos with grinding face convex end to end; concave-surfaced grinding stones; handstones or rubbing stones, occasionally doubling as hammers; polishing stones; full-grooved hammers; hammerstones, often simply unmodified stream pebbles; round stone pot covers; worked sandstone slabs possibly used as covers or even in cooking; scrapers; chipped double-ended drill; chipped knives; stemmed points; utilized flakes; pendants; hematite paint stones; cup-shaped sandstone concretion; unmodified stream pebbles, some of them resembling "floor polishers"; abrading stones; paint pestle.

Bone: Relatively short awls made from split deer elements, especially the metapodials; joint ends are not modified. Perforated deer phalange.

Shell: Oliva shell bead, glycimeris shell button.

Perishables: Wooden scoop of Populus sp.; impressions of coiled baskets on pottery; scallop-toed sandal with double warp.

Economy: Presumably basically agricultural, although the only direct evidence is seen in the corn husks used in roofing Site 107 and charred corn and beans from Site 145. Unworked animal bones found in two of the pithouses may represent objects of the chase: mule deer and turkey. Charred pinyon nuts came from Site 145. There is no definite evidence to indicate domestication of the turkey at any of these sites.

Disposal of the dead: Only five burials can be associated with these sites, four from Site 145 and the one described above from Site 364. Four were flexed and one was

extended on the back; three of the flexed bodies lay partly on
their backs while the fourth was face down. Both preserved
skulls were undeformed. Offerings accompanied the four bodies
facing upwards, including pottery with the extended female from
Site 145 and the flexed male from 364.

Dating: Construction dates have been determined as
follows for most of the structures through dendrochronology:

Site 145, pithouse I	- later than 587
Site 117	- 595
Site 1060	- 608
Site 283	- 612
Site 59 (Pit Structure No. 1)	- later than 626
Site 35, test trench	- 17 dates from 603 to 653
Site 145, pithouse II	- 664
Site 101, first pithouse	- 674
Site 354, (Pit Structure No. 2)	- later than 688
Site 405	- 700

The terminal date of 750 is strictly a guess partly dependent
on the lack of evidence to the contrary.

Pueblo I (Spruce Mesa)

Regional phase: Chapin Mesa.
Time placement: A.D. 750-900.
Sites and/or components: Site 103 (Twin Trees) and
Site 1 Village (O'Bryan 1950; A.S.S. No. 103 has been assigned
to O'Bryan's Site 102 Village) are the only reported excavations to date. A pithouse (Site 353) at Twin Trees was salvage
excavated in 1948 (Lancaster 1968b). There have also been test
excavations at Sites 111 and 786 during the A.S.S. All survey
sites listed in table 2 and quite probably many of those in
table 6 will prove to belong to this phase when excavated.

Site situations: All known house sites are located
along the low ridges of the mesa top.

Architecture: No complete village or cluster of
houses has been dug on Chapin Mesa, although so far all
evidence from surface indications and limited digging suggests
layouts similar to those on Alkali Ridge (Brew 1946: Site 13)
and in the La Plata District (Morris 1939: Site 33). This
would consist of several roughly parallel rows of contiguous
surface rooms with deep pithouses scattered to the south. The
surface rooms are crudely rectangular with walls made out of
wattle-and-daub and apparently plain adobe, often with thin
sandstone slabs set upright at their base. Occasionally roofs

were supported by separate support posts set in the floor near
the four corners. Floors were excavated as much as a foot into
the ground and often contain circular dirt-lined hearths. There
are also outdoor fireplaces. Smaller storerooms may form a
second row behind the larger living quarters. Pithouses (only
two have been completely dug and three others partly dug) are
square in outline with rounded corners, 5 to 7 feet deep and
contain ventilator tunnels, jacal deflectors, wing walls,
circular clay-lined hearths, and various floor pits. The walls
are of earth and the roof, through which entry was effected,
was supported on four posts. A banquette was surely found only
in Site 353. The presence of a sipapu is as yet unknown.
Refuse was generally scattered in a sheet around the houses,
but at least one large trash mound is known.

Pottery: Undecorated Chapin Gray still predominates
in widemouth jar forms, long necked ollas, bowls, and some
exotic forms. Several top coils are frequently unobliterated
in the Moccasin Variety of Chapin Gray producing banded necks.
Chapin Black-on-white persists alongside its successor Piedra
Black-on-white which has bolder designs, polished surfaces,
occasional slipping, and a few more jar forms. Locally-made
red pottery occurs in significant quantities only during this
phase with Abajo Red-on-orange and Bluff Black-on-red.

Objects of clay: Moulded bird head figurine, model
bifurcated basket, sherd disc, tubular pipes, pellets, bead,
burned clay rolls.

Stone: Trough metates made on irregular blocks of
sandstone, uniface manos with grinding face convex end to end,
handstones; smoothing and rubbing stones including "floor
polishers"; polishing stones; abrading stone; full-grooved
hammers; hammerstones, at least some of them pitted; round pot
lids; scrapers; chipped drills; chipped knives; stemmed and
barbed points; utilized flakes; pendants; hematite paint
stones; side-notched axes; galena pebbles; incised (grooved)
pebble; sandstone saw; obsidian core and flake; fossil
gastropod cast.

Bone: mammal-bone awls, eyed needle, spatulas or
spoons.

Perishables: Impressions of coiled baskets on
pottery.

Economy: Also presumably basically agricultural.
Some charred corn cobs were found at Sites 103 and 1 and a
storage room at Site 111 was filled with whole ears and kernels
of corn. Unworked animal bones that apparently represent wild-
food sources include rock squirrel, jack rabbit, cottontail,
and mule deer. Charred pinyon nuts came from Site 103. There

is definite evidence that both turkeys and dogs had been domesticated.

Disposal of the dead: No clearly associated graves have yet been excavated.

Dating: The following tree-ring dates have been derived from various tested and excavated sites:

Site 103   - 25 dates from 804 to 840
                               (16 at 828 to 835).
Site 1 Village   - 9 dates from 814 to 845
                               (5 at 837 to 845).

Because of the very limited chronological data from Chapin Mesa, the time span noted above has been inferred from better known materials in other localities and regions.

Early Pueblo II (Glades)

Regional phase: Mancos Mesa (in part).

Time placement: A.D. 900-1000?

Sites and/or components: Site 102 pueblo (O'Bryan 1950), Site 16 Post-and-adobe village (Lancaster and Pinkley 1954), all survey sites listed in table 5, and probably many of those in table 6. Field house Site 1032.

Site situations: All known house sites are located along the low ridges on the mesa top.

Architecture: No complete village or cluster of houses has been dug either on Chapin Mesa or elsewhere in the Mesa Verde region. Survey distributions would indicate a consistent clustering of perhaps six to eight small, but separate room blocks in much the same manner as the Basket Maker III pithouses. At present it is not known whether each room block had an associated kiva, although the only two excavated units each had one. Ground-surface rooms were built of wattle-and-daub or largely of mud with great numbers of small stones stuck in it. Floors are too poorly preserved to permit notation of floor features. Both excavated kivas are circular, subterranean, earth-lined with stone masonry only where the ground was loose. They contain ventilators, hearths, sipapus, banquettes, and a four-point roof support: in one case upright posts set in the edge of the banquette and in the other low stone-masonry pilasters. Refuse mounds, outdoor fire hearths, and buried corrugated storage jars. One temporary brush shelter is situated apart from the houses.

Pottery: White-slipped decorated pottery of Cortez Black-on-white and Mancos Black-on-white. Corrugated pottery makes its appearance as Mancos Gray and Mesa Verde Corrugated--

Mancos Variety. Chapin Gray persists as does some red ware in Bluff Black-on-red--La Plata Variety. Very little is known about the ceramics of this phase.

Objects of clay: Miniature carrying basket with punctate design, pellets, bob or button.

Stone: Shaped open-end trough metate; flat metate; uniface manos with grinding face convex end to end; uniface mano with flat grinding surface; smoothing handstones and rubbing stones; polishing stones; grooved abrading stones; full-grooved hammer; scrapers; hammerstones; round pot lids; side-notched axes; chipped drills; leaf-shaped knives; stemmed and barbed point; pendants; concretion "cup"; hematite paint stones; fossil.

Bone: Eyed needles; mammal rib awls; splinter awls from mammal bones; split deer metapodial awls; bird bone awls make their first appearance; whole mammal bone awls; flaker; mammal rib scraper; perforated jack rabbit tibia.

Perishables: Impressions of coiled baskets on pottery.

Economy: Presumably basically agricultural. Some charred corn. Unworked animal food bones include deer, jack rabbit, cottontail, squirrel, fox, and turkey. Dogs domesticated.

Disposal of the dead: No clearly associated graves yet excavated.

Dating: Two tree-ring dates of 934 and 947 come from Site 102 Pueblo. The beginning and ending dates for the time placement are strictly guesses based on the estimate for preceding and succeeding phases.

Remarks: This is the poorest known phase in the Chapin Mesa sequence, and much of our knowledge depends on what we know of its predecessors and successors. The survey revealed many early Pueblo II sites, however, so that extensive excavation should be able to alleviate this situation.

Late Pueblo II (Mummy Lake)

Regional phase: Parts of both Mancos Mesa and McElmo.

Time placement: A.D. 1000?-1100.

Sites and/or components: Site 16 Unit Pueblos No. I and II (Lancaster and Pinkley 1954), Site 866 (Lister 1966), Site 809 (Pipe Shrine House) old section, Site 810 pueblo (Far View Tower) (Fewkes 1921, 1923), Site 1 Pueblo (O'Bryan 1950) Site 1914 (Hewett 1968), all survey sites in table 7, and some additional sites in tables 6 and 9.

Site situations: Most house sites are located along low ridges on the mesa top. Several, however, occupy talus slopes, mostly in the northern parts of Little Soda Canyon where broad benches occur, but occasionally beneath cliffs in the deeper canyons toward the south.

Architecture: No complete village or cluster of houses has been excavated. Survey distributions indicate consistent clustering of perhaps six to eight small, but separate blocks of rooms in the same manner as early Pueblo II sites. Kivas accompany several of the units in each cluster. Rooms were built of sandstone masonry walls, one stone thick, occasionally with upright posts. Building stones were generally shaped and dressed by bifacial chipping along both long straight sides. Large thick upright stones (called "megaliths" by Fewkes) formed the base of some walls. Some hearths are present in these rooms. Kivas are still circular, subterranean, partially lined with stone masonry, and contain ventilator, built-in slab deflector, hearth, sipapu, banquette, wall niches, and six masonry pilasters supporting a probable cribbed roof. Shrines, artificial reservoirs, stone check-dams, and field houses were definitely in use. Refuse mounds become more common while outdoor hearths continued in use. At least two specialized ceremonial buildings exist--a kiva-tower unit at Site 1, and towers and kiva at Site 16. One large kiva has eight pilasters and "foot drums." Thick walls and pecked-face stone in ceremonial structures.

Pottery: Mancos Black-on-white dominates all decorated types with nearly equal proportions of bowl and jar forms. Mesa Verde Corrugated--Mancos Variety provided utility ware. Other types occasionally found include Cortez Black-on-white and Chapin Gray--Mummy Lake Variety. A great deal of individual variation and experimentation may be seen in this ceramic complex in the realms of shape, decoration, rim form, paint, and surface treatment. Combinations of normally segregated features, such as black-on-white painting and corrugations, achieve their greatest popularity. Many attributes that become standard in later types were established at this time.

Objects of clay: Bird figurines, pendant, miniature bowl.

Stone: Uniface manos with grinding surface convex end to end; uniface and biface manos with flat grinding surface; smoothing stones; polishing stones; grooved abrader; full-grooved axe; side-notched chipped knife blade; lignite pendant; round stone pot lids; tcamahia; hematite paint stones.

Bone: Tubular beads, disc, perforated jack rabbit

tibias.

Perishables: Impressions of coiled baskets on pottery.

Economy: Presumably basically agricultural--some charred corn and numerous terraced fields. Unworked animal food bones include deer, jack rabbit, cottontail, squirrel, fox, and turkey. Dogs domesticated.

Disposal of the dead: Seventeen associated inhumations exhibit a wide range of burial practices. Bodies were partially flexed or extended and placed on the back, face down, or on the right side. Partial flexing of the knees was most common. Several isolated skulls occur. Offerings of one or two pottery vessels accompany roughly half the burials. Layers of small stones or large pottery sherds covered several of the 14 graves at Site 866 (Lister 1966: 57-59). Cradle-board deformation in the lambdoidal and occipital regions is common (Wade and Armelagos 1966).

Intrusives: Sherds of red wares made in other parts of the Pueblo Southwest occur consistently on these sites and seem to have been prized for the manufacture of pottery pendants. Types represented include Wingate, Puerco, and Tusayan Black-on-reds. In addition Sosi, Dogoszhi, Gallup, Escavada, and Arboles Black-on-whites often occur.

Dating: Two extensive series of dates were derived for two constructions of the Site 1 kiva as follows (O'Bryan 1950):

> 7 dates at 966 to 1014 with probable construc-
> tion at 1014.
> 24 dates at 969 to 1024 with probable construc-
> tion at 1024.

Five dates from Kiva A at Site 866 at 993 to 1060B indicate probable construction in 1060 (Lister 1966: 61). These dates tend to corroborate the estimated time placement based on ceramics, but hardly refine it. Five dates represent a late Pueblo II Component underlying Site 808 (Far View House) at 772 vv, 1039+vv, 1059vv, and 1078vv. At Site 16 Kiva 1, two dates at 1074B probably indicate construction.

Remarks: For the first time, actual occupation of the northern portions of Chapin Mesa takes place both on the mesa top and on benches in the canyon bottoms. These are some of the least desirable agricultural lands and their use may indicate population pressure on the better lands or their partial destruction through erosion.

Early Pueblo III (Far View)

Regional phase: Parts of both McElmo and Montezuma.
Time placement: A.D. 1100-1200.
Sites and/or components: Sites 808 (Far View House)
(Fewkes 1917), Site 809 (Pipe Shrine house)(Fewkes 1923), Site
835 (One Clan House)(Fewkes 1923), Site 119 (Fewkes Unit
Pueblo)(O'Bryan 1950: Appendix E), Site 7 (Sun Point Pueblo)
(Lancaster and Van Cleave 1954), Sites 499 and 875 (Lister 1964
and 1965), Site 810 tower and kivas (Far View Tower)(Fewkes
1921; 1923), Site 790 (Megalithic House)(Fewkes 1923), all
survey sites in table 8, and most of those listed in table 9.
Site situations: Most house sites are located toward
the ends of low distributary ridges on the mesa top which makes
them closer to the rims of the canyons than to the center of
the mesa. Increased numbers occupy situations on the talus
slopes, both at cliff bases in the deeper parts of the canyons
and on the broad benches in the canyon heads near the north
rim. Some cave sites were definitely in use at this time.
Architecture: Complete excavation is not needed to
provide a reasonably clear picture of the clustering of house
sites. In some cases all rooms and kivas were drawn together
into a single structure; in others the pattern seen in the
preceding phase continued; while still others saw several
multiple-kiva sites grouped together. Specialized ceremonial
buildings, such as Far View Tower, seem to be a part of at
least some of these communities. In the great majority of
sites, kivas are wholly or partly enclosed by rooms and walls.
Masonry walls were frequently built two or more stones thick of
sandstone blocks shaped by rough spalling and occasionally
dressed by pecking. Rooms were built in oblong, L-shaped, or
horseshoe arrangements, sometimes two to three stories high.
Kivas are circular, masonry-lined, and have ventilators, built-
in stone-slab or masonry deflectors, hearths, sipapus,
banquettes, southern keyhole recess, wall niches, and usually
six masonry pilasters supporting a probable cribbed roof. Sub-
floor ventilators, of the type common in the Chaco Canyon, were
found in several kivas, but they had usually been replaced by
more typical vents. Elongated floor cists or "foot drums" were
found in the larger kivas. Retaining walls outlining probable
plazas, flights of steps, and refuse mounds are all common.
Shrines, artificial reservoirs, stone check-dams, and field
houses are present. Outdoor hearths continued in use.
Pottery: Almost all utility pottery is corrugated
with a transition in shape taking place from Mancos Variety to
Mesa Verde Variety of Mesa Verde Corrugated (bell-shaped to

egg-shaped jars). In the decorated types, organic paint begins to replace mineral paint as Mesa Verde Black-on-white, particularly McElmo Variety appears, but a fair amount of the Mancos Black-on-white also sport organic pigments. Chapin Gray--Mummy Lake Variety dies out during this period. Mugs tend to replace pitchers, kiva jars supplant seed jars, but bowls, ollas, dippers, and canteens continue unchanged.

Objects of clay: Tublar pipes, stem and bowl pipes.

Stone: Flat-surfaced metates; uniface and biface manos with flat grinding surfaces end to end; mortars; pestles; rubbing stones; abraders; paint-stained slabs; full-grooved hammers; pitted hand hammers; hammerstones; full-grooved axes; waterworn pebbles; chipped knives; small side-notched triangular points; animal figurines; fossils; concretions.

Bone: Awls of mammal and bird bones, eyed and splinter awls, eyed needles, tubular beads.

Economy: Presumably basically agricultural supported by numerous evidences of farming terraces. Unworked animal food bones include turkey, rabbit, deer, antelope, mountain sheep, elk, ground squirrel, and wood rat.

Disposal of the dead: Unknown numbers of inhumations have been disinterred from the refuse heaps and rooms of excavated sites, but about all that can be gleaned from the published reports indicates that both flexed and extended positions were common. Evidence of the reburial of bodies encountered in new construction has turned up several times (e.g., Lister 1965: 13-19). Grave offerings including pottery were encountered to an unknown degree. Lambdoidal skull deformation is reported for at least some skulls.

Intrusives: Sherds of the following foreign pottery types have been identified: Sosi Black-on-white, Gallup Black-on-white, Chaco Black-on-white, Tusayan Polychrome, Tusayan Black-on-red, Houck-Querino Polychrome, Wingate Black-on-red.

Dating: A few scattered tree-ring dates tend to corroborate the estimates, but pose many questions.

```
          Site 875     - 10 dates at 793vv to 987vv;
                          1 date at 1047c
          Site 119     -  2 dates at 1181 and 1190
          Site 499     -  3 dates at 822, 915v, and 1123B
          Site 809 kiva -  2 dates at 898+ and 1214+
```

Probably all pre-1000 dates can be ignored as re-used timbers even through this eliminates 13 of 18 dates. Since Site 809 (Pipe Shrine House) stands on the mesa top, the date of 1214 would suggest that the shift to cave situations during the thirteenth century was either not complete or extended throughout the period.

Remarks: Although it lies outside the bounds of intensive survey on Chapin Mesa and has therefore been excluded from this sequence discussion, Site 34 (O'Bryan 1950) probably belongs with the Chapin Mesa communities and sequence. O'Bryan's published report adds considerable detail to the picture given above.

Late Pueblo III (Cliff Palace)

Regional phase: Montezuma (in part).
Time placement: A.D. 1200-1300.
Sites and/or components: Site 640 (Spruce Tree House)(Fewkes 1909), Site 625 (Cliff Palace)(Fewkes 1911), Site 650 (Square Tower House)(Fewkes 1920), Site 523 (Oak Tree House)(Fewkes 1916a), Site 524 (Mummy House)(Fewkes 1922), Site 522 (New Fire House)(Fewkes 1921), Site 557 (Painted Kiva House)(Nordenskiöld 1893; Fewkes 1922), Sites 520-521 (Fire Temple and Fire Temple Annex)(Fewkes 1921 and 1916a; Cassidy 1960), Site 352 (Sun Temple)(Fewkes 1916b), Site 397 (Cedar Tree Tower)(Fewkes 1921), all survey sites in table 10, and perhaps some remnant occupations in mesa-top pueblos such as Far View House (808) and Pipe Shrine House (809).
Site situations: Almost all house sites are located in shallow rock shelters along the vertical sandstone cliffs near the tops of the canyons. Possibly some mesa-top pueblos were still occupied. Several ceremonial sites occupy mesa-top situations.
Architecture: House sites cluster in groups ranging in size from less than half a dozen small sites to 20 or more ruins that include several quite large structures. The agglomeration of habitation units continued producing more and larger multiple-kiva sites, but the majority of sites still retain one kiva or none. There seems to be less standardization in size and arrangement than in the preceding phase, probably because of space limitations in the caves. Both single and double-coursed masonry walls were built of spalled and often pecked-face sandstone blocks. Buildings stand as high as four stories and either utilized the natural cave roof or were capped with a plain lintel-style roof of wood and earth. Small rectangular or T-shaped doorways, ventilation openings, wallpegs, and hearths characterize the room features. Kivas are circular, subterranean, and masonry-lined, with ventilator, recess, built-in masonry or stone-slab deflector, hearth, sipapu, wall niches, banquette, and usually six masonry pilasters supporting a cribbed roof. None of these characteristics, however, except

perhaps the hearth and ventilator, is seen in every kiva. Some are rectangular, some are built above ground, and any of the various features may be absent. Outdoor hearths are seen in the open courtyards. Refuse was scattered down the talus slopes beneath the ruins. Shrines, specialized buildings of exceptionally fine masonry, artificial reservoirs, ditches, check-dams, and field houses are all known to have been used.

Pottery: The distinctive Mesa Verde Variety of Mesa Verde Black-on-white is the characteristic decorated pottery, although consistent amounts of McElmo Variety are always present. Bowl forms markedly outnumber jar forms. Bowls, dippers, mugs, canteens, kiva jars, and ollas are the common shapes. All utility pottery is Mesa Verde Corrugated--Mesa Verde Variety. There is far less evidence of experimentation and a great deal of standardization.

Objects of clay: Pot lids.

Stone: Flat-surfaced metates; uniface and biface manos with grinding surfaces flat or concave end to end; mortars; small paint pestles; paint-stained slabs; polishing stones; full-grooved and side-notched axes hafted by bending a supple stick twice around the groove and tying the ends together; full-grooved hammers; pitted hand hammers; hammerstones; tcamahias; ground tablets, some in a crude sandal shape; chipped knives; small triangular side-notched points; hematite paint stones; round sandstone pot lids; "corn mounds"; flake drills; lapstones (anvils); buttons, beads, and pendants made from lignite, red shale, and rarely turquoise.

Bone: Humerus scrapers, awls of mammal and bird bones, eyed needles, splinter awls, tubular beads, human figurines, weaving tools, spatulas.

Perishables: Board cradles, wooden spindles and whorls, wooden planting sticks, reed arrows with wood foreshafts, wooden fire drills and hearths, wooden bow, wooden batten sticks, loom rods, prayer sticks, snowshoes, coiled baskets, twilled yucca ring baskets, woven yucca head rests for pots, yucca strip pot rests, hairbrushes, willow withe mats, reed mats, turkey feather blankets, twilled sandals, woven headbands and belts, yucca cordage, leather pouches, wooden hoops, leather moccasins, plaited rush mats, feather wands or headdress, cotton cloth, netting, hickory nut bead.

Economy: Agriculture is clearly indicated by the quantities of all parts of the corn plant, beans, squash, and gourds. Unworked animal food bones include turkey, and probably various mammals, although these are unreported. Accumulations of matted dung indicate turkeys at least were domesticated.

Disposal of the dead: Flexed and extended inhumation

in refuse heaps and in rooms. Evidence of cremation is mentioned by two writers (Nordenskiöld 1893 and Fewkes 1911) but has not been substantiated by more recent work. Mortuary offerings include pottery vessels.

      Intrusives: Sherds of Chaco Black-on-white.

      Dating: The following tree-ring dates provide the most thorough dating for any phase:

      Site 640 - 25 dates at 1020 to 1274 (1 at 1203, 23 at 1230 to 1274); 5 dates at 1038 to 1248 (4 at 1223 to 1248)

      Site 625 - 8 dates at 1210 to 1273 (5 at 1264 to 1273)

      Site 615 - 4 dates at 1190, 1204, 1206, and 1272; 6 dates at 1096, 1128, 1206, 1210, 1279, and 1282

      Site 522 - 2 dates at 1259 and 1260; 2 dates at 1153 and 1263

      Site 523 - 2 dates at 1119vv and 1184c; 3 dates at 1055, 1064, and 1115

      Site 557 - 3 dates at 1199, 1202, and 1271

      Site 650 - 5 dates at 1181+, 1241, 1242, 1243, and 1246; 14 dates at 1114 to 1260 (6 at 1184 to 1223, 5 at 1243 to 1260)

      Site 634 - 2 dates at 1236 and 1252

      Site 538 - 2 dates at 1240 and 1244

      Site 514 - 6 dates at 1013, 1025, 1053, 1176, 1207 and 1208

      Site 515 - 3 dates at 1138, 1178, and 1194

Most of the pre-1200 dates can probably be attributed to re-used timbers, although the consistent occurrence of late 1100 dates suggests a beginning for this phase around 1180 or 1190 or possibly some overlap with the preceding phase. It is also possible that the earlier dates in Sites 523, 514, and 515 indicate earlier occupations there that have been overlain by or obliterated by later use.

      Remarks: A composite view of both Pueblo III phases is presented in Rohn 1963a, although there are many gaps due to abbreviated reporting on many of the excavated sites.

Discussion

      Many of the sites listed under the preceding six local phase descriptions have been used as examples to illustrate various phases described by other authors for the entire Mesa Verde region. It should be possible then to state

rough equivalents between some of these phases and the ones
just described for Chapin Mesa. For one reason or another,
they cannot be considered exactly equal, but the following
notes should permit anyone who is interested to evaluate for
himself the relationships among them.

Basket Maker III on Chapin Mesa most clearly
resembles O'Bryan's (1950) Four Corners Phase and Hayes' (1964)
La Plata Phase, while Reed (1958) would probably include it in
his La Plata Focus. However, the three emphasize different
sites in different districts and apparently are not intended
merely as different names for the same manifestations.

Pueblo I fits well with O'Bryan's Chapin Mesa Phase
and Hayes' Piedra Phase, and it is quite similar to Reed's
Piedra Focus and Brew's (1946) Abajo Phase or Focus. Pottery
typical of both these last two is found on Chapin Mesa where it
was probably locally made.

Early Pueblo II corresponds to Hayes' Ackmen Phase
and possibly the Ackmen Focus named by Brew. O'Bryan and Reed
would probably have included this group in their Mancos Mesa
Phase and Mancos Focus, respectively.

Late Pueblo II would also be placed in the Mancos
Mesa Phase and Mancos Focus by their formulators and in Hayes'
Mancos Phase. Brew's description of a Mancos Focus perhaps
comes closest to the Chapin Mesa material.

Early Pueblo III corresponds best to O'Bryan's and
Hayes' McElmo Phase. Reed and Brew have both preferred to
bypass a separate unit here, including material like that found
on Chapin Mesa in either the preceding or succeeding foci.

Late Pueblo III would be called Montezuma Phase by
O'Bryan, Mesa Verde Phase by Hayes, and Mesa Verde Focus by
Reed. The well-known cliff dwellings that comprise over nine-
tenths of the Chapin Mesa Late Pueblo III Phase sites represent
only one aspect in two of these descriptions, however.

Twentieth-century Navaho sites have been recorded on
Chapin Mesa, but they would properly belong to the modern
American phase of development of the Mesa Verde as a national
park.

VII

SIGNIFICANT CONTINUITIES AND CHANGES

A proper examination of cultural change through time should cover both those aspects of culture that change and those that continue with little or no change. Actually, both change and continuity can be seen in most cultural features between succeeding phases. The distinction between these two processes rests heavily on the point of view of the culture historian who is attacking the problem. If he is trying to define a temporal sequence, the difference between phases or periods will be emphasized. On the other hand a person trying to trace the history of a group or a technique looks for continuities. I need not belabor the point here that many have overemphasized one or the other in an unwarranted manner to foster preconceived notions or to criticize the work of others.

If we are to evaluate or interpret change and continuity, it is essential to recognize the many ways in which these processes may be viewed, and how different views can affect the final interpretations. Generally, we try to determine: How much change took place? What kind of change was it? What changed? When did the change take place? and Why?

Degree of change on any level of complexity can be measured on a linear scale ranging between absolute change and absolute continuity. Absolute change refers to presence versus absence and includes both the first appearances and the complete disappearance of specific traits. When an aspect shows no change so that it is indistinguishable from one phase to the next, there is absolute continuity. It is easy to see that the vast majority of changes would fall somewhere between these two poles.

The description of what changed would seem to be self-evident from the data themselves, but things are not really so simple. Let us assume for example that the decorated pottery in a hypothetical period 2 differs from the decorated pottery of period 1 in temper, technique of applying the decoration, and in design. Each of these attributes can be treated as separate "whats," or they can be combined to define a change in pottery types. Taken together with all other pottery from the two periods, it is possible to talk of a ceramic

change. From another view, we might ask whether the tempering
change represents a new preference for materials, a new source
of temper, or a change in the procedure of preparing the temper
material.

Furthermore, any measurement of the degree of change
can only apply to the unit that has been specifically
described--an attribute, trait, trait complex, or other unit.
An absolute change in one detail might represent only a partial
change in an attribute which in turn does not seriously alter
the basic continuity in decorated pottery. Should the appropriate attributes change enough, it is possible to note an
absolute change in pottery types, even though the one type gave
rise to its successor.

The kinds of changes may be organized under various
groupings. One could distinguish between qualitative change--in
form, technology, aesthetics, etc.--and quantitative change--
absolute or relative increase or decrease in occurrence. The
only significance in these distinctions lies in the realm of
comparison where different weight should be applied to different kinds of change. Of course, change may be both
qualitative and quantitative and often is.

Change itself is a continuing process, so that any
statement concerning when a given change takes place must
depend heavily on the ultimate goal of the culture historian.
Many changes are said to occur within a certain cultural phase
or stage. Frequently the student of chronology actually
describes change in terms of differences between two successive
phases or periods, usually because it is impossible to control
the necessary data more precisely. Unusual preservation,
absolute dating methods, a great mass of data, or a combination
of these are necessary to place the time of a specific change
more closely.

Why a change took place, of course, goes far beyond
analysis of the change itself. Understanding why certain events
took place in the past, why one culture differs from another,
and what processes may have been operating is one of the primary goals for the prehistorian. The "why" of culture change
may not then be satisfactorily explained except as a part of
this larger picture.

I do not propose any objective measures for these
various aspects of change, but I do feel that no analysis of
change can safely overlook them. Descriptions of the cultural
sequence for the Mesa Verde have so far emphasized the differences from one phase to the next (O'Bryan 1950; Watson 1954;
Hayes 1964). I plan to concentrate on continuities within the

Chapin Mesa sequence   and   to balance these   against   the discontinuities.

Site Situations

            Basket Maker III pithouses are found near the center
of   the   mesa   top   on high   ground   formed by the low drainage
divides that separate runoff between canyons.   Usually   primary
ridges   were   chosen, although some   major distributary   ridges
also have pithouses.   Cultivable land was immediately available
all   around them, but   water   sources lay one-half mile or more
distant   in   the   canyons. Building   materials--loessic earth,
timber,   and brush--were all   readily   available.   The mesa-top
soil was also well suited to the excavation of an unlined lower
portion of a pithouse.
            Although the number of buildings and people   steadily
increased, this pattern of preferred   house   location continued
virtually unchanged through Pueblo I, early Pueblo II, and late
Pueblo II.   There was increasing use of distributary   ridges as
time progressed.   This brought some late Pueblo II houses relatively close to the canyon rims, where a much larger proportion
of early Pueblo III houses are found.
            Some use of   rock   shelters is   definitely   known   as
early as Basket Maker III in Wetherill Mesa   sites, and   it may
be suspected on Chapin Mesa from the articles   found   in Spruce
Tree   House   and   other   cave sites.   But there   is no definite
evidence   yet   of   houses   in Chapin Mesa canyons prior to late
Pueblo II.   In that phase several talus sites appear, and   some
shelters may also have been in use.   Again proportions of   this
kind of site situation rise rapidly   in early Pueblo III, until
the nearly   total   occupation   of   cave   locations by   the   late
Pueblo III peoples.
            Most cliff-dwelling and canyon   sites were relatively
nearer water   sources   than their   predecessors, but of   course
they lay farther from their fields.   They were   more   difficult
of   access and   thus   more defensible.   Good building stone was
easily available, but earth for mortar often   had to be   hauled
from   the   mesa top.   Shelter   size and shape, and the frequent
lack of sufficient loose material on the cave floor in which to
excavate for kivas, greatly hampered what building patterns the
Pueblo   III Mesa Verdeans had   developed.   There   can be little
doubt   that   people occupied the   cliff sites   for   reasons   of
defense rather   than   out of   free choice   or   for   reasons   of
comfort.

Architecture

Changes in architecture provide some of the major criteria for differentiating between phases, yet there are many important continuities. Perhaps the most significant is the perpetuation of the Basket Maker III pithouse as the kiva in the later Pueblo phases. Many changes in individual characteristics took place during this development, but the overall structure retained a basic identity throughout.

The partially subterranean pithouse of Basket Maker III becomes a totally subterranean structure in Pueblo I and remains such until environmental limitations of shallow deposits in many late Pueblo III cave locations forced the construction of some kivas above ground. Patches of stone-masonry lining first appear in early Pueblo II to retain sections of loose earth. Kivas completely lined with stone masonry and sporting wall niches became the standard by early Pueblo III, although occasional earth lining still persisted (Lancaster and Van Cleave 1954). Complete masonry-lined kivas characterize all cave and talus sites.

Although the need to hold back patches of loose earth may have prompted the use of stone-masonry lining for kivas, and the loose fill of cave floors and talus slopes required such a retainer, masonry linings achieved popularity in mesa-top soil that could stand vertically unassisted. Thus we can assume that late Pueblo III kivas would have been lined with stone masonry, even if there had not been a pressing need for it.

As pithouses became deeper in late Basket Maker III, the antechamber entranceway degenerated into a ventilator that persisted throughout the rest of the sequence. The opening tended to grow smaller and took on a masonry lining together with the rest of the kiva.

Deflectors, centrally-located circular hearths, sipapus, and banquettes occur from start to finish in the Chapin Mesa sequence. Upright sandstone slabs, set in the floor, give way to stub walls of masonry in early Pueblo III, but never completely disappear. Post-and-adobe deflectors and movable sandstone slabs appear sporadically from Pueblo I through late Pueblo III and probably represent individual experimentation.

Hearths changed least of any trait. They remained circular, mud-lined, and located near the center of the floor. Occasional rectangular slab-lined firepits are found in Pueblo II and early Pueblo III, and ashpits appear in some Pueblo I and Pueblo II structures. When present, sipapus usually had a

clay lining, but necks of broken jars are found in a number of
late Pueblo III examples. Where kivas were dug down to bedrock
in some cliff dwellings, sipapus were often cut into the
sandstone.

Banquettes changed markedly in function, from support
for the sloping side walls of the Basket Maker III pithouse to
the storage shelf and base on which pilasters stood in later
kivas, but they persisted. The functional change probably took
place between early Pueblo I and early Pueblo II when the pithouse became wholly subterranean. There appears to be a
decline in frequency of banquettes in Pueblo I pithouses
(Bullard 1962: 146; O'Bryan 1950: 106). However, banquettes
quickly returned to favor when roof supports were built on
them.

Enlargement of that part of the banquette above the
ventilator into a recess, producing a sort of keyhole shape in
the ground plan, took place in early Pueblo III, but it never
became universal, possibly because of space limitations in the
cliff dwellings. Antechambers or ventilators always faced
toward the south or southeast except where restricted by cave
situations.

These many continuities in the architecture of pithouses and kivas bespeak a strong conservatism in religious
concepts. What changes do take place seem to represent mere
elaboration and sophistication on a basic theme. The sharpest
changes appear at the transition from Pueblo I to early Pueblo
II, when wing walls disappear and a trend toward squarish
shape--possibly without a banquette--yields to circular shape
with banquette. At this time roof supports migrate to the
banquette and stone masonry makes its appearance in some lining
walls. These changes may mark the shift from a structure that
functioned primarily as a dwelling to one with a ceremonial
focus.

Methods of roof support changed considerably,
although there is no evidence that actual roof construction
altered at all. Four posts in the floor gave way successively
to four posts set in the banquette, to four low masonry
pilasters on the banquette, to six and sometimes eight
pilasters (Lancaster and Pinkley 1954: 55-57). Six or more
pilasters denote a cribbing beneath the actual roof. This
complete change takes place from late Pueblo I through late
Pueblo II. Some late Pueblo III kiva roofs rested directly on
the masonry lining wall, even though pilasters were also
present.

Domestic architecture followed a separate line of
development from structures built on the ground surface to

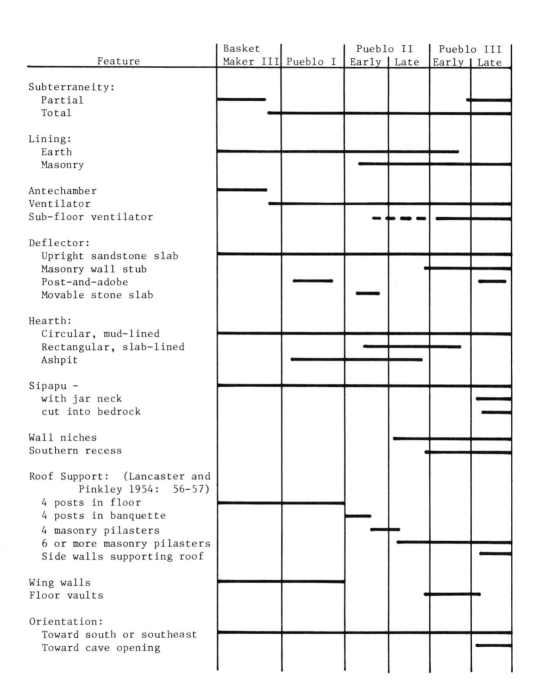

Figure 85.   Pithouse-Kiva Architecture.

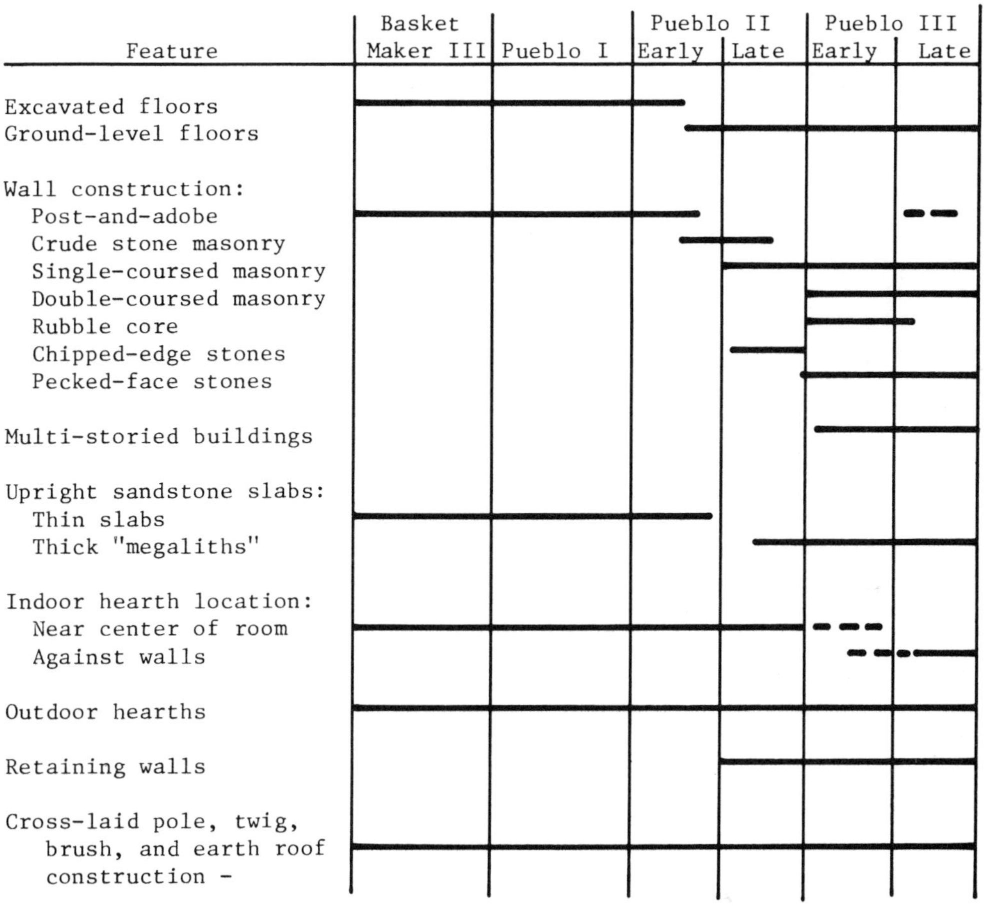

Feature	Basket Maker III	Pueblo I	Pueblo II Early	Pueblo II Late	Pueblo III Early	Pueblo III Late
Excavated floors	▬▬▬▬▬▬▬					
Ground-level floors				▬▬▬▬▬▬▬▬▬		
Wall construction:						
Post-and-adobe	▬▬▬▬▬▬					▬ ▬
Crude stone masonry			▬▬▬▬			
Single-coursed masonry				▬▬▬▬▬▬▬▬		
Double-coursed masonry					▬▬▬▬	
Rubble core					▬▬▬	
Chipped-edge stones				▬▬▬		
Pecked-face stones					▬▬▬▬▬▬▬▬	
Multi-storied buildings					▬▬▬▬▬▬	
Upright sandstone slabs:						
Thin slabs	▬▬▬▬▬▬▬▬▬▬					
Thick "megaliths"				▬▬▬▬		
Indoor hearth location:						
Near center of room	▬▬▬▬▬▬▬▬▬▬▬▬▬				▬ ▬▬	
Against walls	▬▬▬▬▬▬▬▬▬▬▬▬▬▬				▬ ▬▬▪	
Outdoor hearths	▬▬▬▬▬▬▬▬▬▬▬▬▬▬					
Retaining walls				▬▬▬▬▬▬▬▬▬		
Cross-laid pole, twig, brush, and earth roof construction –	▬▬▬▬▬▬▬▬▬▬▬▬▬▬					

Figure 86. Domestic Architecture.

supplement the Pueblo I pithouse. At first, floors were excavated slightly below the ground surface, but in early Pueblo II
they began to rest at ground level. Post-and-adobe walls
characterized Pueblo I and early Pueblo II houses, but contained increasing quantities of stone until true coursed
masonry, one stone thick, replaced jacal in late Pueblo II.
These early building stones were shaped by bifacial chipping.
Pecked-face stones in both single and double-coursed walls
supplanted these in early Pueblo III.

Multiple-storied buildings and some rubble-cored
walls also appear then. Sandstone-spall chinking characterizes
masonry walls from late Pueblo II through late Pueblo III. We
may note that the movement into cliff-dwelling sites occasioned
no significant changes in architecture other than the forced
adaptation to the cramped quarters in the shelters. One jacal
wall is known from the late Pueblo III Site 523, Oak Tree House
(Fewkes 1916a: 105-106). Apparently, roof construction
remained unchanged throughout the sequence. Retaining walls
made their appearance in late Pueblo II sites on the mesa top
and talus slopes.

Upright sandstone slabs in wall construction follow a
continuous distribution through the Chapin Mesa sequence. They
begin as supports set against earth linings in some Basket
Maker III pithouses, continue in the bases of Pueblo I and
early Pueblo II jacal walls, and even are incorporated into the
bases of some incipient masonry walls. By late Pueblo II,
heavy, thick upright stones (called "megaliths" by Fewkes 1923:
110) formed the bases of some masonry walls on the northern
part of Chapin Mesa. "Megaliths" persisted in small numbers
into the cliff dwellings.

Differentiation between living and storage rooms
appears early in Pueblo I and continues through the rest of the
sequence. Outdoor fire places are found in all phases, although
they became more sheltered in courtyards during Pueblo III.
Indoor hearths move from roughly central positions to side-wall
or corner positions with the development of masonry walls in
late Pueblo II.

The building of separate specialized structures other
than kivas, probably for ceremonial reasons, is definitely a
characteristic of late Pueblo II with Site 1 pueblo (O'Bryan
1950) and early Pueblo III. This continues, apparently gaining
in elaboration, into late Pueblo III with buildings like Cedar
Tree Tower and Sun Temple (Fewkes 1921; 1916b). We must not
overlook, though, the possibility of earlier beginnings represented by the large Basket Maker III pit structure (Site 60),
only partly excavated near Twin Trees (Jennings 1968). Too

little is known of the earlier Chapin Mesa phases to permit further speculation.

Round towers follow the same pattern as the special-ized ceremonial buildings. Often towers form a part of them. Many habitation sites of early and late Pueblo III also contain towers, although they probably satisfied ceremonial purposes.

Graphic representation of these continuities is attempted in figures 85 and 86. Only a crude picture can be created in this manner, but it should help in visualizing the longevity of numerous architectural features. I have purposely selected traits for which we have reasonably good information. Actually, a complete listing of all architectural traits would probably look much the same. Do not forget, though, that redefinition of any one feature would alter its apparent life history.

Ceramics

Basic techniques of pottery making change little or not at all through the entire sequence. Vessels were formed and shaped by coiling and scraping from clays apparently derived from shales in the Mesaverde Formation. Except for the relatively few red vessels made during Pueblo I and early Pueblo II, and ignoring periodic accidents, pottery was fired without free access to oxygen.

Choice of tempering material changed in several ways. Crushed rock, mostly igneous and metamorphic rocks from old Mancos River gravels, is found in every pottery type and in every phase. It predominates in plain and corrugated pottery from start to finish. Traces of crushed sandstone and sand appear occasionally, most often in Basket Maker III, and some late corrugated pieces contain sherd temper. This same pattern holds for the red types, and for Chapin and Piedra Black-on-whites. Crushed sherd temper first appears in early Pueblo II Cortez Black-on-white, and gradually increases in popularity, but never entirely replaces rock. Crushed rock occurs in 24% of Mesa Verde Black-on-white--Mesa Verde Variety sherds.

Vessel shapes tend to proliferate through time. Bowls, usually decorated, are found in all phases although they increase in popularity from early to late. Dippers appear in Pueblo I with trough-shaped handles that give the appearance of a scoop to the vessel. In successive phases, dippers assume a significant place among black-on-white shapes and develop solid and tubular handles that are fastened to the bowl exteriors. As these new handle styles evolved, several kinds were always in use at one time.

The many lines of jar development present a most complex picture. There were two main kinds of jar, neither one decorated, made during Basket Maker III: the seed jar without a neck and the wide-mouth jar with a short neck. Pueblo I potters began to decorate seed jars, which thereafter appeared among the decorated pottery types. During early Pueblo III, low raised rims were added around the mouth to contain a lid, and the seed jar became a kiva jar. By late Pueblo III, the kiva jar shape had supplanted the older seed jar.

Necked jars may have originated out of the Basket Maker III plain seed jars. In Pueblo I, necks were made taller and a dichotomy between wide-mouth and narrow-mouth jars arose. Frequently, the last coils added to the neck were not obliterated on the exterior. Separation between body and neck on wide-mouth jars became less evident in early Pueblo II as the overall jar profile was smoothed out. One further change took place during the transition from Pueblo II to Pueblo III as the orifice grew smaller in proportion to the maximum diameter, producing a rough egg shape.

Narrow-mouth jars--ollas or water jars--joined the black-on-white painted ware in early Pueblo II and then remained essentially unchanged through late Pueblo III. Canteens may have developed as smaller water jars or out of the many exotic shapes that began to appear in Pueblo I, probably because of a great deal of individual experimentation. Pitchers also appear first in Pueblo I and continue as an important shape among the decorated types into early Pueblo III. During this phase, mugs began to replace pitchers. Since a mug is essentially a pitcher without the expanded lower body, this is not a particularly significant change.

Rim profiles are closely related to shape. Changes in rims are best studied as a reflection of total shape change--as seed jar to kiva jar--or as variations on a vessel shape of long endurance, such as the bowl. Throughout most of the Chapin Mesa sequence, bowl side walls tapered toward a narrow, rounded lip. As vessel walls began to thicken during late Pueblo II and early Pueblo III, some bowl walls rose straight to broad rounded lips, and ultimately to the flattened lips that predominated in late Pueblo III. Beveled lips, similar to those frequently found on bowls from the Kayenta region, occur rarely during Pueblo III.

There are so many gradations of smoothing on vessel surfaces, that it is difficult to distinguish between degrees of smoothness. We may note, though, that the practice of polishing appears in Basket Maker III and tends to increase both in frequency and quality to the characteristically fine polish on Mesa Verde Black-on-white. Rough, unsmoothed surfaces continue on some pottery, however, from Basket Maker III into early Pueblo III. Slipped surfaces on decorated pottery first appear in late Pueblo I, but assume a majority role in early Pueblo II. Unslipped surfaces, though, may be seen on sherds and vessels of every decorated pottery type and in every phase.

The practice of leaving several construction coils showing on the necks of unpainted vessels appears in Pueblo I. Coil width decreases until by early Pueblo II it becomes true corrugation, with coils built up spirally, rather than concentrically, and with finger indentations. Corrugated pottery accounts for a major proportion of all Pueblo II and Pueblo III ceramic assemblages, and corrugation sometimes is found on parts of decorated vessels. Corrugated exteriors on black-on-white bowls first show up in early Pueblo II, reach their peak of popularity in late Pueblo II, and die out during early Pueblo III. Corrugated necks on black-on-white ollas seem to increase in favor slightly from late Pueblo II into late Pueblo III. Tooling occurs rarely, but most often in Pueblo I and early Pueblo II.

Glaze paint appears only on a few Chapin and Piedra Black-on-white sherds during Basket Maker III and Pueblo I. Mineral matte paint and organic paint vary considerably in relative proportion, but both are found on every black-on-white pottery type in every phase. In Basket Maker III, mineral pigment outnumbers organic pigment by two to one. Nearly exclusive use of mineral paint characterizes Pueblo I and Pueblo II black-on-white pottery, until organic pigment again begins to rise in popularity toward the end of late Pueblo II, and begins to replace mineral substances as the predominant pigment on early and late Pueblo III vessels. Throughout the sequence, mineral pigments were applied in an organic vehicle. Consequently, the addition of powdered minerals to a basic organic mixture represents the only real differences between the two kinds of paint.

Aspects of design are very susceptible to change because they answer only to cultural controls. Furthermore, design has so many variables that a great many pages could be filled by an exhaustive consideration of all of them. I shall limit my comments to a few representative features.

Primary fields of decoration remain essentially the same in all phases. On bowls, for example, the interiors carry the main decoration, particularly on the nearly vertical side walls. Other fields, such as the exterior side walls, rims, and bottom interiors, may be decorated too, but always with

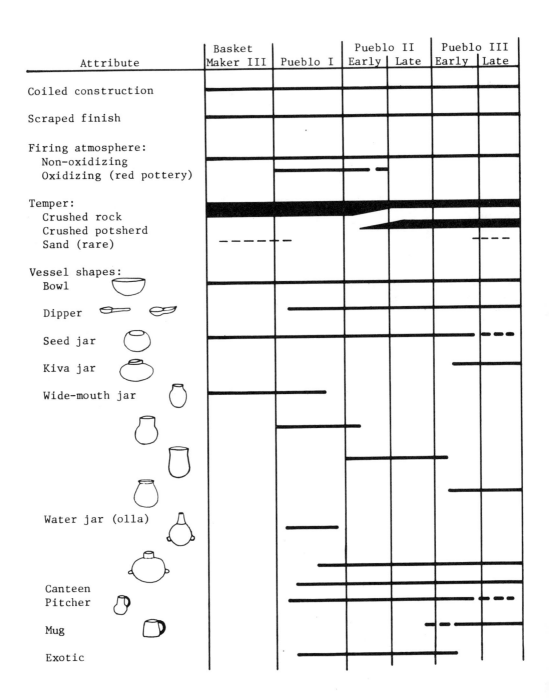

Figure 87. Some Ceramic Attributes - I.

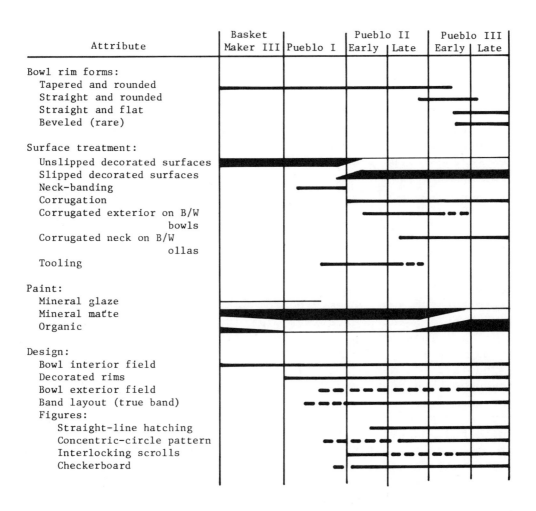

Attribute	Basket Maker III	Pueblo I	Pueblo II		Pueblo III	
			Early	Late	Early	Late
Bowl rim forms:						
Tapered and rounded						
Straight and rounded						
Straight and flat						
Beveled (rare)						
Surface treatment:						
Unslipped decorated surfaces						
Slipped decorated surfaces						
Neck-banding						
Corrugation						
Corrugated exterior on B/W bowls						
Corrugated neck on B/W ollas						
Tooling						
Paint:						
Mineral glaze						
Mineral matte						
Organic						
Design:						
Bowl interior field						
Decorated rims						
Bowl exterior field						
Band layout (true band)						
Figures:						
Straight-line hatching						
Concentric-circle pattern						
Interlocking scrolls						
Checkerboard						

Figure 88.   Some Ceramic Attributes - II.

fewer obvious conventional restrictions than the main design.
Rim decoration becomes common in Pueblo I, begins to elaborate
with the appearance of rim ticking in late Pueblo II, and
appears in wide variety during Pueblo III. Exterior bowl
decoration is found only rarely from Pueblo I through late
Pueblo II, but becomes the predominant practice by late Pueblo
III.

True band layout on bowl interiors occurs rarely
prior to early Pueblo II, but becomes common, actually the
accepted form, from early Pueblo II through late Pueblo III.
It reaches its peak popularity in late Pueblo II and shifts
from a filler for motifs to a background filler in Pueblo III.
Designs made up of series of concentric circles parallel to the
rim appear in late Pueblo II and increase in popularity and
elaboration into late Pueblo III. Interlocking scrolls are
virtually diagnostic of early Pueblo II, are found very rarely
in late Pueblo II and early Pueblo III, but enjoy a minor
resurgence in late Pueblo III. There is little difficulty,
however, in distinguishing between interlocking scrolls of the
different phases. Checkerboard makes its first appearance in
late Pueblo I and occurs regularly in all succeeding phases.

These examples should suffice to illustrate a number
of major points. The foregoing pottery type descriptions have
emphasized the discontinuities between types and how continuing
features have been used differently from one type to the next.
For example, whether or not a bowl rim bears a solid-painted
stripe helps to distinguish between Pueblo I Piedra Black-on-
white and Basket Maker III Chapin Black-on-white. Replacement
of the solid stripe by rim ticking aids in the separation of
Mancos and Mesa Verde Black-on-white, and the great elaboration
of ticked-rim patterns is a hallmark of the Mesa Verde Variety
of the latter type. Thus consideration of bowl rims as a field
of decoration has greater continuity than either of the chief
forms of rim decoration--solid stripe or ticking (dots). Either
of these can be considered separate traits as can the varieties
of rim ticking.

The concentric circle pattern actually first appears
on a few Pueblo I bowls and is quite common in early Pueblo II,
but not as circles drawn with smooth lines. Wavy lines, sometimes smooth lines marked with short dashes at right angles,
were drawn instead. In late Pueblo II and most of Pueblo III,
series of broad lines, all nearly equal in width, were drawn.
Late Pueblo III saw many combinations of narrow and broad
lines, sometimes with secondary elaborations in dot patterns.
Thus, the design tradition of concentric circles beneath the
rim is a long one, but the manner in which the lines were drawn

and the manner in which they were combined changed frequently.

Whether we talk of change or of continuity, then, depends entirely on our choice of traits and on how we limit the definitions of those traits. It is customary to point to the sharp changes that occurred between Pueblo II and Pueblo III black-on-white pottery in Mesa Verde (O'Bryan 1950; Abel 1955) and suggest that strong outside influences are responsible. There are many changes, but perhaps as many or more continuities. In addition, many of the so-called "new" features have antecedents in the Mesa Verde. For the ceramic charts, I have chosen some of the features that clearly cut across this "break" to demonstrate how change may be selectively interpreted as a strong continuum or as a sharp break (figs. 87 and 88).

Stone Artifacts

On the whole, stone artifacts reflect far less change than do ceramics. Many tool types, such as hammerstones, choppers, scrapers, utilized flakes, grooved hammers, grinding stones, abraders, rubbing stones, polishing stones, chipped knives, worked slabs, jar lids, and so forth show no real differences at any time. Others undergo one or two significant changes only. For example, the closed-end trough metates of Basket Maker III persist into early Pueblo II when they begin to change into the flat-topped or slab metate of very late Pueblo II and Pueblo III, passing through an intermediate form where the trough is shallow and open at both ends. Manos reflect this same shift.

Projectile points show two major shifts in style from Basket Maker III through late Pueblo III. The change between Basket Maker III and Pueblo I saw a decrease in weight, an overall elongation and thinning, and the development of long tapering barbs. Both styles had stems that expanded toward the base. During early Pueblo II and in the very beginning of late Pueblo II, the base expanded laterally, the barbs retracted, and the gaps between base and barbs became lateral notches. This time weight remained essentially unchanged. Interestingly enough, large points with side notches are reported from Basket Maker III, Pueblo I, late Pueblo II, and early Pueblo III contexts. These points may have traversed the whole sequence unchanged.

Other Aspects of Material Culture

Bone awls and other tools were used in all phases. Deer were always a preferred source for bone, although by early Pueblo III, bone tools made from turkey elements assume the favorite's role.

Impressions of coiled basketry have been found on potsherds from all phases. Similarly, fragments of charred corn and turkey bones are known from Basket Maker III through late Pueblo III. Clear evidence for the domestication of turkeys and dogs first appears in Pueblo I, although both could have been domesticated earlier.

In spite of the many excavated sites, our knowledge of material culture of the prehistoric Chapin Mesa inhabitants is remarkably incomplete. As yet, we have no excavated sites producing perishable materials for most of the phases. Stone and bone tools are rarely reported as thoroughly as pottery and architecture, and only a few burials have been found for any phases. At this point it is impossible to tell whether many features reported for one phase, or two, occurred exclusively in that phase or whether their true temporal distribution simply has not yet been discovered. (Figure 89 plots known temporal distributions for several non-ceramic characteristics.)

Water and Soil Management

Precise dating is not available on the reservoirs, check-dams, and ditches on Chapin Mesa. We have fairly good evidence, though, that reservoirs such as Mummy Lake were definitely in use by late Pueblo II if not slightly earlier. Agricultural terraces formed by stone check-dams were certainly being built by the same time. Pueblo III people continued the practice of storing water in reservoirs and farming the terrace systems. The oldest known field house dates in early Pueblo II, but these structures are quite common after that.

Settlement Plan and Size

While architecture changed in many ways, some aspects of house arrangement remained rather constant. Orientation toward the south is common to pithouses and to large mesa-top pueblos. Not only are antechambers and ventilators situated on the south side of pithouses and kivas, but these structures themselves lie to the south of any room blocks. Refuse is

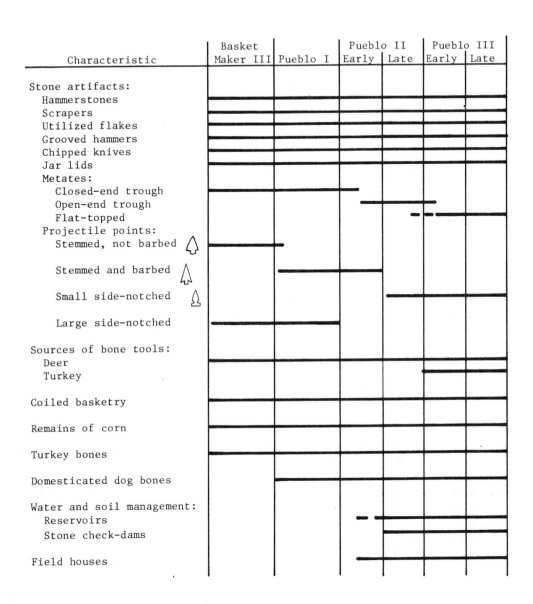

Characteristic	Basket Maker III	Pueblo I	Pueblo II		Pueblo III	
			Early	Late	Early	Late
Stone artifacts:						
Hammerstones						
Scrapers						
Utilized flakes						
Grooved hammers						
Chipped knives						
Jar lids						
Metates:						
Closed-end trough						
Open-end trough						
Flat-topped						
Projectile points:						
Stemmed, not barbed						
Stemmed and barbed						
Small side-notched						
Large side-notched						
Sources of bone tools:						
Deer						
Turkey						
Coiled basketry						
Remains of corn						
Turkey bones						
Domesticated dog bones						
Water and soil management:						
Reservoirs						
Stone check-dams						
Field houses						

Figure 89.   Some Non-ceramic Characteristics.

rarely dumped anywhere but south of the living area. Multiple-storied buildings step downwards toward the south.

Only in the cliffs and on steep slopes can exceptions be found. In these situations, the problems raised by topography apparently overruled whatever reasons there were for southern orientation. Most cliff and talus sites are arranged as if the ground sloped south, with kivas and refuse placed on the downslope side of the room blocks. In small caves and ledges, all structures are oriented solely by the demands of space.

It is possible that southern orientation represents nothing more than southern exposure to take full advantage of the sun's warming effects. But the attempts to retain as much southern orientation as possible in the caves, where cave exposure alone determines the effect of sunshine, seems to indicate some cultural value.

Until early Pueblo III, pithouses and kivas usually stand well apart from the blocks of living and storage rooms. From then on, they are usually partially or wholly surrounded by rooms.

The vast majority of pre-Pueblo III house sites represent single habitation units (Bullard 1962: 101). By this, I mean the associated group of living and storage rooms with a single pithouse or kiva. Some longer rows of contiguous rooms with several associated pithouses or kivas, in Pueblo I and late Pueblo II especially, represent several habitation units. During Pueblo III, many of these habitation units had begun to agglomerate into relatively large pueblos such as Far View House and Cliff Palace, although many more were still built as detached units.

In all phases, habitation units are found in clusters. I think there are good reasons for identifying many of these clusters as communities whose separate histories can be traced to some extent at least. It is necessary first to plot and examine the distribution of sites by phases to satisfactorily delineate communities on Chapin Mesa. Following this we can reconstruct the lines of development for some of them.

VIII

POSTULATION OF LOCALIZED SOCIAL GROUPINGS

Separate outline maps portray the distribution of habitation sites on Chapin Mesa, within Mesa Verde National Park, during each of the six local phases (figs. 91, 93, 95, 97, 98, and 99). It is impractical to show on these outline maps non-habitation sites, such as check-dams or shrines, because too few of these can be satisfactorily assigned to any one phase, and because they would tend to confuse the view of settlement pattern.

On the distribution maps, a black dot represents each site at which an occupational component can be recognized as belonging to the particular phase. Thus, some multi-component sites, such as 16 and 299 are marked on two or more maps. Most site numbers have been omitted to avoid cluttering.

Unfortunately, affiliation with any one particular phase could not be adequately determined for many single-component sites and they could not be plotted on the maps. These are most of the miscellaneous burned stone mounds in table 6. Even though their absence certainly affects some distributions—primarily those of Pueblo I and early Pueblo II—their haphazard inclusion would jeopardize such conclusions as may be drawn from the distributions. The Basket Maker III pattern undoubtedly suffers from virtually total natural obliteration of many pithouse sites. There is no way to tell how many sites of this phase have not yet been detected. An unknown number of Pueblo I and Pueblo II houses probably lie hidden beneath the remains of later structures. Only the distributions of the two Pueblo III phases can be considered even reasonably complete, and the full picture for both of them cannot even be approached until they have all been excavated.

The site serves as the primary unit of distribution, although a considerable difference separates the extremes of what has been recorded under a single site number. During the Chapin Mesa Survey, each distinguishable building, or presumed building, was assigned a separate site number, with some exceptions. On the mesa top, each site consists of the mound formed from a collapsed masonry or mud-walled structure and its associated rubbish. Occasionally, more than one structure,

particularly inferred pithouses, may be present where the
surface indications are blurred. In the canyons one site number
generally applies to the contents of one rock shelter, ledge,
or group of associated ledges, even though these may include
several separate buildings. All check-dams in a single system
have been covered under one number.

Few readers will find this usage of the concept of
site identical to their own practice or general preference.
Virtually every archaeologist speaks of sites, yet the concept
remains a most difficult one to define. Maybe a definition is
undesirable. A site is a working unit of ground space to which
the archaeologist refers his records, his photographs, and his
artifacts. Before he excavates it, he can only guess about its
constituent parts and its contents.

In spite of the difficulties concerning delineation
of individual sites, the black dots on the distribution maps
point up several patterns of settlement. Not only are there
shifts in site concentrations from one phase to the next and
changes in the choice of site location, but the recurrent
clustering of sites during all phases suggests that some communities can be recognized.

The community is a local group determined not by
kinship but by spatial proximity that brings its individual
members into face-to-face contact almost daily (Linton 1936;
Murdock 1949). This means that settlements once occupied by
communities should be recognizable archaeologically by the
relative proximity and separation between contemporary habitation sites and by observable routes of access between houses.

I believe that village-size settlements can be
identified during all phases of the prehistoric Pueblo occupation of Chapin Mesa, although several weaknesses in the
available data must be understood. The inference of contemporaneity depends mostly on surface observations and on evalua-
tions of ceramic assemblages. Occasionally, testing and
excavation have provided supplementary clues. Settlement
limits are rarely clear, because human activity does not cease
at the physical boundaries of the village. Finally, even though
settlements, or villages, might be discrete at any one point in
time, the archaeologist sees the remains from all the points in
time lumped together, and as he separates them, the absence of
absolutely accurate dating forces him to treat a whole time
period as the nearest approach to a single point in time.

Because of these difficulties, as well as the certainty that many ancient remains have eluded the notice of the
Chapin Mesa Survey, I shall attempt to delineate only a
restricted number of the more apparent village-size settle-

ments. This need not mean that only these few sites belonged
to one or another such settlement and the rest did not. Rather,
the incomplete state of our knowledge permits us to perceive
only the most clear-cut examples--those whose make-up has not
been obscured by subsequent events.

     Population estimates are offered for most of the
delineated settlements. These estimates are based on actual
counts of rooms, kivas or pithouses or estimates of such units
from the size of visible rubble mounds. Unusually good preservation in the cliff dwellings permits quite accurate room and
kiva counts, even in unexcavated sites. Comparisons then with
historic Pueblo census data (e.g. Rohn 1971: 262;   Parsons
1923; White 1962) suggest rough averages of one person per room
(about half the rooms were used for storage) or two persons per
living room. Extensions of these figures suggest approximately
ten to twelve persons per kiva and probably per pithouse.
Separate population ranges were estimated for each site and
totaled for settlement estimates.

     For Chapin Mesa as a whole, an approximate population
curve can be drawn using the · sums of room-kiva-pithouse
estimates for all habitation sites belonging to each local
phase. Such a curve shows an increasing rate of population
growth from Basket Maker III reaching a peak in late Pueblo
III. Even though earlier sites are less obvious, and many are
obscured by later structures, the growth rate from one phase to
the next would probably not be significantly affected were all
components known. This is especially true of the difference
between early and late Pueblo III. ·At its peak, some 1200 to
1800 persons lived on Chapin Mesa. Then, around A.D. 1300,
this number fell to zero as all the Pueblo peoples moved away.

     All of the following site clusters have been examined
as potential settlements on the ground, where they frequently
appear to be more easily distinguishable than the distributions
of black dots would imply. It would be foolish to pretend that
each delineation presents a perfectly accurate picture of a
centuries-old community, or that these are the only recognizable examples. They will, however, help demonstrate that such
local groupings were in existence among the prehistoric
Puebloan inhabitants of Chapin Mesa. Furthermore, they will
give us some idea of the nature of these groupings.

     Earth   Lodge   B   Settlement (Basket Maker III).
Widespread testing in the immediate vicinity of the excavated
pithouses A and B (Sites 117 and 118) revealed evidence of six
more similar structures (Sites 68, 112, 113, 114, 115, and
116). That all eight houses (fig. 90) were occupied contemporaneously is strongly suggested by the exclusively Basket Maker

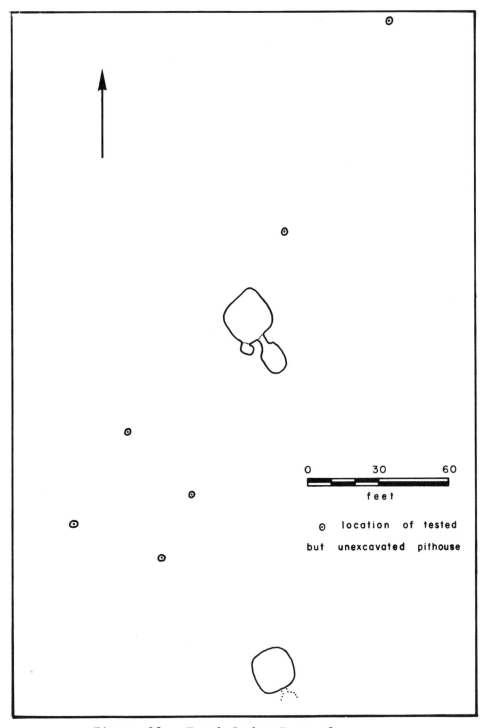

Figure 90.   Earth Lodge B settlement.

III pot fragments gathered from the small test holes and from the surface of an incipient wash located downslope; by the nearly constant depth at which floors were encountered; and by the complete absence of indications for any other kind of structure within the same space or nearby; and by the absence of observed instances of architectural stratification.

Presumably, all eight houses were basically alike in size and construction, although the differences between the two excavated pithouses forewarn us to expect no two to be identical in all details. I think it safe to presume that each house sheltered the members of one household and that the total community population ranged around 40 to 50 persons. There is yet no evidence of any community-wide features such as a common dump or burial place or of special structures. Site 60, located about 500 feet southeast, might be such a building, but unfortunately it has only been partially excavated, and no thorough analysis of it has been conducted. Tree-ring dates from Site 117 and the ceramics suggest a time placement in the first half of the seventh century A.D. for this settlement.

Twin Trees I Settlement (Basket Maker III). Remains of many structures occupy the Twin Trees area, but they can be quite readily sorted chronologically using both architectural and ceramic data. Once again, extensive testing discovered floors of seven probable pithouses (Sites 101, 104, 105, 106, 108, 109, and 110). Excavation of Site 101 brought to light two separate houses, but since one had been built partly in the ruins of the other, both could not have been occupied simultaneously. An eighth structure (Site 354), perhaps too small to be a house, was excavated during road widening operations.

Seemingly this group closely resembled the Earth Lodge B group except for a slight shift in architectural details (e.g., reduction of antechambers to ventilators, increased depth of floor beneath ground surface, etc.). It had a lesser number of houses (seven) and a somewhat later date of occupation. A late seventh century-early eighth century time placement is indicated by tree-ring dates and typology of architectural and ceramic features. Site 60 lies about 500 feet to the north and could be associated with this group just as easily as with the preceding one, if it is associated with either.

Other possible Basket Maker III settlements. I am inclined to suspect that most, if not all, pithouses once belonged to village clusters. Only through investigation, including excavations (e.g. Rohn 1975), can we verify or refute such a hypothesis. For example, Sites 283 and 1061 may represent only part of a group we might tentatively designate the

Earth Lodge C Settlement.

Farther north, where surface indications are more prominent, two groups of four sites each are located west and north of Cedar Tree Tower (fig. 91). Sites 412, 414, 416, and 433 form one group; Sites 405, 435, 442, and 443 form the other. Neither group engenders much confidence without thorough testing in the vicinity.

A considerable quantity of Basket Maker III pottery and artifacts seem to suggest the former presence of a settlement near an isolated plum tree about one mile south of Far View. However, only two concentrations have been distinguishable as sites--787 and 792. Because of the potential importance of this group in interpretation, I have designated it the Plum Tree I Settlement.

Twin Trees II Settlement (Pueblo I). The densest occupation of the Twin Trees locality took place during Pueblo I. It seems doubtful to me that all of the Pueblo I site numbers here represent structures that were occupied exactly contemporaneously. Sites 1, 103, 111, and 58 appear to represent typical rows of slab-based jacal-walled rooms with deep pit structures set just south of them. Pit structures known from excavation and testing include three at Site 103 and one each represented by Sites 353 and 107. Surface indications suggest the presence of a fourth pithouse at Site 103 and two at Site 58, while O'Bryan (1950) suggests that a later kiva at Site 1 had been built inside still another. I strongly suspect excavation would disclose still more, especially at Site 111.

Sites 57, 62, and 69 have been included within this settlement because of their general contemporaneity within the Pueblo I phase, although they could represent either a beginning development of the phase or merely temporarily occupied houses. Evidence for structures at these three sites is sparse and perhaps no more than six to ten rooms and an unknown number of pit structures are represented at all three. Experience at Sites 111 and 786, however, has demonstrated that some Pueblo I houses leave no traces visible on the ground's surface.

Tree-ring dates from Sites 1, 103, and 58 place the most evident Pueblo I occupation here during the ninth century A.D. Assuming contemporaneity of all but Sites 57, 62, and 69, we have evidence for at least 9 pithouses--with a strong probability for more--and 11 excavated rooms plus an estimated 16 to 30 more that have left some surface traces. I would estimate the population of this village between 50 and 100.

Site 370 Settlement (Pueblo I). Site 370 seems to form the nucleus of an extensive Pueblo I concentration south of Cedar Tree Tower (fig. 92). Rows of contiguous rooms are

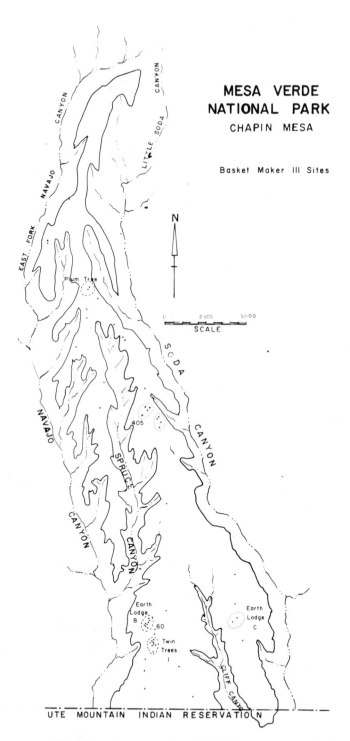

MESA VERDE
NATIONAL PARK
CHAPIN MESA

Basket Maker III Sites

Figure 91.   Basket Maker III sites.

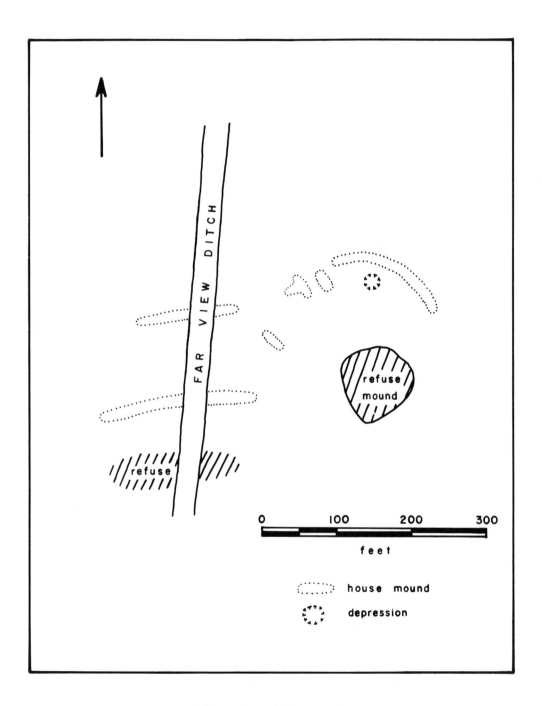

Figure 92.   Site 370 settlement.

discernible at this site and at Sites 376, 386, 389, and 1047, with small blocks of rooms at Sites 387 and 371. Extent of the surface evidence suggests an estimate of 75 to 100 total rooms that could have housed 100 to 150 people. Four or five slight depressions may mark pithouses, but most of these structures probably left no traces whatsoever on the ground surface. A very large trash mound between Sites 370 and 376 appears to have served as a common dump for the entire community.

Here, too, a group of six sites (373, 398, 419, 420, 423, and 431) to the north seems to be slightly earlier. Typically Pueblo I pottery types Piedra Black-on-white and Chapin Gray--Moccasin Variety were missing from all of these except Site 373, which lies closest to the Site 370 group. Chapin Gray body sherds, Chapin Black-on-white, and red sherds were plentiful. There may once have been 25 to 35 rooms. I would guess that this smaller cluster housed the immediate ancestors of the inhabitants of the Site 370 Settlement.

Plum Tree II Settlement (Pueblo I). This large group of ten sites (704, 705, 754, 785, 786, 793, 795, 796, 797, and 494) again may include several that are only grossly contemporary. It is impossible to distinguish accurately from the hazy surface indications how much of this group was inhabited at any one point in time. A conservative estimate, based only on visible evidence, gives a total of 40 to 60 rooms. Limited testing encountered one pithouse that had left no mark at all on the ground surface.

Spruce Mesa Settlement (Pueblo I). About one mile south of the Plum Tree sites, on the northern end of Spruce Mesa, is another cluster of eight Pueblo I sites. Three long rows (Sites 742, 745, 748) account for most of the estimated 40 to 55 rooms, while the remainder are scattered in small blocks of 2 to 3 rooms apiece (Sites 756, 757, 759, 760, 775).

Other probable Pueblo I settlements. The plotted distribution of Pueblo I sites on Chapin Mesa (fig. 93) provides strong indication of several other village-like clusters. Encircling the headwaters of Cliff Canyon are at least four, possibly five, such groupings. A short distance southwest of Far View is a group of five sites, and there may well be others in the intervening ground. None of these has been investigated directly, however, so I would prefer not to dignify them with names at this time.

Some of the scattered and partly isolated sites, especially Site 937 in the bottom of Spruce Canyon and Site 271 near Balcony House, may be only temporary outlying shelters or the isolated homes of marginal members of the society. They are all small in size. Certainly, the vast bulk of the Pueblo I

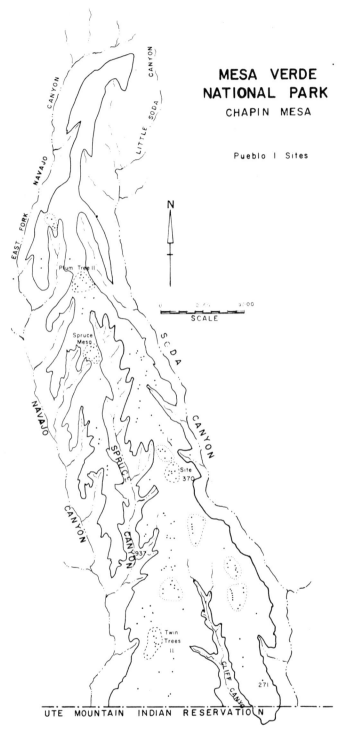

Figure 93.   Pueblo I sites.

population occupied the numerous village-size settlement.

Sun Temple Ridge I Settlement (early Pueblo II). The probability that many early Pueblo II sites are concealed by later masonry buildings makes it difficult to distinguish village-like clusters. Perhaps the best group is located near the north end of the distributary ridge leading to Sun Temple (fig. 94). The ten sites (126, 144, 146, 147, 148, 150, 157, 162, 163, 351) account for a possible total of 35 to 50 rooms. The largest room block may have contained 6 to 10 rooms; the smallest probably had only 2. No kiva depressions have been found, although excavation should certainly reveal several kivas. Refuse was concentrated into three small mounds. I would estimate a maximum population of about 50 to 60.

Mummy Lake I Settlement (early Pueblo II). Permanent occupation of the Far View area seems to have begun with this group of 13, possibly 14 sites (806, 813, 814, 815, 816, 817, 823, 824, 825, 827, 829, 886, possibly 841). More imposing later masonry buildings obscure the early Pueblo II components on most of these sites, making it impossible to estimate the numbers of rooms for each. There may also be other components not yet discovered beneath still other late sites. Some kivas and some of the refuse mounds almost certainly were in use at this time.

The seemingly sudden appearance of a relatively large population in this area provides a strong argument for the development of some artificial supply of water. There is good evidence that Mummy Lake was in use at least by middle Pueblo II, and I would suspect that its first construction enabled this early Pueblo II community to settle here. Although we cannot adequately estimate the population of this group, the average house size seems to have been slightly larger than on the Sun Temple Ridge, and hence the population was probably greater in the Mummy Lake I group.

Other possible early Pueblo II settlements. Although they have not yet been delineated on the ground, the distribution map (fig. 95) suggests that other settlements might be found, again encircling the headwaters of Cliff Canyon, especially near Twin Trees and Site 297, in the Plum Tree area, and on Spruce Mesa. This last group would be unusually widely scattered.

It would appear that the early Pueblo II Chapin Mesa Indians had begun to build and use field houses such as Site 1032. Thus several of the sites here plotted as habitations may well have been only seasonally-occupied outliers, confusing the picture still further. This phase is the poorest known of all Mesa Verde occupations.

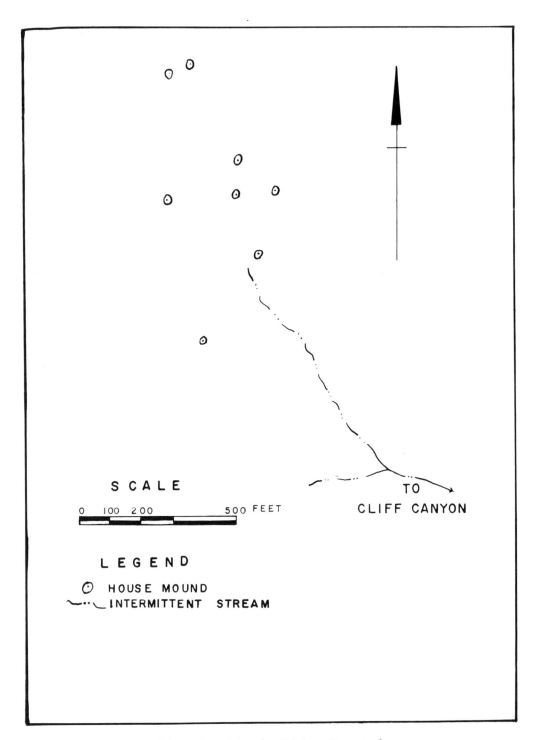

Figure 94.   Sun Temple Ridge I settlement.

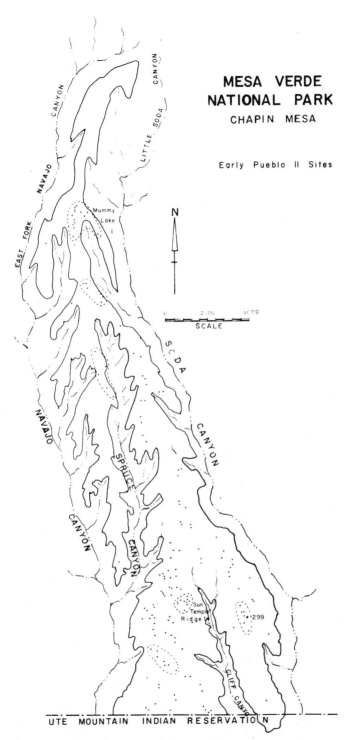

Figure 95.   Early Pueblo II sites.

Sun Temple Ridge II Settlement (late Pueblo II). This group consists of nine closely spaced sites (124, 125, 127, 128, 129, 130, 132, 133, 135) with two possible outlying members (Sites 143 and 151). The nine nuclear sites contain an estimated 50 to 80 rooms plus 5 to 8 kivas. Sites 143 and 151 would only add about six more rooms if they belonged to this same cluster. Such a settlement would roughly equate with the late Pueblo III Square Tower House (Site 650) both in size and in estimated population--perhaps 75 to 100. The occupants of each house had their own separate refuse dump nearby.

The various structural units of this community have been laid out lineally along the crest of the ridge in a northwest-southeast direction (fig. 96). The three or four larger sites near the center formed a sort of nucleus where the kivas were located. In the small wash immediately to the east of these sites is a series of stone check-dams (Site 134) that once formed agricultural terraces. The proximity of these terraces would suggest they were at least used by this group, although they may originally have been constructed by their early Pueblo II predecessors, possibly of perishable materials. The stone walls could be a subsequent modification.

Mummy Lake II Settlement (late Pueblo II). Some 36 sites were apparently inhabited in the Far View area during late Pueblo II. Once again many of these were masked by larger Pueblo III structures. In several instances, Site 809 for example, Pueblo III builders simply added rooms to the late Pueblo II buildings and continued to use them, so that only excavation revealed the full picture. Excavated units at Sites 809, 810, 866, and 875, and those sites that were least disturbed suggest that each house block may have contained an average of slightly more rooms than those on Sun Temple Ridge. This would mean an estimated population of several hundred persons, perhaps 200 to 400.

At this time, the Mummy Lake water system was definitely in operation and undoubtedly supplied domestic water to this budding urban settlement. Systems of stone check-dams in the gullies that form immediately to the south mark some of the agricultural field locations. However, the now vacant mesa top south to the head of Spruce Canyon provided the largest quantity of tillable land within easy range of this settlement.

It seems likely that the Mummy Lake II people utilized temporary shelters and other outbuildings in the more distant field areas and possibly while tending the Mummy Lake collection system on Navaho Hill to the north. Structures of this sort have been found in both areas, but it is impossible, of course, to link them positively to this settlement.

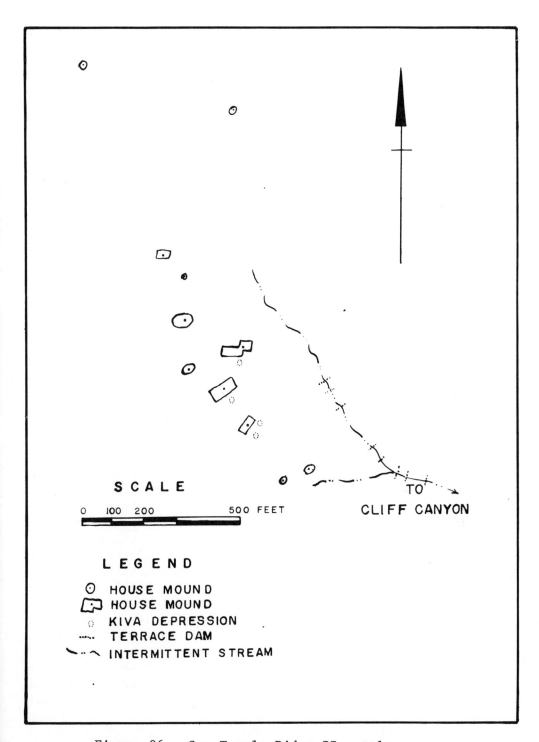

Figure 96. Sun Temple Ridge II settlement.

Other possible late Pueblo II settlements. Once again
the plotted distribution (fig. 97) suggests that other late
Pueblo II settlements may be found near the north end of Spruce
Mesa, to the east across Spruce Canyon on the main ridge of
Chapin Mesa, between the two head tributaries that form Cliff
Canyon, and around Site 299. Three sites in Little Soda Canyon
probably represent the vanguard of the subsequent heavier
occupation in that area. There is also evidence of increasing
use, perhaps only intermittently, of several cliff and canyon
situations: for example, at Sites 508 and 626 in Cliff Canyon.

Far View Settlement (early Pueblo III). While there
are only half as many sites here as before, the total
population may have increased, since each building contained
more rooms. The 18 sites account for an estimated 300 to 375
rooms and at least 32 kivas, suggesting a possible population
of some 400 to 500 if all sites were occupied at the same time,
and they seem to have been. At least three sites (808, 820,
821) contained 30 to 50 rooms and 5 kivas apiece; four others
(200, 809, 823, 840) fall in the size range of 20 to 30 rooms;
there are eight (Sites 499, 818, 828, 835, 851, 867, 872, 875)
with 10 to 20 rooms; only three (Sites 790, 822, 864) have less
than 10 rooms, and only the smallest of these, Site 822, lacks
any evidence of a kiva. Each site has a sizeable refuse mound
near it. Four have circular masonry towers that may have served
some ceremonial purpose. In addition, Site 810 was probably a
special ceremonial site embodying a round tower and at least
two kivas, erected on and in the ruins of a late Pueblo II
house.

Like their predecessors, the Far View people relied
on the Mummy Lake catchment and reservoir system for water to
serve both domestic and agricultural needs. They probably
farmed the same lands, too. An excellent reconstruction of life
in the early Pueblo III Far View Community was painted by
National Geographic Society staff artist Peter Bianchi for the
February 1964 issue of National Geographic Magazine.

The numerous field houses of early Pueblo III date
located in the vicinity of the fields around the head of Spruce
Canyon and on Navaho Hill can probably be identified with this
group. If the outlying Sites 881, 1909, 856, and 857 housed
people who participated in Far View Community activities, we
may wonder if these were not marginal members of the society.

Little Soda Canyon Settlement (early Pueblo III). The
incentive for moving into Little Soda Canyon at this time may
have been a desire or a need to cultivate the relatively large
flat terrace found there. The numerous stone check-dams found
in the small tributary washes certainly indicate that farming

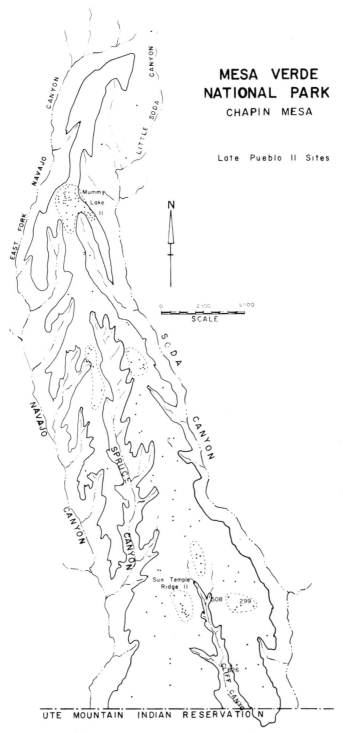

Figure 97.   Late Pueblo II sites.

was pursued. Sites 898, 906, 907, 911, 912, 913, 914, 915, 919, and 920 form the core of this group and contain a total of about 150 rooms, 10 kivas, and 3 towers. Site 907 alone accounts for half of this total. Five other small sites strung along the narrower canyon to the north may have been outliers occupied only sporadically.

Because occupation of canyon bottoms like this one lasted for only a relatively brief time, the Little Soda Canyon group may well have participated in the construction and use of an, as yet, unsurveyed isolated great kiva situated on the south side of Battleship Rock, a short distance to the south. There are other contemporary sites to the east and north, all, like the kiva, beyond the coverage of the Chapin Mesa Survey, that are just as closely associated.

Other possible early Pueblo III settlements. The relatively large size of many early Pueblo III sites makes it difficult to recognize other possible communities from site distributions alone (fig. 98). Four scattered sites (728, 747, 751, 773) near the north end of Spruce Mesa have a combined estimate of 55 to 70 rooms, 7 kivas, and 3 towers. Farther south on the same distributary mesa, Site 782, with 40 to 50 rooms, 2 kivas, and a tower, may be a small settlement by itself. Similarly, Sites 325 and 328 together boast enough size--45 to 55 rooms and two kivas--to represent another small settlement. Five sites (72, 74, 75, 79, 119) straddling the wash leading to Little Long House combine for an estimated 30 to 35 rooms and 4 kivas.

Even though we cannot yet accurately estimate the degree to which early Pueblo III Chapin Mesans had begun to move into rock-shelter situations in the cliffs, the distribution map shows that a smaller proportion of the population lived in the neighborhood of Cliff Canyon than during both earlier and later phases. Large numbers of field houses were in use by early Pueblo III, and the Indians appeared to place less value on living near their farmlands than they formerly did.

Cliff-Fewkes Canyon Settlement (late Pueblo III). This large and extensive group is united by the common need to share a few (8 to 10) routes of access between the mesa-top farmlands and their canyon site situations at the base of the vertical sandstone cliffs. Travel between sites, along the top of the steeply sloping talus and next to the cliff, is considerably easier than ascent to the mesa top. A sheer cliff between Sites 632 and 618 obstructs communication around the point of the spur mesa between Cliff Palace and Balcony House.

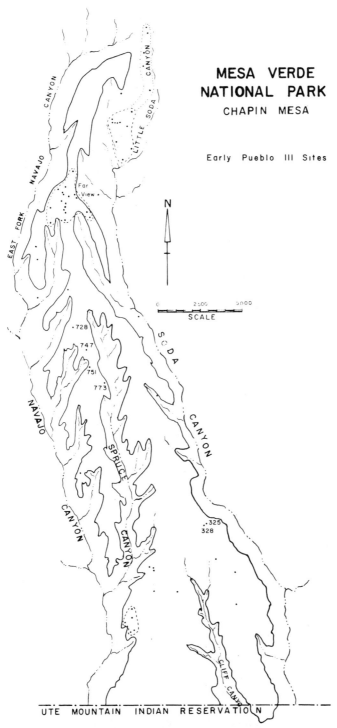

Figure 98.   Early Pueblo III sites.

This group consists of 33 habitation sites, ranging in size from one room to the largest site on Chapin Mesa, Cliff Palace (Site 625), with an estimated 220 rooms and 23 kivas. Some 530 to 545 rooms and 60 kivas belong to this community. An estimated 600 to 800 persons probably inhabited them, accounting for approximately half of the total population estimated to have lived on Chapin Mesa during the thirteenth century. Although many sites are small, half the rooms and kivas are found in the two largest sites (625 and 523), two-thirds in the five sites of 20 or more rooms each, and nine-tenths in the fourteen sites containing 10 or more rooms each. There is a marked tendency for these larger sites to be located nearer the spatial center than the periphery of the settlement.

Two large non-residential structures (Sites 520 and 352--Fire Temple and Sun Temple), located among the sites of this group, may have been built for and used by members of the community as a whole. Strong cases have been made in support of a ceremonial function for each (pp. 115-116 above; Fewkes 1916a, 1916b, 1921; Cassidy 1960).

Both artificial and natural sources of water were developed. Springs at the base of the cliff below Sun Temple and in the head of Fewkes Canyon were probably the most reliable local sources, although several seeps were quite likely developed in the two heads of Cliff Canyon and near Cliff Palace (Site 625) and Sunset House (Site 626). I have already stated my hypothesis (pp. 107-108 above; Rohn 1963b) that the Far View Ditch was constructed to lead water collected by the Mummy Lake catchment system to the large artificial reservoir (Site 26) situated above the head of Fewkes Canyon. If this is correct, then Sites 52 and 388, which I feel are associated with the ditch, may also have been built by members of this community. We may wonder if the situation of Sun Temple, directly above the strongest natural spring, and the position of Fire Temple in the cave shelter closest to the artificially augmented source in the head of Fewkes Canyon are more than coincidence.

It is probably safe to assume that the Cliff-Fewkes Canyon people farmed the mesa top in the immediate vicinity of their houses. If my guess that many of these people moved here from the Far View Settlement is correct, there is also a strong possibility that they continued to till the old fields around the head of Spruce Canyon. Many of the field houses associated with check-dam systems in this area have yielded late Pueblo III pottery.

In the sense that I have just described it, the Cliff-Fewkes Canyon Settlement appears to have been a small urban settlement scattered among the rock shelters in the cliffs of these two canyons. Its members seem to have cooperated in the building, use, and maintenance of a water supply system and of specialized ceremonial buildings. I would like to suggest further that this community, together with the three smaller ones located closest to it and to be described next in order, formed the main-stream segment of thirteenth century Chapin Mesa society, and that they continued to function actively until near the time of final abandonment of the Mesa Verde.

Balcony House Settlement (late Pueblo III). This small settlement of nine sites consists of 72 rooms and 6 kivas. It probably provided homes for no more than 60 to 100 persons, almost all of whom lived in two sites (515 and 615). Six other sites contain 2 or 3 rooms each and probably represent small isolated houses. Site 617 appears to be a specialized defensive structure on the entrance trail to Balcony House (Site 615). Interestingly, three kivas are clustered with only 11 rooms in Site 515, while the majority of people lived in the 44 rooms of Balcony House, which has only two kivas. Water was available from two strong springs at Balcony House and from what appears to be a catchment basin in the tributary canyon head below Site 515. Adequate farmland could be found on the mesa top within a mile to the north.

Square Tower House Settlement (late Pueblo III). A similar situation exists in this group of seven sites comprising some 111 rooms and 12 kivas. Here too, most of the population and 11 of the kivas concentrated in two sites—Square Tower House (Site 650) and Little Long House (Site 647). A strong spring in the steep canyon wall below Square Tower House and a seep augmented by two reservoirs—one natural and one artificial—near Little Long House provided water. Excellent farmland occupies the adjacent mesa top. Some 120 to 150 people may have belonged to this group.

Spruce Tree House Settlement (late Pueblo III). This cluster differs from the preceding three in two primary ways. Of the estimated total 160 to 175 rooms and 11 kivas, 114 rooms and 8 kivas are concentrated in the large, centrally-located Spruce Tree House (Site 640). Secondly, eight sites (530, 642, 644, 645, 651, 653, 654) consist of a single storage room apiece, while Site 643 has two rooms. Four more sites complete the group, one of which—Site 531—was a talus pueblo. Approximately 150 to 200 people may have lived in this settlement.

Water was obtainable from the strongest spring on Chapin Mesa at the head of Spruce Tree Canyon. The Indians may have built an artificial reservoir above this spring, undoubtedly enhancing its flow. Again the adjacent mesa top would provide adequate farmland.

Other late Pueblo III settlements. Even though we know more about late Pueblo III sites than about sites belonging to any other phase, we should not expect to find all sites clearly associated with one another in settlements. We know that temporary shelters were employed frequently, but we do not yet know how elaborate some of these might have been. The evidence from Site 981 (Luebben, Rohn and Givens 1962) suggests some were quite large. Thus, relatively small and isolated sites, such as Sites 540 (2 rooms) or 1054 (6 to 8 rooms with 2 possible kiva depressions), may have been either seasonally-occupied field houses or the outlying homes of persons who did not participate fully in society and who preferred to live apart from the main group. Would we not expect to find such individuals in any society, especially one where the food quest does not require constant moving about?

In spite of these limitations, I have attempted to combine almost all late Pueblo III habitation sites into settlements. I am inclined to think this listing of clusters with total room estimates (table 13) presents a reasonable picture and does not force the data.

In each of the first eight site clusters, one or two relatively large sites form a nucleus for the whole group. Consequently, I am inclined to consider these eight as true residential settlements. The next three clusters have no such nuclear site, or, for that matter, no site containing more than five rooms. Because of this and the somewhat scattered marginal positions of these three groups (fig. 99), I do not believe any of them can be considered as permanent residential units. Perhaps these and the seven left-over sites represent seasonal or temporarily occupied sites, which cluster only by chance.

At this point, I should remind the reader of the inequality of the dots shown on the distribution maps. Clusters of dots alone cannot indicate the existence of a settlement. Each should be examined firsthand, not from written records alone.

TABLE 13

Late Pueblo III Site Clusters

Site Cluster	No. Sites	Est. Rooms	Est. Kivas	Est. Pop.
1) Cliff-Fewkes Canyon	33	530–545	60	600–800
2) Spruce Tree House	14	160–175	11	150–200
3) Square Tower House	7	111	12	120–150
4) Balcony House	12	81	6	65–110
5) Middle Navaho Canyon	20	92–100	8	100–150
6) Upper Soda Canyon	12	56–64	3–4	50–70
7) Painted Kiva House	9	31	2	30–40
8) Site 596	8	20	2	20–35
	115	1081–1127	104–105	1135–1555
9) Spruce Canyon	8	17–20	2	20–30
10) Upper Navaho Canyon	8	16–17	1	15–25
11) Sites 599–609	11	25	0	25–40
	27	58–62	3	60–95
Left-over sites	7	18	1	19–32

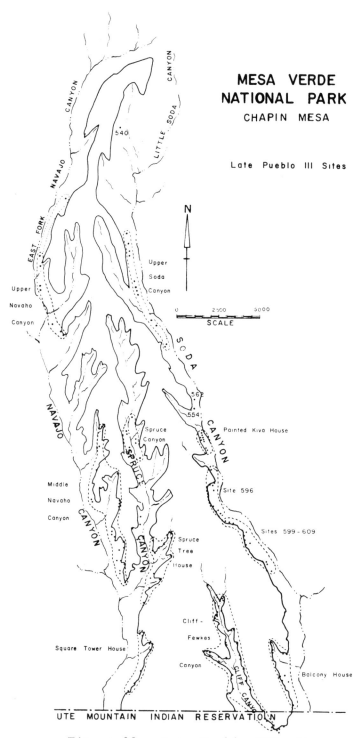

Figure 99.   Late Pueblo III sites.

IX

CONCLUSIONS AND PERSPECTIVE

The settlement-oriented view I have taken of Chapin Mesa site distributions helps in visualizing population distributions. The figures in table 13 indicate that half the late Pueblo III population lived in the Cliff-Fewkes Canyon Settlement alone. Indeed, approximately 95% lived on only the southern half of our Chapin Mesa study area, in contrast to the concentration found in the more northerly Far View Locality during the preceding several centuries. This major population shift, as well as several lesser ones, can be examined in the light of changes apparent in some of the village-size settlements through time.

Several kinds of changes may be inferred. Again, I will make no attempt to be all inclusive, but I will only discuss the clearer cases, organized as examples of the several kinds of changes. My evidence consists mainly of the distributional data presented in the preceding chapter, which in turn depends on the temporal conclusions drawn from ceramics and inferred architectural details.

Continuity in the Twin Trees-Square Tower House Locality. All six prehistoric cultural phases known from Chapin Mesa are represented by habitation sites in this locality. During Basket Maker III, the Earth Lodge B Settlement—occupied in the early 600's A.D.—was succeeded by the Twin Trees I Settlement with several tree-ring dates around A.D. 700. Both units appear to have been roughly equal in size and both may have used the large possibly ceremonial structure at Site 60.

The many Pueblo I sites in the Twin Trees II Settlement suggest an increase in population, even though they were almost certainly not all inhabited contemporaneously. During early and late Pueblo II, the house sites are scattered more widely here than at any other time, making it difficult to define clearly any particular settlements. Pueblo II sites of both phases are definitely found in this locality, however, although there probably was a diminution in population.

By early Pueblo III, the locus of the house sites had shifted westward to both sides of the wash that leads to Little Long House (Site 647). Population was still low. Another shift

289

led to the construction and occupation of the Square Tower House Settlement cliff dwellings during late Pueblo III, when population in this locality seems to have reached its peak.

Even though the position of house sites shifted through time in this locality, their inhabitants presumably continued to use the same farmlands and water sources because of their proximity. The mesa top around Twin Trees was the closest farmland to house sites of all phases. Similarly, the nearest source of water for all house sites lay in the spring below Square Tower House. Only during the two phases of Pueblo II did the distances between house sites within this locality approach those distances separating them from house sites in adjacent localities.

Population appears to have reached two distinct peaks--one during Pueblo I and one during late Pueblo III--with a relative low between them, sometime during Pueblo II (table 14). The absence of any evidence for precursors certainly suggests that a group of people moved into the locality together, perhaps settling in the Earth Lodge B Settlement. The apparently steady growth through the later part of Pueblo I might well be explained by normal biological increase with few or no individuals moving in from elsewhere. A reversal of this trend, or some calamity, would have to account for the Pueblo II drop in population, unless many families moved away. I favor the idea that some families moved away, because there is evidence that the total population on Chapin Mesa was increasing and that many Chapin Mesans were shifting their site locations at about this time.

The rise in population between early and late Pueblo III I would similarly attribute to movements of families into the locality from elsewhere on Chapin Mesa or from still farther away. The increase seems too sharp for normal biological processes, and it, too, coincides with a period of major shifting of house locations all over Chapin Mesa. Almost certainly the termination of occupation here involved the movement away of all the then living members of the community (we cannot overlook the possibility that aged and infirm individuals were left behind, but I regard this as highly unlikely).

Cultural continuity in this locality, then, is represented by the continuous habitation of at least some people, by the recurring exploitation of the same land and water resources, and by the lack of overlap at any time with other adjacent settlements. Perhaps there was a constant movement of a few families into and out of this settlement, but on two occasions this flow was seemingly unbalanced, resulting in

TABLE 14

Population Trend in Twin Trees Locality

Settlement or phase	Est. Rms.	Pithouses or kivas	Est. Pop.
Earth Lodge B	-	8	40-50
Twin Trees I	-	7	35-45
Twin Trees II	27-41	9+	50-100
early Pueblo II	17-25	2+	20-35
late Pueblo II	15-20	4-5	20-30
early Pueblo III	30-35	4	35-45
Square Tower House	111	12	120-150

marked changes in community population. Other changes took place in the choice of house site locations, in architectural styles, ceramics, kinds of tools, and in water management practices.

Similar continua in other localities. No other Chapin Mesa locality contains positive evidence of continuous habitation through all six known cultural phases. On Spruce Mesa, this may only reflect a lack of data for Basket Maker III. The relative isolation of this locality suggests continuity from the Pueblo I Spruce Mesa Settlement through the late Pueblo III mid-Navaho Canyon Settlement. Here, too, the population seems to have fluctuated in much the same way and probably for the same reason as at Twin Trees.

There was apparently continuous occupation from Basket Maker III through early Pueblo III in the vicinity of Earth Lodge C and Site 299. It is not clear, however, where these people moved during late Pueblo III. Aside from these instances, there appears to be no other case of continuous community occupation in one locality through more than three successive phases.

Effect of artificial water sources in the Mummy Lake Locality. Basket Maker III and Pueblo I house ruins have not been found in the Mummy Lake Locality, but they are relatively plentiful to the south around the head of Spruce Canyon, including the Plum Tree Locality, where good farmland is also plentiful. Compared to the latter, the Mummy Lake area is not a particularly desirable location in which to live. It occupies the northern edge of the rich loess mesa-top soils. The only natural water source was a spring in the bottom of Soda Canyon, which yielded alkaline water.

Construction of the Mummy Lake water system in Pueblo II almost surely coincides with the seemingly "sudden" appearance of early Pueblo II house sites (Mummy Lake I Settlement) in the vicinity of the reservoir. Thus, it would appear that development of a good water source stimulated the development of a sizeable settlement. This particular situation continued to attract additional settlers until, during early Pueblo III, it had become the largest settlement on Chapin Mesa, containing perhaps one-third to one-half of the mesa's total population. During this same time, the areas to the south were decreasing in population; some of them, such as the area around the head of Spruce Canyon, were abandoned altogether. I think it probable that these two events are directly related.

Effect of terracing in Little Soda Canyon. It seems reasonably certain that the development of agricultural terracing on the flat benches in the bottom of Little Soda Canyon accompanied the establishment of an early Pueblo III settlement there. I also suspect that no settlement would have grown up there without the concurrent reclaiming of farmland through terracing. Since the most practical route of access to Little Soda Canyon leaves from near Far View House, there is an excellent possibility that this canyon-bottom unit formed as an offshoot from the Far View Settlement.

The Movement Southward. During the transition from what is designated early to late Pueblo III on Chapin Mesa, the focus of population shifted from the Mummy Lake Locality to Cliff and Fewkes Canyons. I have previously advanced the opinion that the Far View people actually moved to Cliff Canyon, taking their artificial water supply with them by constructing the Far View Ditch. Even if all persons on Chapin Mesa relocated their residences at this time, the large proportions of the total population found in these two local- ities would virtually ensure that some people moved directly from one to the other. The strong suggestion of continuity in the Square Tower House and Spruce Mesa localities would argue against such a hypothetical universal relocation, however.

In one sense, nearly all the people on Chapin Mesa did relocate their homes, by moving to a cliff-face situation from a mesa-top situation. Those inhabited localities that contained suitable rock shelters continued to be occupied. However, few such shelters are found in the Mummy Lake area, while Cliff and Fewkes Canyons contained many. Cave locations obviously influenced the redistribution of population, especially since the same lands were still farmed. Since the only significant value to be gained by living in these shelters is protection against surprise raids, the desire for defense would appear to underlie this general movement southward.

Local Groupings larger than village-size. From the preceding discussion of probable population movements as reflected by changes in village-size settlements, there would seem to be a kind of unity among the inhabitants of Chapin Mesa, including the unsurveyed south part located on the Ute Indian Reservation. There is no indication that new information from this unsurveyed area would materially alter the general conclusions stated in this study. Most population shifts seem to have occurred within the confines of this physiographic unit.

From late Pueblo II through Pueblo III, one large settlement has dominated the picture for the entire mesa. The Mummy Lake II Settlement first assumed prominence during late Pueblo II followed by the even larger Far View Settlement. In late Pueblo III the Cliff-Fewkes Canyon Settlement held sway with about half of Chapin Mesa's total population and the two large, communally-built ceremonial structures, Fire Temple and Sun Temple. The absence of comparable structures elsewhere on Chapin Mesa would also tend to support this concept of unity.

The kind of local grouping represented by the whole of Chapin Mesa need not have had formal political significance. It may simply have been a reaction to existing subdivisions in local topography. The position of large ceremonial structures at the center of population density does remind one of the ceremonial-center pattern of settlement so common in regions of high cultural development within the Western Hemisphere.

Let me close these speculations with the suggestion that this type of settlement pattern may have been recently emergent in the Northern San Juan Region of the Puebloan Southwest during late Pueblo III. It seems to me possible to view Wetherill Mesa as another such unit focused on Long House with its Fire Temple-like structure (forthcoming publications of the Wetherill Mesa Archeological Project will help us visualize this pattern). Intensive work elsewhere in the region may well reveal additional groupings of this sort at such places as Hovenweep, Yucca House, Lowry Ruin, and Aztec Ruin, and it may also indicate such units existed earlier than I have suggested here. The large pit structures found with Pueblo I sites in the Ackmen-Lowry district (Martin 1939) could be analogous in function to Great Kivas, and they may have antecedents in Basket Maker III. But, it is unwise to speculate too much where our knowledge of distributions is still very incomplete.

That a true ceremonial-center settlement pattern never developed further may well be a result of the several severe crises that beset Pueblo culture in subsequent centuries. First among these was the wholesale abandonment of the San Juan drainage by Puebloan peoples following Pueblo III. As the effects of this redistribution of population were dissipating, Spanish conquerors entered the Southwest, commencing over four centuries of contact with and accultura- tion to the technologically more advanced western European civilization. During this same period there were constant conflicts with non-farming neighbors such as the Comanche and Navaho, even if such hostility had not taken place earlier.

Summary and Perspective

Throughout the descriptions and interpretations of the findings of the Chapin Mesa Archaeological Site Survey I have assumed that it is essential to view culture change in terms of the interrelationships between continuity and alteration, or change. I have also assumed that my rather extensive interpretations concerning the composition of this one particular segment of prehistoric Puebloan society will augment our overall view of the cultural development that took place within that society.

Because so many previous writers have emphasized the changes that occurred through time, I have concentrated on some of the continuities. The changes are quite evident, in any case, without the need to draw special attention to them. I have further concentrated on the kinds of change that can best be analyzed using the data derived through intensive archae- ological survey. This has led to the lengthy treatment of site distributions and specific situations, from which the existence of two kinds of local groupings has been inferred. Village- size settlements are the easiest to define and trace. It is tantalizing, though, to postulate the emergence of a ceremonial-center kind of larger settlement pattern, which could never achieve fruition among the numerous crises that have confronted Pueblo culture from that time to the present.

Until our knowledge of other portions of the Puebloan Southwest reaches a comparable state, and until more complete excavations are carried out, I can contribute nothing more to general question of external influences. The pottery study has argued against the once hypothetical migration of peoples from the Kayenta, Arizona, Region to the west into Mesa Verde at the beginning of Pueblo III.

Aside from this and the overall approach to the subject of culture change, this study has, I think, tended to demonstrate two significant characteristics of prehistoric

Puebloan society. From the time Basket Maker III peoples arrived on Chapin Mesa until their descendants left about 700 years later, they lived in typical village-size settlements, even during Pueblo II. Secondly, even though they were sedentary peoples, they frequently built and occupied new homes, often in new locations.

We should not envision any regular mass movements of whole communities, coinciding neatly with the transitions between cultural phases, or the simultaneous adoption of new architectural design. Instead, it would seem more likely that every year some individual households or family units moved to new homes. They probably constructed new houses according to then current styles. Even the population shift from near Mummy Lake to Cliff and Fewkes Canyons probably took place in this manner rather than as a total community migration at one time.

Only under conditions such as these could we expect to see such rapid changes in architecture. Understanding these two characteristics of prehistoric Puebloan society on Chapin Mesa makes it somewhat easier to visualize the mass exodus from the Mesa Verde at the end of Pueblo III.

REFERENCES

ABEL, LELAND J.
  1955. San Juan Red Ware, Mesa Verde Gray Ware, Mesa Verde
          White Ware, and San Juan White Ware. In "Pottery
          Types of the Southwest," ed. by Harold S. Colton.
          Ceramic Series 3 B, Museum of Northern Arizona.
          Flagstaff.
BRETERNITZ, DAVID A., ARTHUR H. ROHN, JR., and ELIZABETH A.
  MORRIS
  1974. Prehistoric Ceramics of the Mesa Verde Region. Museum
          of Northern Arizona Ceramic Series, no. 5. Flagstaff.
BREW, JOHN O.
  1946. Archaeology of Alkali Ridge, Southeastern Utah,
          Peabody Museum Papers, vol. 21. Cambridge.
BRYAN, KIRK and JOSEPH H. TOULOUSE, JR.
  1943. The San Jose Non-ceramic Culture and Its Relation to
          a Puebloan Culture in New Mexico. American Antiquity,
          vol. 8, no. 3, pp. 269–280. Menasha.
BULLARD, WILLIAM R., JR.
  1962. The Cerro Colorado Site and Pithouse Architecture in
          the Southwestern United States Prior to A.D. 900.
          Peabody Museum Papers, vol. 44, no. 2. Cambridge.
BURGH, ROBERT F.
  1934. The Far View Group of Ruins. Mesa Verde Notes, vol.
          5, no. 2, pp. 32–36. Mesa Verde.
CASSIDY, FRANCIS
  1960. Fire Temple, Mesa Verde National Park. In "The Great
          Kivas of Chaco Canyon and Their Relationships"
          by Gordon Vivian and Paul Reiter. Monographs of
          the School of American Research, no. 22. Santa Fe.
COLTON, HAROLD S.
  1932. A Survey of Prehistoric Sites in the Region of
          Flagstaff, Arizona. Bureau of American Ethnology
          Bulletin 104. Washington.
  1939. Prehistoric Culture Units and Their Relationships in
          Northern Arizona. Museum of Northern Arizona
          Bulletin 17. Flagstaff.
  1946. The Sinagua. A Summary of the Archaeology of the
          Region of Flagstaff, Arizona. Museum of Northern
          Arizona Bulletin 22. Flagstaff.
  1953. Potsherds: An Introduction to the Study of Prehis-
          toric Southwestern Ceramics and Their Use in Historic

297

Reconstruction. <u>Museum of Northern Arizona Bulletin</u> 25. Flagstaff.

1955.   Tusayan Gray and White Ware, Little Colorado Gray, and White Ware. In "Pottery Types of the Southwest," ed. by Harold S. Colton. <u>Ceramic Series 3A, Museum of Northern Arizona</u>. Flagstaff.

_____ and LYNDON L. HARGRAVE

1937.   Handbook of Northern Arizona Pottery Wares. <u>Museum of Northern Arizona Bulletin</u> 11. Flagstaff.

CUSHING, FRANK H.

1886.   A Study of Pueblo Pottery as Illustrative of Zuni Culture Growth. <u>Fourth Annual Report of the Bureau of American Ethnology</u>, pp. 467–521. Washington.

DOUGLASS, ANDREW E.

1938.   Southwestern Dated Ruins: V. <u>Tree-Ring Bulletin</u>, vol. 5, no. 2, pp. 10–13. Tucson.

ERDMAN, JAMES A., CHARLES L. DOUGLAS and JOHN W. MARR

1969.   Environment of Mesa Verde, Colorado. <u>National Park Service Archeological Research Series</u>, no. 7–B. Washington.

FEWKES, JESSE W.

1898.   Archaeological Expedition to Arizona in 1895. <u>Seventeenth Annual Report of the Bureau of American Ethnology</u>, pt. 2, pp. 519–742. Washington.

1906.   Hopi Shrines Near the East Mesa, Arizona. <u>American Anthropologist</u> n.s., vol. 8, no. 2, pp. 346–375. Lancaster.

1909.   Antiquities of the Mesa Verde National Park, Spruce Tree House. <u>Bureau of American Ethnology Bulletin</u> 41. Washington.

1911.   Antiquities of the Mesa Verde National Park, Cliff Palace. <u>Bureau of American Ethnology Bulletin</u> 51. Washington.

1915.   Prehistoric Remains in Arizona, New Mexico, and Colorado. <u>Smithsonian Miscellaneous Collections; Explorations and Field-Work for 1915</u>, vol. 66, no. 3, pp. 82–98. Washington.

1916a.   The Cliff-ruins in Fewkes Cañon, Mesa Verde National Park, Colorado. <u>Holmes Anniversary Volume</u>, pp. 96–117. Washington.

1916b.   <u>Excavation and Repair of Sun Temple, Mesa Verde National Park</u>. Department of the Interior, Washington.

1916c.   Prehistoric Remains in New Mexico, Colorado, and Utah. <u>Smithsonian Miscellaneous Collections; Explorations and Field-Work for 1916</u>, vol. 66, no. 17, pp. 76–92. Washington.

1917.   A Prehistoric Mesa Verde Pueblo and its People.
        Annual Report of the Smithsonian Institution - 1916.
        pp. 461-488. Washington.

1920.   Field-Work   on   the   Mesa   Verde   National   Park.
        Smithsonian Miscellaneous Collections; Explorations
        and Field-Work for 1919, vol. 72, no. 1, pp. 47-64.
        Washington.

1921.   Field-Work   on   the   Mesa   Verde   National   Park.
        Smithsonian Miscellaneous Collections; Explorations
        and Field-Work for 1920, vol. 72, no. 6, pp. 75-94.
        Washington.

1922.   Archeological Field-Work on the Mesa Verde National
        Park. Smithsonian Miscellaneous Collections; Explo-
        rations and Field-Work for 1921, vol. 72, no. 15, pp.
        64-83. Washington.

1923.   Archeological Field-Work on the Mesa Verde National
        Park. Smithsonian Miscellaneous Collections; Explo-
        rations and Field-Work for 1922, vol. 74, no. 5, pp.
        90-115. Washington.

FRANKE, PAUL R. and DON WATSON
1936.   An Experimental Corn Field in Mesa Verde National
        Park. The University of New Mexico Bulletin, October,
        1936. Albuquerque.

GETTY, HARRY T.
1935a. New Dates From Mesa Verde. Tree-Ring Bulletin, vol.
        1, no. 3, pp. 21-23. Tucson.

1935b. New Dates From Spruce Tree House, Mesa Verde. Tree-
        Ring Bulletin, vol. 1, no. 4, pp. 28-29. Tucson.

GLADWIN, WINIFRED and HAROLD S.
1934.   A Method for the Designation of Cultures and Their
        Variations. Medallion Papers, no. 15. Globe.

GIFFORD, JAMES C.
1960.   The Type-Variety Method of Ceramic Classification as
        an Indicator of Cultural Phenomena. American
        Antiquity, vol. 25, no. 3, pp. 341-347. Salt Lake
        City.

HARGRAVE, LYNDON L.
1936.   Notes on a Red Ware from Bluff, Utah. Southwestern
        Lore, vol. II, no. 1, pp. 29-34. Gunnison.

HAWLEY, FLORENCE M.
1936.   Field Manual of Prehistoric Southwestern Pottery
        Types. The University of New Mexico Bulletin (Revised
        1950). Albuquerque.

HAYES, ALDEN C.
1964.   The Archeological Survey of Wetherill Mesa. National
        Park Service Archeological Research Series, no. 7-A.

Washington.

_____ and JAMES A. LANCASTER

1962.   Site 1060, A Basket Maker III Pithouse on Chapin
         Mesa, Mesa Verde National Park. Tree-Ring Bulletin,
         vol. 24, nos. 1-2, pp. 14-16. Tucson.

HAYES, ALDEN C. and JAMES A. LANCASTER

1968.   Site 1060, A Basketmaker III Pithouse on Chapin Mesa.
         In: Contributions to Mesa Verde Archaeology: V,
         Emergency Archaeology in Mesa Verde National Park,
         Colorado, 1948-1966; ed. by Robert H. Lister.
         University of Colorado Studies, Series in Anthro-
         pology, no. 15. Boulder.

HEROLD, JOYCE

1961.   Prehistoric Settlement and Physical Environment in
         the Mesa Verde Area. University of Utah, Anthropo-
         logical Papers, no. 53, Salt Lake City.

HEWETT, ARTHUR F., JR.

1968.   The Salvage Excavation of Site 1914, Navajo Hill. In:
         Contributions to Mesa Verde Archaeology: V, Emergency
         Archaeology in Mesa Verde National Park, Colorado,
         1948-1966; ed. by Robert H. Lister. University of
         Colorado Studies, Series in Anthropology, no. 15.
         Boulder.

HOLMES, WILLIAM H.

1886.   Pottery of the Ancient Pueblos. 4th Annual Report of
         the Bureau of American Ethnology, pp. 257-360.
         Washington.

JENNINGS, CALVIN H.

1968.   Archaeological Excavations at Site 60, Chapin Mesa.
         In: Contributions to Mesa Verde Archaeology: V,
         Emergency Archaeology in Mesa Verde National Park,
         Colorado, 1948-1966; ed. by Robert H. Lister.
         University of Colorado Studies, Series in Anthro-
         pology, no. 15. Boulder.

KIDDER, ALFRED V.

1924.   An Introduction to the Study of Southwestern Archae-
         ology. Department of Archaeology, Phillips Academy,
         Papers of the Southwestern Expedition, no. 1.
         Andover.

1927.   Southwestern Archaeological Conference. El Palacio,
         vol. 23, no. 22, pp. 554-561. Santa Fe.

1936.   The Pottery of Pecos, Vol. II. Department of Archae-
         ology, Phillips Academy, Papers of the Southwestern
         Expedition, no. 7. Andover.

LANCASTER, JAMES A.

1968a.   The Salvage Excavation of Sites 353 and 354, Chapin

Mesa. In: Contributions to Mesa Verde Archaeology: V, Emergency Archaeology in Mesa Verde National Park, Colorado, 1948-1966; ed. by Robert H. Lister. University of Colorado Studies, Series in Anthropology, no. 15. Boulder.

1968b. An Archaeological Test at Site 80, Chapin Mesa. In: Contributions to Mesa Verde Archaeology: V, Emergency Archaeology in Mesa Verde National Park, Colorado, 1948-1966; ed. by Robert H. Lister. University of Colorado Studies, Series in Anthropology, no. 15. Boulder.

_____ and LELAND J. ABEL
1968. Test Excavation of Site 391, A Typical "Burned Rock Area" on Chapin Mesa. In: Contributions to Mesa Verde Archaeology: V, Emergency Archaeology in Mesa Verde National Park, Colorado, 1948-1966; ed. by Robert H. Lister. University of Colorado Studies, Series in Anthropology, no. 15. Boulder.

_____ and JEAN M. PINKLEY
1954. Excavation at Site 16 of Three Pueblo II Mesa-top Ruins. In "Archeological Excavations in Mesa Verde National Park, Colorado, 1950." National Park Service Archeological Research Series, no. 2. Washington.

_____ and PHILIP F. VAN CLEAVE
1954. The Excavation of Sun Point Pueblo. In "Archeological Excavations in Mesa Verde National Park, Colorado, 1950." National Park Service Archeological Research Series, no. 2. Washington.

_____ and DON WATSON
1942. Excavation of Mesa Verde Pithouses. American Antiquity, vol. 9, no. 2, pp. 190-198. Menasha.
1954. Excavation of Two Late Basketmaker III Pithouses. In "Archeological Excavations in Mesa Verde National Park, Colorado, 1950." National Park Service Archeological Research Series, no. 2. Washington.

_____ JEAN M. PINKLEY, PHILIP F. VAN CLEAVE, and DON WATSON
1954. Archeological Excavations in Mesa Verde National Park, Colorado, 1950. National Park Service Archeological Research Series, no. 2. Washington.

LINTON, RALPH
1936. The Study of Man. D. Appleton-Century, New York.
n.d. The Small Open Ruins of the Mesa Verde. Unpublished Manuscript in archives, Bureau of American Ethnology, Washington.

LISTER, ROBERT H.
1964. Contributions to Mesa Verde Archaeology; I, Site 499,

Mesa Verde National Park, Colorado. _University of Colorado Studies, Series in Anthropology_, no. 9. Boulder.

1965.   Contributions to Mesa Verde Archaeology: II, Site 875, Mesa Verde National Park, Colorado. _University of Colorado Studies, Series in Anthropology_, no. 11. Boulder.

LISTER, ROBERT H.

1966.   Contributions to Mesa Verde Archaeology: III, Site 866, and the Cultural Sequence at Far View Villages in the Far View Group, Mesa Verde, Colorado. _University of Colorado Studies, Series in Anthropology_, no. 12. Boulder.

_____ and FLORENCE C.

1969.   The Earl H. Morris Memorial Pottery Collection. _University of Colorado Studies, Series in Anthropology_, no. 16. Boulder.

LUEBBEN, RALPH A., LAURENCE HEROLD, and ARTHUR ROHN

1960.   An Unusual Pueblo III Ruin, Mesa Verde, Colorado. _American Antiquity_, vol. 26, no.   , pp. 11–20. Salt Lake City.

_____ ARTHUR ROHN, and R. DALE GIVENS

1962.   A Partially Subterranean Pueblo III Structure. _El Palacio_, vol. 69, no. 4, pp. 225–239. Santa Fe.

MARTIN, PAUL S.

1936.   Lowry Ruin in Southwestern Colorado. _Anthropological Series, Field Museum of Natural History_, vol. 23, no. 1. Chicago.

1938.   Archaeological Work in the Ackmen-Lowry Area, South-Western Colorado, 1937. _Anthropological Series, Field Museum of Natural History_, vol. 23, no. 2. Chicago.

1939.   Modified Basket Maker Sites, Ackmen-Lowry Area, Southwestern Colorado, 1938. _Anthropological Series, Field Museum of Natural History_, vol. 23, no. 3. Chicago.

_____ and ELIZABETH S. WILLIS

1940.   Anasazi Painted Pottery in Field Museum of Natural History. _Field Museum of Natural History Anthropology Memoirs_ vol. 5. Chicago.

MASON, C. C.

1918.   The Story of the Discovery and Early Exploration of the Cliff Houses at the Mesa Verde. Unpublished paper given to The State Historical Society of Colorado. Denver.

MCNITT, FRANK
   1957.   Richard Wetherill: Anasazi. University of New Mexico
            Press. Albuquerque.
MERA, HARRY P.
   1935.   Ceramic Clues to the Prehistory of North Central New
            Mexico. Laboratory of Anthropology Technical Series
            Bulletin, no. 8. Santa Fe.
MINDELEFF, VICTOR
   1891.   A Study of Pueblo Architecture: Tusayan and Cibola.
            8th A   the Bureau   of   American
            Ethnol   .hington.
MOHR, ALBERT and
   1959.   San Jo   es in Southeastern Utah. El Palacio, vol.
            66, no. 4, pp. 109-119. Santa Fe.
MORRIS, EARL H.
   1919a.   The Aztec Ruin. Anthropological Papers   of   the
            American Museum of Natural History vol. 26, pt. 1.
            New York.
   1919b.   Preliminary Account of the Antiquities of the Region
            Betwee   Mancos and La Plata Rivers in South-
            western colorado. 33rd Annual Report of the Bureau
            of American Ethnology, pp. 155-206. Washington.
   1939.   Archaeological Studies in the La Plata District,
            Southwestern Colorado and Northwestern New Mexico.
            Carnegie Institution of Washington Publication, no.
            519. Washington.
        and ROBERT BURGH
   1954.   Basket Maker II   Sites near   Durango, Colorado.
            Carnegie Institution of Washington Publication, no.
            604. Washington.
MURDOCK, GEORGE P.
   1949.   Social Structure. Macmillan Company, New York.
NORDENSKIÖLD, GUSTAF
   1893.   The Cliffdwellers of the Mesa Verde, Southwestern
            Colorado, Their Pottery and Implements. Trans. by D.
            Lloyd Morgan. P. A. Norstedt & Soner, Stockholm -
            Chicago.
NUSBAUM, JESSE L.
   1911.   The Excavation and Repair of Balcony House, Mesa
            Verde National Park. Abstract of paper presented to
            the 12th General Meeting of the Archaeological
            Institute of America, Decmeber 27-30, 1910. American
            Journal of Archaeology, vol. 15, p. 75. Norwood.
O'BRYAN, DORIC
   1950.   Excavations in Mesa Verde National Park, 1947-1948.
            Medallion Papers, no. 39. Globe.

OSBORNE, DOUGLAS
    1964.   A Prologue to the Project. In The Archeological
             Survey of Wetherill Mesa, National Park Service
             Archeological Research Series, no. 7-A. Washington.
PARSONS, ELSIE C.
    1923.   Laguna Genealogies. American Museum of Natural
             History Anthropological Papers, vol. 19, pt. V. New
             York.
    1939.   Pueblo Indian Religion. The University of Chicago
             Press, Chicago.
PHILLIPS, PHILIP
    1958.   Application of the Wheat-Gifford-Wasley Taxonomy to
             Eastern Ceramics. American Antiquity, vol. 24, no. 2,
             pp. 117-125. Salt Lake City.
REED, ERIK K.
    1944.   Archeological work in Mancos Canyon, Colorado.
             American Antiquity, vol. 10, pp. 48-58. Menasha.
    1958.   Excavations in Mancos Canyon, Colorado. University of
             Utah, Anthropological Papers no. 35. Salt Lake City.
ROBERTS, FRANK H. H., JR.
    1929.   Shabik'eshchee Village: A late Basketmaker site in
             the Chaco Canyon, New Mexico. Bureau of American
             Ethnology Bulletin 92. Washington.
    1930.   Early Pueblo Ruins in the Piedra District, South-
             western Colorado. Bureau of American Ethnology
             Bulletin 96. Washington.
    1935.   A Survey of Southwestern Archaeology. American
             Anthropologist n.s., vol. 37, no. 1, pp. 1-35.
             Menasha.
ROHN, ARTHUR H.
    1963a.   An Ecological Approach to the Great Pueblo Occupation
             of the Mesa Verde, Colorado. Plateau, vol. 36, no. 1,
             pp. 1-17. Flagstaff.
    1963b.   Prehistoric Soil and Water Conservation on Chapin
             Mesa, Southwestern Colorado. American Antiquity, vol.
             28, no. 4, pp. 441-455. Salt Lake City.
    1966.   Cultural Continuity and Change on Chapin Mesa, South-
             western Colorado. Ph. D. Dissertation, Harvard
             University, Cambridge.
    1971.   Mug House. National Park Service Archaeological
             Research Series, no. 7-D. Washington
    1975.   A Stockaded Basketmaker III Village at Yellow Jacket,
             Colorado. The Kiva, vol. 40, no. 3, pp. 113-119.
             Tucson.
_____ and JERVIS D. SWANNACK, JR.
    1965.   Mummy Lake Gray: A New Pottery Type. Society for

American Archaeology Memoir no. 19, pp. 14-18. Salt Lake City.

SCHULMAN, EDMUND
  1946.   Dendrochronology at Mesa Verde National Park. _Tree-Ring Bulletin_, vol. 12, no. 3, pp. 18-24. Tucson.

SHEPARD, ANNA O.
  1939.   Technology of La Plata Pottery. Appendix to Earl H. Morris, Archaeological Studies in the La Plata District, _Carnegie Institution of Washington Publication_ no. 519. Washington.
  1948.   The Symmetry of Abstract Design with Special Reference to Ceramic Decoration. Carnegie Institution of Washington _Contributions to American Anthropology and History_ no. 47. Washington.
  1957.   Ceramics for The Archaeologist. _Carnegie Institution of Washington_ Publication 609. Washington.

SMILEY, TERAH L.
  1949.   Pithouse Number 1, Mesa Verde National Park. _American Antiquity_, vol. 14, no. 3, pp. 167-171. Salt Lake City.
  1950.   Miscellaneous Ring Records, II. _Tree-Ring Bulletin_, vol. 16, no. 3, pp. 22-23. Tucson.

SMITH, ROBERT E., GORDON R. WILLEY, and JAMES C. GIFFORD
  1960.   The Type-Variety Concept as a Basis for the Analysis of Maya Pottery. _American Antiquity_, vol. 25, no. 3, pp. 330-340. Salt Lake City.

STEVENSON, MATILDA C.
  1904.   The Zuni Indians: Their Mythology, Esoteric Fraternities, and Ceremonies. _23rd Annual Report of the Bureau of American Ethnology_. Washington.

STEWART, GUY R.
  1940.   Conservation in Pueblo Agriculture. _The Scientific Monthly_, vol. 51, pp. 201-220 and 329-340. Lancaster.
  n.d.   Conservation Practices in Flood Water Agriculture at Mesa Verde. Unpublished report to the National Park Service, Mesa Verde National Park, Colorado.

_____ and MAURICE DONNELLY
  1943a.   Soil and Water Economy in the Pueblo Southwest, I. Field Studies at Mesa Verde and Northern Arizona. _The Scientific Monthly_, vol. 56, pp. 31-44. Lancaster.
  1943b.   Soil and Water Economy in the Pueblo Southwest, II. Evaluation of Primitive Methods of Conservation. _The Scientific Monthly_, vol. 56, pp. 134-144. Lancaster.

SWANNACK, JERVIS D., JR.
　1969.　Big Juniper House. <u>National Park Service Archaeolog-</u>
　　　　<u>ical Research Series</u>, no. 7-C. Washington.
TURNER, CHRISTY G., II
　1963.　Petrographs of the Glen Canyon Region. <u>Museum of</u>
　　　　<u>Northern Arizona Bulletin</u> 38. Flagstaff.
WANEK, ALEXANDER A.
　1959.　Geology and Fuel Resources of the Mesa Verde Area,
　　　　Montezuma and La Plata Counties, Colorado. <u>Geological</u>
　　　　<u>Survey Bulletin</u> 1072-M. Washington.
WATSON, DON
　1954.　Introduction to Mesa Verde Archeology. In Archeolog-
　　　　ical Excavations in Mesa Verde National Park,
　　　　Colorado, 1950, <u>National Park Service Archeological</u>
　　　　<u>Research Series</u> no. 2. Washington.
WENDORF, FRED and TULLY H. THOMAS
　1951.　Early Man Sites Near Concho, Arizona. <u>American</u>
　　　　<u>Antiquity</u>, vol. 17, no. 2, pp. 107-114. Salt Lake
　　　　City.
WHEAT, JOE BEN, JAMES C. GIFFORD, and WILLIAM W. WASLEY
　1958.　Ceramic Variety, Type Cluster, and Ceramic System in
　　　　Southwestern Pottery Analysis. <u>American Antiquity</u>,
　　　　vol. 24, no. 1, pp. 34-47. Salt Lake City.
WHEELER, RICHARD P.
　1954.　Two New Projectile Point Types: Duncan and Hanna
　　　　Points. <u>The Plains Anthropologist</u> no. 1, pp. 7-14.
　　　　Lincoln.
WHITE, LESLIE A.
　1962.　The Pueblo of Sia, New Mexico. <u>Bureau of American</u>
　　　　<u>Ethnology Bulletin</u> 184. Washington.
WILLEY, GORDON R. and PHILIP PHILLIPS
　1958.　<u>Method and Theory in American Archaeology</u>. University
　　　　of Chicago Press, Chicago.
WOODBURY, RICHARD B.
　1961.　Prehistoric Agriculture at Point of Pines, Arizona.
　　　　<u>Memoirs of the Society for American Archaeology</u> no.
　　　　17. Salt Lake City.

INDEX OF SITE NUMBERS